A Place
in the Country

Also by
Laura Shaine Cunningham

Memoir

SLEEPING ARRANGEMENTS

Novels

THIRD PARTIES

SWEET NOTHINGS

TAMARA

Plays

BEAUTIFUL BODIES

BANG

I LOVE YOU, TWO
(WHERE SHE WENT, WHAT SHE DID
and
THE MAN AT THE DOOR)

CRUISIN' CLOSE TO CRAZY

THE WIVES

THE FALL OF THE HOUSE OF GLASS

RIVERHEAD BOOKS

NEW YORK

2000

For June —
with fond
memories
of the
reading group!

Laura Shaine Cunningham

A Place
in the Country

Laura Shaine Cunningham

RIVERHEAD BOOKS
a member of
Penguin Putnam Inc.
375 Hudson Street
New York, NY 10014

Portions of this work first appeared in *The New Yorker*.

Library of Congress Cataloging-in-Publication Data

Cunningham, Laura.
A place in the country / Laura Shaine Cunningham.
p.   cm.
ISBN 1-57322-157-0
1. Cunningham, Laura—Homes and haunts—New York (State)—
Shawangunk Mountains.   2. Country life—New York (State)—
Shawangunk Mountains.   3. Shawangunk Mountains (N.Y.)—
Social life and customs.   4. Authors, American—20th century—
Biography.   I. Title.
PS3553.U478 Z466   2000   99-059914
813'.54—dc21

Printed in the United States of America
1   3   5   7   9   10   8   6   4   2
This book is printed on acid-free paper. ∞

BOOK DESIGN BY DEBORAH KERNER

For

my daughters,

Alexandra Rose

and

Jasmine Sou Mei

A Place
in the Country

Introduction

This book is dedicated to all the city people who crave the country, who love nature with a passion that is near demented in its innocence. I am thinking of my friend the actor who visited me for the weekend and ended up buying a cabin in spite of the fact that he doesn't have a car, or even a license to drive. (He plans to commute by taxi, two hundred miles round-trip.) I am also thinking of the family man who came upstate to "look for a place" and fell through the rotted floorboards of the first house he was shown. "I'll take it," he cried out from the basement. And, of course, I am remembering my own relatives, especially my uncle Gabe, who always ventured into the woods wearing his business suit and shined shoes. He led me, as an eight-year-old girl, up the steep side of Mount Beacon. We climbed up rock face and tore through thorned underbrush. When, muddied and scratched, we reached the summit, Gabe stretched out his arms to embrace the vista and the emotion: "This is living!"

The love of city people for the country is a mad love; it feeds on impulse and pays no attention to fact. We, the buyers of country places, don't really want to know too much about them before we take possession. We don't want our joy deflated by such details as *E. coli* counts, carpenter ants, and logging rights-of-way. Often, in the heat of purchase, we don't even want to know the actual location of the country house or how long it will really take to get there from the city. We never dwell on the nasty mathematics of cost or hear the "mort" in "mortgage." We want that house, that plot of land, and we are as unstoppable as the blade of city grass that cracks through concrete (and which may well have been our first exposure to nature).

We city folk who conduct crazed love affairs with the country are often only a generation or two in time and distance from another country, the old country. We are the children and grandchildren of the *Bubbas* and *Zaydas*, the *Nonnas* and *Poppas* who climbed onto their rooftops to plant tomatoes in crates, who grew lemon trees in their living rooms and harbored hyacinths in their closets.

My own grandmother Etka from Minsk loved to remember the dacha where her family had summered. In Russia, at their "place in the country," my grandmother's parents had grown plums, cherries, pears; they brewed these fruits into a liquor that flamed the spirit and induced an ecstasy that could still make my grandmother glow eighty years later when she felt the sun warm her through the window glass of our New York City apartment. "This is the time of the year when we would pack up everything and go to the dacha."

So, perhaps, a seed was sown and took root in my subconscious. As a child, I wasn't aware of paying homage to my grandmother's reminiscences, but I must have cared, for I spent the next three decades searching for my own version of that dacha. Now I inhabit my dream place. In truth, this farm surpasses my fantasies. I would not have presumed to envision such a generous, pretty house, set on an estate landscaped by Frederick Law Olmsted (a designer, too, of Central Park, a place with which I was far more familiar).

But here I am, in the center of several hundred acres, on the property that was named Willowby Park in 1892 and is even now known to locals as Willowby. My house has a name, The Inn, and a history—as the Shawangunk Inn, it was a stopping place on the old carriage roads through the Shawangunk Mountains, southeast of New York's more famous range, the Catskills.

The Inn actually consists of two houses—The Inn proper, an 1820 center-hall colonial, and The Innlet, a smaller, perhaps older, guest house. In 1899, the two houses were joined like Siamese twins, at the head. Upstairs, I must walk through a Victorian linen closet to reach the three back guest rooms.

On the west side of the wraparound porch, a carriage step still awaits visitors, whom I envision as ladies wearing Victorian dresses and high-buttoned shoes. I spend some time imagining their existence, the spinsters who ran The Inn, the guests. Clues to the way they lived remain throughout the house—buzzers to summon the butler (would that he were still here). The bedroom doors have transoms for ventilation, and the fittings for awnings remain on the porch. It's easy to imagine fragrant summer afternoons, guests relaxing in the shade.

Some days, I feel I inhabit the past. In many ways, I live a nineteenth-century existence even as the twenty-first has overtaken me. Now as I look out my bedroom window, I see a view that might have been enjoyed a century ago—a herd of Holstein cows posed in the frosted pasture. The cows stand still, as if in a Hudson River School landscape painting. The ground is covered with the first snow of the season. Steam rises from the cows, wafting upward to combine with the fine flakes to form fog. The cows exude an aura I think of as "bovinity." They have what I still seek: perfect peace. Time is slower here, slow as the snow, and reasons for leaving become less urgent by the minute.

This place has a history of attracting people, seducing them into staying. Legend has it that the founder of the estate, Willowby Park, was an American businessman who visited The Inn and was so soothed by the surroundings that he acquired them. He purchased several colonial farmsteads, then hired the Olmsted firm to unite the properties into an English-style park. His grandson, a British lord, sold The Inn to me and my husband, ninety years later. As country "sellers" do, His Lordship did not leave the property but remained in the manor house his grandfather built.

The animals have stayed on, also—herds of white-tailed deer, flocks of wild turkey, predators such as fox, weasels, coyote. There has even been a black bear, spotted during a summer drought, on the run, paws dripping honey from a neighbor's hives. Now, in late winter, I see the turkeys, thirty-eight of them, walking single-file in the hoofprints left by the procession of cows. The turkeys nibble on grain left intact in the cow patties. As I watch, the turkeys start and flutter in the discombobulated way that turkeys do—not quite flying away. I see what caused their distress—the diagonal run of a coyote crouched for the kill. This time, the coyote is not quick enough—the turkeys squawk and escape. The coyote slinks off. The cows, unperturbed, continue their gustatory march, the lifelong procession toward an endless lunch. Meanwhile, above them, two hawks circle, searching for the occasional mouse snack. They are a hunting pair, white-feather-bellied, and close enough that I can see the curve of their beaks, the arch of their talons.

In my view, there are only two spots of color—the red of the farmer's barn below, and to the south, the soft yellow ("Jersey Cream") of the Manor. All the rest is shades of gray and white, the air dotted by widely spaced snowflakes. I can see my neighbors coping with the snow. The lord's station wagon is gliding at the ten-mile-per-hour speed limit along the Avenue, the gravel drive Olmsted designed for horse and carriage and which is so expensive to maintain for cars. Every spring, the lord sets down costly gravel; every winter, the snowplow shovels it up. Downhill, to the east, sits the dairy farm. My pasture leads to the barns; the farmer and I are connected by a back road, separated only by a wire of electric fence.

4

From the bedrooms of The Inn, the farm proper appears reduced in the distance; the tractor pouffing smoke is a Tinker Toy image of the continual work that goes on down below. Today, the farmer has driven his truck up my back road to hang high-tech maple syrup buckets on my trees. Some of the trees wear what I consider the more charming traditional sap buckets, but others are dressed with white plastic sacks that resemble oversize IV bags. As I watch, three generations of the farmer's family—father, son, and granddaughter—run from tree to tree. They move fast and not in especially good humor. It is cold, the light is fading, and fifty cows with swelling udders wait in the barn for the twice-daily ritual of milking. The farmers are costumed as one would expect—in plaid flannel shirts, blue denim overalls, even snug milking caps—but they don't exude the overt cheer of fictional farm families like the Waltons. The real farmers' faces are blanched gray-white by the wind, and when they stumble, carrying buckets, I can hear them curse. The farmers often yell at the cows. The cows accept criticism; they stare back, impervious, their mouths moving in the continuous chewing of the cud.

It's always beautiful to be here on the farm; it isn't often easy. Even as I write, my hands stiffen from the cold, and I hear the roar of my generator, hooked up this dawn, at the start of one of the frequent power failures that afflict my dream place.

My two daughters are home from school—the third snow day in a week. At the moment, they are playing, but soon, I know from experience, they will lose patience with their game and each other, and I will have to run downstairs to summon up another diversion for the long indoor day. Still, for now, all is peaceful in the playroom, which was once the formal dining room of The Inn but today houses a collection of stuffed animals and three real ones—two parakeets and a pet mouse.

So I am allowed to remain at my desk by the window for the time being, to continue the daydreams my view inspires. In a little while, I will have to pull on my snow boots and go out to my own small barn, to tend what I laughingly call my "livestock," a crowd of forty-five fat animals who do little but exist in a digestive trance.

At the moment, I can hear them—the distant cluck of the chickens, the honk of the geese, and the occasional *thud* of the dairy goats as they ram the walls of the barn, a portion of which they devoured in their one episode of mating. None of my farm animals does an honest day's work; they don't provide me with what their species are supposed to produce—eggs, milk, cheese. Instead, it is I who provide for them, catering every snack. Twice a day, I lug fifty-pound sacks of chow out to this group, and they thank me by clucking or snorting for more, then firing off their little beebies.

I know a large-animal veterinarian whose right arm is outsized; I fear my own right arm has become enlarged also with all the heaving and lifting I do. My marriage ended five years ago—since then, I have done both woman's and man's work here. Each day brings its harsh surprises—the failure of the furnace, some new irritation. Today, I have what is known as a "weeping rash" between my fingers, the result of gathering bouquets of a gray-white weed that I thought would make an attractive winter arrangement but which turned out to be dead poison sumac. Thus I have combined the agonies of winter and summer.

While I live on the farm of my dreams, I wonder: in fulfilling my childhood fantasy, have I mistaken a form of migrant labor for recreation? Am I deluded in insisting this lifestyle of medieval inconvenience has some charm? I cannot even call my herd or flock decorative, as they appear overweight and ungainly, waddling from one meal to the next.

In essence, I've created a spa for useless animals. The idea was that I would somewhat live off the land, not that the land would live off me. But that's what has happened. I even buy dirt for my dirt from the garden center. My main accomplishment as a city-person farmer has been the gentrification of a generation of groundhogs, who love mesclun mix now that I've introduced it to them. The fantasy that I would raise food for my table has literally bitten the dust. (Stay on the farm long enough and you will appreciate the truth to every country cliché—"You can lead a horse to water but you can't make it drink"; "In a pig's eye"; and "Got my goat.") After seventeen seasons of roto-tilling, fertilizing, fencing, and back-dislocating labor, I produced the six-hundred-dollar tomato. It was a good tomato, a golden tomato, spared by the rodents that left their dental impressions on all the other tomatoes.

Each year, I repeat the mistakes of the past and reap this harvest of shame. This past summer, I struck a new low. I took so long to prepare the soil for the spring planting that by the time the earth was ready, it was no longer spring but midsummer. To cover my lapse, I bought seedlings instead of seeds, only to discover that before I could transplant my storebought baby vegetables, the wild critters had eaten them straight from the greenhouse six-packs. I had finally provided the animals with the ultimate city treat—takeout.

So here I am, in the country, surrounded by proof that I don't know what I am doing. I've hung on for eighteen years, through crop failures, blizzard, divorce, heatless holidays, and a waterless swimming pool. Today, I share my home with two little girls and an eighty-four-year-old uncle. Every day, I am tested—yet I will not give up. Not since Scarlett O'Hara clawed the red earth of Tara has a woman clung to her clods of earth with more tenacity. I will do anything to keep my place in the country, and I have.

As I segue from catastrophe to disaster, the true quest is for answers. Why do I, a woman born on East Twenty-seventh Street in Manhattan, persist in these fruitless endeavors? And why, oh why, does it mean so much?

Having arrived here, at this farm, my destination, it may be possible to retrace my steps, discover the reasons. Looking back, I can see that certain aspects of my early life led me to take a series of actual and spiritual moves to the north. I suspect that, along the way, everyone I've loved has been connected to this one-foot-in-front-of-the-other, near-blind-but-somehow-never-off-course journey. Now I must dig to uncover how deep the green-tendrilled ache does reach.

o n e

Desire was there first, before memory. I can't remember a time when I didn't long for "a place in the country." From the beginning, I can recall the warmth of my mother's handclasp as we toured model homes on sequential Sundays, seeking, always seeking, the house of our dreams. Those dreams wafted a specific scent: fresh shellac and new paint.

"Someday," my mother, Rosie, would say, as we walked through the vacant rooms full of hope, "we'll have a place of our own. A private house outside the city."

"A private house." Even today, those words hold a potent magic for me. Then, they were more than enough to propel us every weekend on buses and trains to differing destinations we called the "country." On the buses, I commandeered the window seat, the better to scan the roadside, my eyes searching for the corridors of evergreen, the hidden paths that led to some ultimate, secret oasis. It seemed to me that the scenery flashed by too fast. Was that a house, set back in the woods? A haunted house, abandoned. Perhaps available? I hunted for the shadows, too, for pure adventure—was that rock overhang hiding a cave?

I flush to realize how close the "country" was then. We seldom left the city limits, except in spirit. Wherever the shade extended for more than a few feet and sunlight dappled the leaves—that was our "coun-

try." I'm embarrassed to admit I confused the Mount Vernon that borders the Bronx with the "real" Mount Vernon, where president George
Washington lived, down in Virginia. Both my mother and I regarded
suburbs like Rockville Centre, Long Island, as rustic.

One of the country homes we coveted stood in pitiful proximity to
our Bronx high-rise apartment building, AnaMor Towers (named for
its owners, Anna and Morris Snezak). My first dream house of record
was a cottage a block away, a clapboard house that had been left after
the construction boom of the fifties leveled most of the South Bronx.
While the rest of the neighborhood had given way to tall brick apartment houses with deluded names ("Roxy's Mansion," "The Alber-
marle"), one small white farmhouse remained. The cottage stood,
constricted between high rises, so squeezed by progress that it looked
as if its windows would pop.

A little girl lived in the private house. She seemed as unlikely as
the cottage itself, as if she, with her pigtails and gingham jumper, had
been transported along with her house, like Dorothy to the Land of Oz.
This impression was heightened by the angle at which the house
seemed to tilt, following the descent of the street.

Every morning, on my way downhill to the public school, I passed
this house. I never ceased to marvel at the way the girl—who had the
equally unlikely name of Orietta—flew from her own front door and
raced down a set of plank steps to the sidewalk. It may not be easy for
people who have always lived in private houses to understand how exotic this simple action appeared: a girl, flying through her own front
door, straight to the outside, without having to navigate the usual
urban intermediary zones—the hallway, the elevator, the lobby, the
foyer—before finally reaching the street. She never needed to be
buzzed in. Her door seemed always to be unlocked.

Orietta had her own flower garden, albeit a skinny urban version—a lone line of tulips bracketed by a metal guard to keep out poo-

dles who might lift a leg on her blossoms. Sparse and endangered as it was, it was still a flower garden, and Orietta could be spotted watering it, even plucking the occasional bloom. In summer, the entire house appeared trimmed in morning glory vines, a living valentine to the past. In winter, her narrow yard seemed to accumulate more and better-textured snow. Orietta had her own shovel, and we could see her dig a white-walled path to her front step. She could, with her brothers and sisters, pack the excess snow into a bona fide snowman, complete with corncob pipe jutting from his chill mouth.

During every season, the country house seemed to emit a light different from that of ordinary dwellings, one more lemon-colored. Warm drafts of odor wafted from the ever-baking oven inside—the aromas of hot bread, cookies, and cakes. Some days the scent was so strong, so spicy and enticing, it anesthetized me in midstep; I would have to stop halfway up the hill on my walk back from school.

The world of the country house struck me as another culture. There always seemed to be someone inside, calling out that supper was ready or to remember your hat or your gloves. Every time the door flew open, I could glimpse a center hall and a wooden staircase. Children could be seen running down that staircase, pell-mell, from what I imagined to be a warren of bedrooms in the even more exotic territory of the upstairs.

To me, an upstairs was the height of luxury. Everyone I knew lived in apartments. You were judged by the size of your apartment. I envied girls who had their own rooms, who inhabited a junior four instead of a one bedroom or a studio. My mother and I lived in what was called an efficiency—a studio with a kitchenette along one wall, and a bath. Because my mother worked long hours in the netherworld of downtown, I often spent my after-school weekday afternoons alone in that one-room apartment that my mother had decorated for us.

Life inside that frame house must be very different, I thought. Countless children seemed to run in and out, without any need of keys. As I watched them, I felt a pressure in my chest, right behind the dog tags that I had to wear, the tags that bore my name, my mother's name, my birthdate, and which linked me, bead by bead, to the unwritten fate of my father, who, I was told, had been "lost in the war." The tags themselves were a little scary. They would be used to identify me if some unknown, awful thing were to happen to me. The tags related, too, to the frequent atomic bomb drills at P.S. 35, when, at the wail of a siren, all the children had to duck under the desks to await possible annihilation.

The bomb never landed on me, but those tags continued to hang heavy, along with my set of keys, which hung from the same chain. I carried three keys—one to the lobby of AnaMor Towers, and one each to the top and bottom locks of 3M, the studio I shared with my mother, Rosie.

I used my keys to let myself into 3M, dense in its atmosphere of solitude. More than once, I forgot to wear my keys and dog tags, and when I reached AnaMor Towers, stood on the welcome mat and wept. Even though I knew, at age six, that my fear was unrealistic, I was afraid that without the keys I might never again be admitted to a home I could call my own. The sanctuary of 3M had been too hard won. Before we could afford that apartment, my mother and I had lived in a holding pattern, moving from one relative's apartment to another, being accommodated in odd slices of space. We'd slept in foyers, entry nooks, living rooms. For a time, we slept under a long mahogany dining table. For the first four years of my life, Rosie and I had been transient, taking up as little space as possible in other people's homes.

These apartments were already cramped. My aunt Tessa lived so tight, we had to squeeze sideways through her living/dining room, passing through a crevasse created by looming bookcases and an upright piano. Living there was an exercise in compression. The apartment was set into a complex of subsidized buildings called the Dorchester Houses. The design had been inspired by feudal times and captured the repression of that era. A half-dozen buildings were grouped around a sunless courtyard that held limp, dying trees. The trees were supported by girdles, as were most of the women tenants. The daytime population on view were stocky housewives who seemed to have rolled over from the Slavic countries pushing loaded carts.

The gimlet-eyed apartment buildings were vast, but they had been designed without generosity. There was no main entrance or gracious lobby. Each "sector" had its separate entry, a narrow door at the top of a stoop that was pitched too steep. Entering, one had the sensation of lurching into the building, then being constricted into an elevator packed with pregnant women pushing prams. The buildings smelled of cooking cabbage and garbage incineration.

We lived in 5R, my aunt Tessa's apartment. We were seven people in three rooms. Because of the number of people and the oversized furniture, 5R seemed more storage unit than habitat. The living room was lined with the ceiling-high bookcases, piano, and a breakfront. The dining table filled the center of the room, seven chairs jammed against it. There was no space for the sofa, so it sat, wedged against the window and the radiator, becoming in winter, a literal hotseat.

At the rear of 5R were two tiny bedrooms—the master, where Aunt Tessa slept with her husband, Saul, a young Russian-born rabbi. They lay on twin beds, surrounded by stacks of books (his) and recipe files (hers). My aunt Tessa collected recipes, hundreds of recipes that she planned to try someday, just as my mother and I planned to move to a private house. The second bedroom held their three teenage sons, my boy cousins, who lay stacked on bunk beds amidst the chaos of basketballs, hockey sticks, bats, and an inanimate fourth brother, the dummy Charlie McCarthy. Every time my aunt screamed, "Go to your room!" her boys had the perfect retort—"How?" The door to their room could open only partway.

There was a single bathroom for all seven of us. Every morning, a conga line of urinary urgency formed outside the door. "Emergency!" was a cry that was often heard; everyone else crossed their legs and danced. Every evening, the adults tended to find a position and remain in place. The boys bounced basketballs against the ceiling and ricocheted off the walls.

Adding to the general confusion was the punctuation provided by actual alarms—5R faced a fire engine company. Night and day, fire trucks roared forth, sirens screaming, giving vehicular voice to our frustrations. From age one to three, I lived there, accustomed to emergency, to the constant need for more air, more space. My aunt was always opening the windows to take advantage of 5R's single virtue, what she called its "excellent cross-ventilation." Every day, the adults cried out for more *Luft*, *Luft* being a breeze of fresh air or something indefinably better—a draft of hope, a whiff of escape. "*Luft*," they said. "We need more *Luft*."

All spring and summer, the windows were kept open. The windows led to exterior extensions of our living space—the fire escapes and the tarry subroof. Every day, my uncle Saul, always attired in his rabbinical yarmulke and summer outfit of undershirt and suspendered trousers, would climb out the bedroom window to the asphalt terrace beyond. Often, he lifted me over the windowsill so that I could help him tend his vegetable garden.

This was my first farm—Uncle Saul's rows of balsa-wood boxes packed with dug-up park dirt. We had no gardening tools, so we used urban substitutes from 5R—we watered with a juice pitcher, dug with a soup spoon or a kiddie shovel. In spite of our equipment, we produced bumper crops. By midsummer, the tomato plants stood high and tangled, drooping under the weight of their red fruits. The tomatoes were so big and juicy that they split under the pressure of their own growth. I was told that I could pick and eat the "broken" ones straight from the vine. I can still taste their salt-sweetness, feel their skin burst to the bite. As exciting as their flavor was the tomatoes' green perfume, the fragrance of farms far away.

Uncle Saul hovered over his vegetables. He walked that outdoor aisle between his balsa-wood boxes, watering here, pinching there, picking here. He was a sweet man, with brown eyes liquid with intellect: a gaze that addressed you more often than his voice did. He was so quiet, I cannot hear him, even in memory. But I do remember him holding me, helping me over the window ledge, guiding my hand with the water pitcher.

Saul was the opposite of his wife, my aunt Tessa, who shrieked, "Don't make me scream! I'm hoarse from shouting!" She yelled continually, trying to discipline her three sons, who leaped away from her, mischievous, rebounding off the confines of our constricted world. Tessa had two verbal styles—the yelling and a monologue on her own cheerfulness: "They call me Mrs. Sunshine. Wherever I go, I brighten every room." In the crowded living/dining room, Uncle Saul sat at the table, sometimes resting his cheek on his Talmudic studies. In summer, weather permitting, he climbed out the window to tend his crops.

There was something off with Aunt Tessa and Uncle Saul's eldest son, Willy. Willy slurred his speech; he dragged his feet. His face appeared sloped, distorted, like the reflection on the back of a spoon. His big brown eyes were like his father's, but they protruded slightly, showing the whites. It made him appear melancholic; his eyelids drooped. His hands hung heavy, too, and it seemed he did not know what to do with them, until he took my hand in his: for a time, when I was three and Willy was thirteen, we were inseparable, and it was he who led me closer to what we regarded as the country.

Most afternoons, Willy took me for a walk. He seemed not to have any friends, and I needed minding. Our needs meshed. Every day, we walked farther and farther, until we reached a place where the pavement ended and marsh grass began.

These vacant lots were not pristine. Refuse and rubble, even the rusted shells of wrecked cars, lay hidden in the grass. Willy and I would explore, poking through the underbrush for interesting bits of trash. One afternoon, we walked farther than we had ever gone before and discovered an old steamer chest. We unlocked the chest, and it exhaled a musk to match any mushroom. Inside the trunk, papers had almost turned to compost. But the chest had once held items of value; it was beribboned within, divided into tiny drawers and compartments. Willy and I called it the "treasure chest."

Just past the treasure chest, the marsh grass began to grow in earnest, high enough to hide the trash, even the old stoves that lay scattered like dominoes. As we walked on, the garbage receded and the grass and scrub bushes dominated. Birds nested, and an occasional rabbit hopped past. For the first time, I could see a horizon, detect a curve to the globe of our earth.

We walked and walked, aware that we were out too late but unable to deny the pull of that horizon line. In the violet urban dusk, the sky fired hot with the magentas of pollution. Willy and I reached a spot where the land seemed to roll down away from us into an expanse of gray-buff wilderness.

"This is it," he said. "This is the end of the city."

From that evening on, this place became our destination.

"Oh, take me there," I'd beg Willy, and he would. And each time we reached that high ground with the view, he said in exactly the same important tone, the voice of the explorers Lewis and Clark at the Continental Divide:

"This is it. This is the end of the city."

t w o

What was the city, I wondered, but the country covered over? The evidence was everywhere underfoot: those blades of grass that cracked the concrete, the asphalt that buckled as the earth tried to shed its tarry mantle. As soon as buildings were demolished, nature reasserted itself, growing up through the tumbledown bricks and hunks of mortar.

I had seen other strong signs of the countryside that had once existed here. For example, there was a bus route my mother and I took from Aunt Tessa's. This bus traveled past a Revolutionary War–era farmstead now hemmed in by a major thoroughfare and a chain of department stores. The place was still owned by a descendant of the original family, a ninety-eight-year-old woman who could be seen moving about in broken-backed shoes, chopping wood and growing corn in her yard, inches from a windowless cement-block shopping center.

There were frequent news stories regarding this country woman in the city: how she had refused to sell when the stores first "went in" and how the commercial giants had been forced to build around her. The pioneer woman and her stone home remained, a living time capsule, a fortress of the past. Her wash waved like victory banners in the increasingly sooty wind of change.

"They offered her *millions*," people would say as the city bus roared past. No matter who made the remark, there was always a chorus of respect from the other bus passengers. "They," the forces of so-called progress, had offered her a fortune, but her way of life had been worth more, was the consensus. The woman resembled Spencer Tracy, but even as a child, I was impressed by her tenacity. I saw her often, as this bus route was our favorite; it led to the New York Botanical Garden. So we arrived at what had been lost: paradise.

Even the entry to the Garden was exciting: my mother and I had to run across the highway that separated the Garden from the Bronx Zoo. It was always a mad dash, a take-your-life-in-your-mother's-hand run. But across the thoroughfare was the lacy iron gate that led to a shaded country lane, a cathedral quiet. I don't recall the flowers as much as I do the shadows; they felt like luxury in summer, when the asphalt could (and did, for the benefit of the tabloids) cook an egg.

When we entered and felt the coolness of the longed-for shade, I would begin to skip and sing: "We're off to see the Wizard, the wonderful Wizard of Oz" and "Follow the yellow brick road." The Garden seemed a suitable stand-in for a mythical Oz. I was drawn at once to a tunnel of shade that led down to the river and, from there, to a series of short waterfalls. I sought and found rock formations that suggested the mouth of a cave. That shadowed entry seemed to invite us into an ancient, half-forgotten past, to crystal mysteries hidden within.

My mother and I had a history with the Botanical Garden. Our interest was perhaps inherited. Rosie's mother, my grandmother, the woman who dubbed herself "Etka from Minsk," as if she were visiting Russian nobility, had spent so much time in the Botanical Garden that she almost qualified as a resident.

Sometime in the late 1930s, my grandmother, a petite, iron-backed woman, was diagnosed with a painful condition similar to arthritis. The doctor prescribed a "hot, wet climate." Instructed to move south, Etka instead moved into the hothouse—the crystal dome, the great Victorian conservatory that featured the Garden's most exotic ferns and tropical plants. For years, she commuted daily between her apartment and a verdigris bench beneath the tallest palms. "Why should I stay home when I can sit here?" she wrote in her leatherbound journal. "Here I am surrounded by beauty, and that influences my thoughts."

Etka's prose reflected the humidity of her surroundings—the purple ink seeped from the pages as she recounted her "philosophy." She likened herself to Plato and Socrates (modesty was not an Etka virtue). "I have my own quotations," she wrote. She was an immigrant who had been forced to abandon a city mansion and a dacha in Russia to take up an existence in New York's tenements, finding versions of the same "railroad flat" in slums of three separate boroughs. Somehow, she had preserved her pride during these humiliating transfers and arrived with it intact at the Botanical Garden. The glassed-in Victorian elegance was the perfect display case for Etka, who wore pert suits and often her ermine stole.

"I was famous not only for my beauty," she wrote in the greenhouse, "but also for my intellect." Etka from Minsk had so much presence that I'm sure no guard dared challenge her long-term use of the greenhouse as her private study. She had a way of looking over her eyeglasses and pursing her lips that could, czarina-like, banish any dissenter to a figurative Siberia. Her hot-house cure was effective: she finished her book, *Philosophy for Women*, and cured her sciatica. One day she walked out and left her pain behind, amid the fragrant fronds of the fern forest.

Was it any wonder that, decades later, her daughter Rosie and her granddaughter would walk into the Botanical Garden with a similar sense of entitlement? The Garden was ours. The weekend excursions there and to similar verdant country-in-the-city beauty spots were our most cherished times. We combined the recreational outing with the ongoing house hunt. Most of our day trips included a stop at a "For Sale" sign and a tour of a model home.

We explored the open houses at the end of our day, possibly to forestall returning to our actual home, the cramped 5R. Mentally, we inhabited every house that we saw—one weekend, it was a square Dutch Colonial on Pelham Bay Parkway; the next, a Tudor near Riverdale. "This is my room," I'd cry out on every tour while my mother followed, whispering, "And this could be mine."

We always lingered in the backyards, where we might inhale the mixed aromas of someone else's roses and a neighbor's barbecue. Someday, we knew, we would live that way, too.

Sometimes, we journeyed slightly farther afield—to Westchester County or Long Island, where our "rich" relatives already had what we regarded as country homes. It's almost funny now to look back and see that even our rich relatives were poor, living in ten-thousand-dollar ranch-style houses or jerry-built split levels in developments. But whatever the house, we pronounced it beautiful and looked with longing at the owners' many rooms and sodded lawns. To dig in your own dirt, to plant a personal flower—I wanted to grow roses in honor of my mother's name—seemed the height of happiness and glory.

"Someday," we always said, as we rode home on the city bus, "someday."

Until that time, we contented ourselves with our day trips to the future. If the house hunting held only a distant promise, at least the public parks offered us immediate pleasures. We would walk and walk until my mother could sustain herself no further on her high heels, and then we'd happily collapse for our inevitable picnic, the high point of every weekend or holiday.

I played scout, seeking out the perfect picnic place. My instincts led me to value privacy over panorama: I found the most secluded glades, remote meadows or groves. "This," I would say when I found our private place, "is the spot."

Then Rosie would spread out our picnic cloth, a classic red-and-white-checked square, and we would settle inside its borders and share the lunch she had packed. Why were those early picnics such bliss? Why did the food taste so much better outside? Why did these meals nourish our dream of the country when, in reality, we sat only a few blocks' distance from the screaming city sidewalks?

I still want my life to resemble those interludes. The series of weekends was nothing less than a love affair. My mother, Rosie, was unmarried—but wed to the idea of romance. Eating in nature, she said, was romantic, a word I mispronounced as roman*tick*, anticipating the tick panic that would mar so many picnics of the distant future.

But this was the 1950s; we were innocent of ticks—we dealt only with ants. And nothing could mar the glories of those first alfresco meals. Our checked cloth set new boundaries around us, defined our state of grace. Within the red-and-white-checked world, we munched what I called "samwiches" and nibbled from a bag of washed fruit and crushed cookies. We didn't have the accoutrements of a high-style picnic—our hamper was just a plain brown paper bag that would inevitably weaken and show stains from the fruit hemorrhaging inside it. If we broke bread, it was only packaged white bread. Poor stuff, but we did not live by Wonder Bread alone. On these occasions, my mother nourished me with her dream of romance.

Her relatives had long criticized Rosie for staying single. They said she refused to "settle," as indeed, she did. At thirty-eight, she might be unmarried with a child and little cash, but she still resisted the marriage of convenience to the dentist or the accountant who offered her a safety that must have scared her more than the precarious life she led with me. It was during our weekend picnic expeditions that I began to have a sense of her reasons, which were really not reasons at all, but a condition of desire.

During these meals on the grass, I came to understand that my mother and I were refugees, not of the war but of the peace: my father had been a soldier, but he had not, as first reported to me, been killed in the war. But neither had he survived, at least in the sense that he would ever return to us.

While we nibbled on our fresh fruit, Rosie treated me to more private conversation than we might share in our transient home. Dining while reclining seemed to evoke memories of her love affair, the great unfinished romance with the man who became my father.

She spoke in a voice that was softer than the one used for ordinary conversation; a huskiness crept into her whispers. Larry had been so handsome, such a good dancer. They had shared picnics, too—once beside a rushing river. He had had a car, and he'd often driven Rosie out to the country so that they could be alone. Gradually, over a series of picnics, I came to realize that I was a hybrid; the daughter of a city girl and a country boy. My father, Larry, had been from the South, from Alabama.

Where exactly was Alabama? I'd wanted to know.

Alabama, my mother told me, was in the far, far country, the deep, deep South. Alabama became a distant, dream destination. My father's family had a private house, she said. She might have even used the word "plantation," for the South was as mythic to Rosie as it was to me. We never went south except once, to Miami Beach, which wasn't the true South at all but an outpost of Jewish New York.

Together, we conjured up an antebellum world (*Gone With the Wind* being our main inspiration). We envisioned my father's house as a mini-Tara. In my mind, I visited my father, Larry, in his multi-columned white house. I could see him, wearing country white to match the portico, a Tennessee Williams lead playing out the tragedy of his own life.

If my father was country, my mother emphatically was not. Rosie was a self-described city girl, a wearer of smart suits and high heels that had carried her out of the tenements of Brooklyn down to Manhattan and then into economic exile in the outback of the Bronx, to her sister Tessa's apartment.

Although they were sisters—my mother the younger by two years—Rosie and Tessa did not resemble each other at all. Tessa had married at nineteen and cheerfully costumed herself in the uniform of the housewife—a shapeless dress called a duster. She did, in fact, spend a lot of time dusting. She even liked to talk about dust—where she'd found it, how much came in through the windows. She was good at getting rid of it, too.

Rosie was different—she was the "career girl." Despite her modest ways and means, Rosie did not lack glamour. In summer, she sported all-white suits, picture hats, and spectator pumps. Even as a child, I noticed that Rosie caught many a man's eye on our excursions. She had a come-hither look, but turned shy when they actually came hither. If a man stared too long and began an actual approach, she flushed and looked down at her lap. She had what I now think of as a wanton shyness.

Rosie was undeniably passionate. Sometimes I caught her gazing after an attractive man. I could feel the draft of her desire, as palpable as her "Fleur de Lis" perfume. And I knew the kind of man she wanted—not the accountant or the dentist. At home, those men might have seemed prudent choices. Out here on the wild grass, I could see Rosie would have none of them. She was after Adonis.

While my mother extolled the joys of love and nature, I agreed, but couldn't help noting that nature looked pretty whipped from where we sat. Our neighborhood parks were flat, cemented places, more pavement than grass, bracketed by streets and racketing overhead subway rails. In the Bronx, even alfresco was not so fresco: cinders as large as snowflakes fluttered on the incinerator-accelerated breeze.

But the soul of the picnic, the communion with the earth, always survived. With the ground beneath us, Rosie and I felt closer to heaven and the soil. We looked up at the skies, charted cloud formations. We returned to our original animal selves and became woodland spirits. Even in the Bronx, it seemed likely that nymphs and naiads were afoot.

Inspired, I would leap to my feet and do a "dance of the samwich," a celebration of grape jelly that was, well, a bit Dionysian. My mother's hushed invitations, even when pertaining to peanut butter and jelly, always heralded our best times. "Let's have it outside," she would say. And I'd never refuse. *Oh, let's.*

We'd return to Aunt Tessa's apartment in a state of grace. Hand in hand, we'd skip up Eastchester Road, singing, "Skip, skip, skip to ma-loo, skip to ma-loo, my darling." In the narrow hall, before we entered 5R, Rosie would give me a special kiss, signaling the temporary farewell to our secret selves. She wore cherry red lipstick and pink pressed face powder. When she kissed me, she passed along the imprint of her lips and a pink dust, the scent of safety and feminine love.

How Rosie managed such élan while residing under her sister's dining table, I'll never comprehend. I know only that she did; that she turned the situation upside down and flipped exigencies into excitement. If we had to sleep under a table, then that could become part of our games: the tablecloth could be our canopy; we played peekaboo through the lace. If my mother ever felt defeat, she concealed it from me in her real-life version of hide-and-seek.

Often we pretended that the heavy table legs that surrounded us were still part of a living wood. We were campsite mates in what we called the "carved forest." Amidst the polished mahogany trees, we whispered of adventures we would have when we found our true place in the country.

When, one night, we moved—suddenly and by subway, carrying lamps in our hands—it seemed a push in that direction. Finally, we could afford a small place of our own. We rode the train to the first outdoor stop on the line. The subway cars tore from the tunnel, and we felt a breakaway rush. In fact, our new neighborhood was better than Aunt Tessa's. There were more trees, more parks. The fire company's sirens were replaced by Yankee Stadium's megaphoned moans of defeat or roars of applause. We lived in the aura cast by the radiant arena, an insomniac violet glow at night. By day, if I stood on the elevated train station, I could look down and see the hyper-green playing fields and the miniaturized players.

We had moved not to a house but to a tiny "efficiency," 3M, a studio apartment that was, despite its size, a huge improvement over living with relatives. The studio encapsulated our privacy, and my mother filled it with signs that our hopes would be realized. She even brought the country into its corners: a parakeet that chirped in its cage, a turtle that sunned itself on a miniature plastic island on the windowsill, and a small jungle of snake plants that tilted, as we did, toward the light.

We could love 3M because it was the first stop on our journey. This was the beginning, we thought, of a series of moves that would take us to the real place in the country we never doubted we would find. If we had any failure of vision, we had only to look down the street, to the perfect farmhouse that remained intact and beckoned, with its lemon-colored lights, to our future.

The new neighborhood offered more fresh air, *Luft,* a commodity all our relatives and neighbors often discussed. The need for fresh air was frequently stated, and the parks were the places we went to get it. They were lined with benches that held whole segments of our society:

young mothers sat out their days, rocking prams while the babies took in the touted fresh air. And grandparents, too, sat and breathed deep, able to relax for the first time in their lives.

The neighborhood offered two main parks, separated by the gray granite cake box of the Bronx County Courthouse that sat squarely on the Grand Concourse. The boundary separated the legal from the illegal, the tame from the wild. On the north side of the court was Joyce Kilmer Park, where cement and civilization prevailed. The park was named for the poet who wrote: "I think that I shall never see/A poem lovely as a tree." The trees, young maples, wore the required city girdles, and the fields were bracketed, too, by black-enameled railings that contained orderly games of catch. There was a single, spectacular centerpiece that promised a bit more eros: a marble fountain that featured naked stone mermaids, whose bare breasts provided the only titillation in this otherwise plain of the mundane. As a child, I had played on the Lorelei, using their laps as footholds and getting a grip on their chipped nipples.

Joyce Kilmer Park was always open and could be found filled with people as late as midnight on a hot summer night. The street lamps would illuminate the green-veined leaves and cast the silver hair of the elderly bench sitters into coronas of light. The Good Humor man patroled the aisles, his wagon atinkle, vapor rising from his frozen cart each time more Humorettes were dispensed.

On the south side of the courthouse, the other park, Franz Siegel, cast a psychic as well as a physical shadow. The citizenry did not venture into its hilly, wooded terrain, where the foliage and rock formations provided cover for alleged primitive misdeeds. There were tales of people screaming and disappearing in there. It was a place where girls, especially, were told not to go.

Of course, this forbidden forest beckoned me. I soon had a partner in crime—Diana, the "dirty girl" down the block. Diana was a savage spirit, untamed by parents or school. At five, she did as she pleased. Diana led me on a wild chase. Her "I dare you, I double dare you" was a challenge I couldn't resist. She introduced me to what we called the Dark Park and its many mysteries.

Inside the glens, we played Indians and later, a game of hide-and-seek with the perverts who seemed to be the only other habitués of our secret places. They may have been hopping in and out of the court-house next to the park, between arraignments. Whatever the expla-nation, these men wandered "our" woods, moving silently behind the trees. Diana, giggling, stalked them as they stalked us.

"Ssssh," she would whisper. "Look." And she would part the foliage to offer me a peek. The sight was so startling that I denied, even to my-self, what I saw. The motion of a hand on an engorged organ in the deep gloom under a hemlock tree could be confused with the play of light and shadow.

Until, one late afternoon, what we saw became unmistakable, the threat too direct. We spied a young man, wearing glasses, walking in agitated circles. He wandered, holding his inflamed penis like an in-jured part. We escaped without serious harm. (In fact, we escaped with a dollar, Diana's reward for touching it.) But after that, the shadows held dread for me, and I stayed away from the Dark Park.

The Hudson also called to us. Diana and I, wearing Davy Crock-ett hats and singing "King of the Wild Frontier," ventured down to the docks. There, the river moved past, sullen, bearing rainbows of oil and floating hunks of foam and trash—a raft of refuse in perpetual motion. It stank. Strange men frequented the riverfront. The same tensions as in the forest of the Dark Park prevailed. Diana "dared" and "double dared," but soon I beat a sneakered retreat to my mother, who preferred a walk on the light side, on the literal sunny side of the street. So I grew to age eight a combination—not as fierce or fearless as my friend Diana, but perhaps more daring than my mother. Maybe I had inherited my unknown father's capacity for flight. Whatever, the push/pull within me, the city/country blend of my parents, two lovers who had not stayed together, remained a force to tug me toward what we called "wild country." Wherever the grass was not cultivated, the paths not preordained, I continued to run wild. I played Indian, wearing a costume my mother provided—a deerskin dress with embroidered symbols: the rising sun and the crescent moon. At play, I assumed a second identity; in the deep trance of make-believe, I was Deer Girl, Iroquois maiden, expert scout.

Every weekend, we explored more terrain as I searched for what I called the "happy hunting grounds." Rosie, her high heels sinking in the sod, followed me down a hundred footpaths. Never altering her career girl costume, she chased me in full regalia. There came an afternoon when we picnicked in the most secluded section of Central Park, the part named the Ramble. I raced ahead of Rosie into a natural amphitheater created by boulders and towering evergreens. The shade fell upon me with a sudden chill. I realized I had run too fast ahead of my mother and that I now stood alone in this dark place. I called out, and then, as if by magic, she appeared. I didn't know it then, but after that day, we did not have too much time left together. I began to hear my mother whisper the word "hospital" in late-night telephone conversations. One morning she walked out of 3M to go there and never returned home.

Just before she left, I made my first attempt to buy a house. I thought I had scored a terrific coup. Overnight, in the deserted lot across the street, a wooden house had been erected. I imagined Rosie moving our few furnishings, our kitten, our bird, the turtle into it.

One afternoon, my life savings of seven dollars crumpled in the palm of my hand, I approached the man who seemed to own the little gray house. He laughed when he heard my offer. It wasn't a house, he told me, it was only the watchman's shack, a construction hut to oversee the building of yet another high-rise. It was not for sale, or even for keeps.

I went back up to 3M and told Rosie what had happened. I had wanted so much to surprise her with that little house. She kissed me and said that it was all right that I hadn't been able to buy it; it was better, even, because one day, we would find a prettier house, a yellow one, in a nicer setting.

We planned a trip to the country for when she came home. The next morning, Rosie left the efficiency that had so compactly held us and our dreams. I couldn't have known that morning when she waved good-bye with a smile that we had no future, only our past. In the end, I remember our hopes, our endless house hunt, and the yearning for the country place without ever feeling that we had failed to find it. Weekend after weekend, we'd enacted our future, play-acting on all those empty stages in a kind of real estate repertory. We'd discovered beauty everywhere and mentally inhabited dozens of homes. So I was left with Rosie's legacy—not of an actual place but of our shared search for one. Our journey had become our destination—the string of beautiful days linking us in ongoing adventure. We had looked forward too long to be disappointed.

With my mother, I had had a home.

three

In the weeks following the loss of my mother, a turn of fate sent me north to true country for the first time. Where we had planned to go together, I now went alone—to a camp high in the mountains. This period formed an interval between two lives—the life I had shared with Rosie and the life I would live in the care of her two bachelor brothers, my uncles Len and Gabe.

My uncles had materialized in 3M almost as soon as my mother had disappeared into the hospital, but it was decided two weeks after her death that I should join my friend and neighbor Susan for the summer at the camp where she had just started the season. I had campaigned to join her—more than campaigned, I begged and threatened in the relentless way of an eight-year-old—until one morning, I found myself on board a bus, heading to the mountains a hundred miles north of the city.

Camp Ava was situated in the Catskills, in a dark, forested mountainscape that must have been reminiscent of the "old country" to the Polish and Russian Jews who had set up the camp there. The area was already popular with Jewish groups. Some rambling hotels and bungalow colonies had been established by working-class New York Jews and refugees from the not-so-distant war in Europe. There, they created a seasonal way of life that celebrated their liberation (from the city, from the war) yet still recalled the hardships of life as they had known it. The children's camps were poor places, set on rough terrain: Camp Ava, for example, occupied a mountainside so Bavarian in character that the sun set on it an hour before light faded from nearby pastures and the local village of Upper Cragsdale. I, at eight, knew none of this, of course—I had a clear image in my mind of the Camp Ava I wanted: a series of Hansel-and-Gretel cottages set into misted meadows afire with wildflowers, bisected by babbling brooks. I pictured a "fairy-tale" woodland, and, with the magical thinking experienced by children in my situation, it seemed not impossible that somehow Rosie was waiting for me there.

I boarded the bus with my uncle Gabe, Rosie's youngest brother, a bachelor who even at thirty-eight seemed suspended in permanent boyhood. He wore sneakers and, like my boy cousins, liked to bounce a basketball against walls. Gabe had come to mind me while my mother was in the hospital, and I had grown accustomed to his strangeness. Gabe was many things, most of them contradictory—he was a grownup, but he played like a child. He chased me around the parks, in a game he invented, called Birdie and the Giant. He seemed to enjoy the chase as much as I did, and we would collapse, laughing, gasping at the conclusion, when I'd be cornered under full-blooming forsythia. Like me, Gabe loved nature. He was a poet and a songwriter, and he claimed to find inspiration at every turn of the footpath. He actually wrote on his notepad while leaning against a tree. An Orthodox Jew, he had somehow combined his faith with a love of black gospel singing and set many of his poems to a soulful rhythm. Gabe sang as we explored the mini-forest of the Cement Park.

I had another uncle, Uncle Len, who was more mysterious. Len was two years older and a head taller than Gabe, his kid brother. At six feet, six inches, Len towered over everyone, but, despite his size, managed to be elusive. Len had no permanent address. He costumed himself in trench coats and slouch hats and alluded to secret missions, as if he were a CIA agent. Complicating his image, Len often referred to Abraham Lincoln, whom he somewhat resembled. He was a Lincoln buff and could recite many of the late president's most famous speeches. Other than the Lincoln speeches, Len maintained significant silences. When asked a direct question, he replied with an indirect answer. "That remains to be seen," was his favored response. Len, too, had appeared in 3M, but briefly; when I would see him again "remained to be seen." It was left to Gabe to prepare me for the trip to summer camp.

We bought the requisite camp tee-shirts and green shorts and had name tags sewn in by a tailor. At last, a week behind my friend Susan, I headed for camp on an ancient bus that seemed to splutter exhaust at the thought of climbing the mountainous road to Upper Cragsdale.

The city we left behind was sweltering. We slept in the blast of floor fans that sent our bedsheets billowing. Some nights, the heat could not be defeated indoors, and entire families slept on fire escapes or rooftops. We needed *Luft,* and *Luft* was scarce in the city summers. Among many families, it was customary to send the children to the country; often, the mothers went, too. "Summer bachelors" were a common sight: men who trudged alone to and from work through July and August. They suffered the subways—rumbling rides through hell. But the spirit of self-sacrifice was considered normal. "All is for the children" was the saying, and the threat of polio was not distant enough to relax the precautions: even I knew a boy at school whose leg dragged in a clanking brace. It was considered healthy, desirable to depart for the mountains if one could possibly escape. For the first time, I was part of the seasonal exodus.

The bus pulled out of the Bronx on a memorably muggy day— there seemed little difference between the air and the exhaust. A vapor rose from the softening asphalt. As the old bus backfired, rudely passing more black gases, I had the sensation I was getting out of town just in time. The minute we hit the open road, my uncle Gabe began to suffer from motion sickness. Although he often wrote and sang songs that celebrated travel, he vomited at fifteen-minute intervals throughout the trip. I saw more margins of greenery as the bus pulled over so that my uncle could alight and retch. Between incidents, he commented on the scenery as I scanned the roadside for my longed-for caves and haunted houses. The last leg, the vertiginous climb to Camp Ava, was taken by taxi. We pulled up at dusk.

What I saw should have warned me: the camp was situated on a slope so steep that it seemed as if the bunkhouses could slide down the mountain. Everything listed to the left, including the Camp Ava sign. This tilt reflected the camp politics—it had been founded by socialist labor union leaders.

We arrived in the rosiness of sunset. Uncle Gabe was dispatched to the infirmary, where his nausea did not abate but gained recognition as a chronic condition. He was put under observation. Gabe loved the country, but he was, in fact, allergic to it. He suffered hay fever, sinus irritation, and skin rashes. Even a minor bug bite ballooned into a deforming lump. Insects seemed to seek him out. "I have the sweet skin," he said. Nothing diminished his pleasure: "I'm so glad to get out in the fresh air," he wheezed on his way to the infirmary.

Gabe would spend the better part of the summer in that camp shack, where, the single adult patient, he recuperated. Whenever he came out, he'd gaze at the mountains in rapture and sing country songs: "Oh, my darling, oh my darling, oh my darling Clementine/You are lost but not forgotten, oh my darling Clementine."

Meanwhile, I was left on my own to check out the camp. At the height of the season, the place appeared abandoned. Even the crabgrass had died. The center playing field was denuded. The advertised swimming pool turned out to be a slime pit, dammed by concrete, that leached turquoise paint chips.

Of course, I could not take all this in at first sight. As night fell, throwing the silhouettes of the hemlock trees into relief, I stood in the main field, holding my clothes, packed into a pillowcase (my uncles' substitution for a suitcase).

I could not quite grasp that this was the real Camp Ava. I had envisioned the camp so completely that I was certain that my notion of it had to exist somewhere—maybe on the other side of the mountain. The weeks that followed were an encapsulated version of my future country experiences: I went into "nature shock"—stung by bugs, inflamed by rashes, and more susceptible to fear than delight when I found myself alone in the longed-for wilderness. But I would also find what I sought—solace in a sylvan setting. I had arrived a week late in a ten-week season—I might as well have arrived in the next century. In the abbreviated social time span, the week I missed could never be made up. Friendships had formed, rivalries flared. Bunks were divided, and the bunk wars had begun.

Camp Ava had advertised swimming, nature hikes, horseback riding, but the actual activities at camp were diarrhea, masturbation, stripping, and attempted escape. During my nine-week stay, I would experience most of the highlights, with a few personal detours.

Later, I discovered that the camp fee was one hundred dollars—ten dollars a week. A collection had been taken up at Rosie's office to finance my expedition. Special entrée had been gained by my friend Susan's father. All these good intentions came to naught only minutes after my arrival, when the camp managers, Ava and Manny, greeted me with bad news. Ava told me, "There is no bed." There had been a mistake.

Although they were probably middle-aged, Manny and Ava appeared ancient. They had seemingly exchanged sexes—Ava, though dressed in gypsy skirts and a ruffled blouse, had chin whiskers and barked commands in a deep voice. Manny had softened, with breasts drooping onto the ledge of his belly. He spoke in a high, piping voice, squeaking out double negatives. He knew nothing about registration "procedures" we had followed down in the city. There was no bed for me at Camp Ava. They had not been prepared. Every bunk was filled.

A blue light suffused the clearing in the forest. A white mist, an extension of the sugared-looking needles of the spruce trees, infiltrated the air. It was a warm night, but low white clouds settled like an out-of-season frost. The night song of the woods began; crickets sang and insects chittered. The children joined in, with a half-hearted rendition of "Michael, Row Your Boat Ashore." The campfire sputtered and died. It was too late to return to the city. I was left in the care of Ava herself, who, gypsy skirt swinging, led me to her cabin, "just for tonight."

My first-ever night in the country. Ava snapped open a canvas cot covered with Rorschach-suggestible stains and positioned it next to an open window. She pointed out the window to a cherry tree hung with ripe fruit. "You will want to reach out and pick those cherries," she predicted. "Don't do it. I know how many are there." The minute Ava fell asleep, I leaned out and plucked those cherries. And, of course, they were the most juicy cherries I had ever tasted, their flavor enhanced by their being nothing less than forbidden fruit.

I could not sleep in such strange surroundings, far from my familiar city. I passed my first country night in near delirium, a fevered semi-consciousness in which dreams and reality were confused.

Ava awoke at dawn—this was something people did in nature, I assumed, rather than ducking under the covers to postpone the day, as you did at home. Here, there were no high-rise barriers to the sun. Light slashed through the windows sooner than I was accustomed to seeing it. Ava crooked her finger—"Follow me"—and led me from the cabin to the still-dark woods. The grass felt wet, and I saw my first dew—diamonds sparkling on each spare blade of grass. I followed Ava on a narrow footpath that seemed to retravel a dream I had had, down to a pond, hidden far below camp. Rabbits hopped past. Apparently, this was the time to spot wild animals. They got up early, too. We reached the lower end of the pond, draped in mist. Ava stepped onto a rough wooden deck and dropped her clothes. I couldn't believe it. Except for my mother, I had never seen a woman in the nude. Ava was older, more angular—her bones supported her skin, which was like a leather casing. Her breasts dangled empty, twin sacks that had once held something more. Her buttocks were shriveled, too, and reflected the droop of her breasts. Despite her lack of muscle tone, Ava assumed the perfect diver's pose, then disappeared beneath the fog.

When she emerged, Ava said that I could swim, but I declined. I loved to swim, but without a bathing suit and in this fogged, exotic atmosphere, I could not imagine myself imitating Ava—stripping and jumping into that unseen water.

Nudity became a theme of the "torture vacation," as I came to regard my stay at Camp Ava. I was kept constantly on the run by the older girls, who pursued the younger campers with intent to strip them. I ended up living a semiferal existence on the edges of the camp. I was having a memorably miserable time, save for two events that redeemed the summer—and, possibly, my soul.

After much debate, Manny and Ava let me stay in a bunkhouse for my age group, the eight-year-old Bluebells. I had only one goal in life—to be reunited with my friend Susan. Susan was ten years old and in an off-limits bunkhouse for older girls; she was a Dandelion. Susan had not exactly forgotten me, her little friend from AnaMor Towers, but she seemed a bit vague and very uncommitted to having me in her bunkhouse. She had already made a new friend—Roberta, plump and pink as a piglet, stuffed into her Camp Ava tee-shirt and bermudas. Susan's lack of interest did nothing to dissuade me; I waged a campaign to get into her bunkhouse, which ended in a sit-in on the basketball court one July night. I reached a stalemate with Manny and Ava: they would not let me join Susan's bunk, and I would not go to bed with the baby Bluebells. The moon was rising, the mosquitoes were whining, and no one knew what to do.

My uncle Len was summoned and arrived by Checker cab from Manhattan. He emerged as if he were attending a spy convention, in complete costume—fedora, trench coat, and carrying a single piece of luggage: a manila envelope. Uncle Len disembarked from the taxi and strode onto the basketball court. He was the ultimate in urban style: he had never even contemplated driving.

Wearing his oxblood lace-up shoes, Len walked slowly with purpose to where I sat cross-legged, glaring at Manny and Ava. He loomed large and cast an even longer shadow. With the moon rising at his back, Uncle Len appeared at least nine feet tall. "I must remonstrate with you," he addressed Ava and Manny. They conferred under the hoop. He spoke of "détente" and the "possibilities of negotiation." Manny and Ava argued—if they gave in to me, all the campers would want the same thing. Uncle Len suggested that they must make a single exception. "After all," he pointed out, "we are dealing with special circumstances here. We are talking about a child who lost her mother two weeks ago." Could they declare an exception, in this one case? No, they couldn't. Voices were raised (although not Len's—like a great actor, he knew that lowering his voice would command more attention). He spoke in his gravest, most Lincolnesque manner: "We are gathered here tonight on this basketball court to decide the fate of one small girl." Still, they resisted. Len offered his urban solution to the problem—check into a hotel.

I lay down on the court—the asphalt had rippled, resisting the thrust of the earth beneath it. "No," I said. "I'm not going anywhere except into Susan's bunkhouse."

A boy counselor appeared, cajoling: "Do it for me. I taught you how to swim and dive."

"I knew how to swim and dive before I met you!" I spit back.

"Negotiations," as Uncle Len would express it, broke down. Manny and Ava retired to their respective rotting bungalows, leaving me on the basketball court to "freeze my tushie off" if that's what I wanted. Of course, it was not what I wanted, and the shadows of the night forest were already encroaching. After a few minutes, when the campers dispersed to their bunks, all that stood between me and the wilderness was the tall form of Uncle Len.

Len had warned Ava and Manny that their actions were ill-advised and there would be "serious repercussions." I didn't know what repercussions were, but I liked the sound of them. But how long, realistically, could I last out here in this alien dark and cold? Already, there were rustlings in the woods, the distant howl of a coyote. The mountain air chilled fast; soon the radiant heat left the asphalt court. I started to shiver.

Uncle Len took off his trench coat and covered me. Then, in a surprise move, he lay down on the court, too. "They are a tough bunch," he told me, but we would prevail. He quoted my remark to the boy counselor: "I knew how to swim and dive before I met you." We laughed together.

That night was my introduction to the true outdoors. The moon rose and stars sequined the sky, in sequence. As Uncle Len pointed out the constellations, I began to grasp the "big picture"—where we were in the solar system. Back in the Bronx, the stadium lights and the urban glow had blanched out the heavens.

For the first time since losing my mother, I dared voice the questions that haunted me: Was it possible that when people died, they didn't entirely vanish but went to other planets? Could souls soar free in space? I imagined my mother among the stars, or living on Mars with a duplicate daughter. Uncle Len and I lost ourselves in these speculations, lost our sense of time, but not of place. With my back to the ground, I felt a part of the globe, turning toward the next day. I had the feeling of being at once diminished and enhanced, part of the glittering infinite above me.

We were brought up sharp to the reality of our situation when Ava and Manny, emissaries from the land of the gross and ordinary, clomped out in flapping bedroom slippers to announce an end to the standoff. They didn't need lawsuits if we got pneumonia. They would break with precedent: I would be allowed to join Susan in the older girls' bunkhouse.

Uncle Len rose and led me to the plank steps of Dandelion House. I inhaled the scent of honeysuckle and listened to the crickets, night critters who, I now knew, chirped by rubbing their hairy legs together.

I tiptoed into the bunkhouse and took my place on a cot beside the sleeping Susan. When I took a final look out the bunkhouse window, I saw Uncle Len, walking backward across the basketball court. He waved his fedora.

His diplomatic mission completed, Uncle Len vanished as he had appeared—in a Checker cab. That left my other uncle, Uncle Gabe, "incapacitated," as he would say, in the children's infirmary. Uncle Gabe recuperated among the children with sprained ankles, poison ivy rashes, and infected wasp bites. His illness was complicated by its cure: the refugee camp doctor turned out not to be a doctor at all. He was a dentist. "He made up the part about the medical degree," Manny and Ava admitted. But the man was a Holocaust survivor, and it was deemed acceptable to allow him to practice whatever he could.

By the time Gabe tottered out of the infirmary, the camp season was nearing conclusion. He emerged with a classic case of city-person-in-the-country euphoria. He sang full-out in the meadows and under the pines. "Oh, love is a river, flowing forever, while by your side, I stumble a-long." In his striped pajamas, Gabe looked like an inmate, which, in a sense, he was, as he "stumbled a-long" on his daily nature hike to build up his strength. He made a point of pausing every few steps to gulp the fresh air—inhaling the ragweed that aggravated his sinuses. He seemed to overdose on *Luft*, keeling over and reeling back to bed.

Gabe fit in well at Camp Ava, socializing with the adult camp counselors and the talent adviser. The grownups at Camp Ava, led by Ava herself, had imported familiar city foods and customs. The menu leaned heavily on tuna fish, caraway-seeded rye bread, challah, sardines, and a steady supply of bagels and deli food driven up each weekend by visitors who nourished the Catskills colony. If we had traditional camp events, such as cookouts, the campfire featured Hebrew National hot dogs—definitely not *trafe*. And no marshmallow was speared without a search on the plastic sack for its kosher "U" rating and its "P" for "pareve." The meals were served in accordance with Orthodox procedure: one did not mix "meat" (*fleishig*) with dairy (*milchig*), which led to incongruous rules at our rests: on Indian Day, the braves and squaws were forbidden to have their ice cream until six hours after the *flesischdekeh* lunch.

Many of the parents and visitors brought signs of the city with them: Roberta's father, a shoe manufacturer, actually peddled his wares from an open car trunk. Mr. Zolotow took sandal orders one weekend and returned with the shoes for his junior clientele a few weeks later. He was supposed to have complicated relationships with Ava and Manny and was later accused of skimming sandal profit. Meanwhile, union leaders had frequent flare-ups over who would get the contract for the next season's tee-shirts.

If the city-country combination evolved into a climactic experience, it occurred on Talent Night, when adults and campers competed in the social hall, displaying a variety of gifts. Uncle Gabe belted out his Jewish gospel, the lone spotlight glaring off his eyeglasses: "Oh, how did Moses ever know, Over ten thousand years ago. About love and charity, clean living with so much clarity." He won second prize: a pressure cooker.

Like Hans Castorp in *The Magic Mountain*, Uncle Gabe evenly divided the remainder of his time at camp into daily hikes to promote strength and sessions of suffering. I began to slip away from my bunk to walk with Gabe. I taught him the camp songs as I learned them. He sang full-out, charging along a footpath lined with daisies.

Uncle Gabe ultimately left Camp Ava, too, following in Uncle Len's large footsteps. Gabe said they would be setting up a new home for me for when I returned to the city.

I spent what time remained at camp delving deeper into the actual woods and also into my alter ego, Deer Girl. Whenever possible, I darted away from the group to explore on my own: this was the forest I pictured. If the camp itself fell short, the terrain did not. There was a great granite outcropping whose shadows, I was sure, hid caves and forests so dark, the green appeared black.

Hearing the echo of my own last dare to my mother—"I'm off to the happy hunting grounds"—I set forth to explore in earnest and one afternoon wandered farther than I ever had before, inching along a rock crevice—my belly against the stone, my back to a gorge spiked with evergreen trees.

I felt the cold breath of the cave before I saw it. Sideways, I wedged myself into the crevice. Once inside, I saw that I stood on a natural balcony. I looked down at a full cavern, complete with permanent icicles and a conical pile of ash at its center. I caught my breath and lowered myself, inch by inch, down the side of the cave, using the creases in the rock as sneakerholds. My heart beat against my tee-shirt. *This was it,* what I had been searching for.

It was freezing inside, and I was shaking from the cold by the time I reached what must have been an ancient campfire site. I reached down and touched the conical pile—it turned to finer dust at my touch. I bent to examine what I was holding and saw traces of color on beads that disintegrated between my fingers. Indian beads? I tried to collect a few, but each time I touched one, it turned to powder. Then, in the midst of the pile I felt something firmer. It was made of metal, silver perhaps—I looked—it was a bracelet. I slipped it on my wrist and knew that I would not take it off for a long time.

The discovery of the Indian cave and the bracelet led to two new pleasures—I wrote down the details of my discovery in my first short story, "The Bracelet," and I also began to confide in my first true boyfriend, a kindred spirit named Frankie who had also broken from the pack and whom I encountered in the shadowy world of my forbidden walks to the cave.

One hot afternoon, I led him down to the secret crevice and showed him how to hold his breath and slide inside the cavern. He gasped—from the chill as well as from wonder. Inside, we held hands, and he gave me my first sweetheart kiss.

We were both eight years old. It would be many years before I knew such perfect love again. I soon returned to the city, to start my new life with my uncles. We lived in the same building, AnaMor Towers, but moved up in the floors and in the hierarchy. While my mother and I had shared the simplest accommodation, a studio, with Gabe and Len I moved into a junior four.

Seven G was located on the top floor. The next flight of stairs led to the roof. I would climb those stairs and open the fire door to step out onto the tarred roof of the building. From there, I could see the roof-scape of the South Bronx, across Grand Concourse to the straight rows of more apartment buildings and the squares of greenery that were our parks. It would be ten years before my next interlude in what I think of as true country. But I often stared up at the night skies, trying to discern the constellations that I now knew were up there. In the insomniac violet glow cast by Yankee Stadium, only one or two of the brightest stars could ever prevail. From that year onward, however, I knew the configurations of the heavens, however hidden, and the greener glades and rock gorges that lay just north of the city. I had the sense of a great unexplored territory that waited and ultimately held a place for me.

f o u r

How many days, months, years does it take for a life to seem "normal" again? After Rosie's death, I lurched awake every day for more than two years. Every dawn, I had to reacquaint myself with the tragedy; why she was gone and how it was that I remained. All that stood between me and the abyss were my two uncles, Len and Gabe, guardians of my fate.

We searched for a way to be together that did not reflect, at every moment, the tragic reason and short history of our being the "family." My uncles continued all the Rosie traditions as best they could.

Every weekend, we went on outings or picnics. We rode buses to the green borders of the city, got out, and walked. We found new outposts of country in the city. Uncle Gabe took me to Poe's cottage, on the Grand Concourse. The cottage was so tiny, it seemed in scale for an eight-year-old. When I walked into the miniature green-and-white house that seemed barely protected from the roaring thoroughfare, I tried to imagine Edgar Allan Poe living there with his child bride, Virginia, who died of consumption. Poe's poems hung, framed, on the walls. Uncle Gabe would read "The Raven" out loud, and Uncle Len would paraphrase Poe's greatest short stories. His favorite was "The Cask of Amontillado." The cottage seemed dark as well as small, as if it existed in some shadow of a sad past. Inside the cottage, I always shivered, but I felt its pull, too—it was hard to leave. And when Gabe and Len led me back to the bustle of the Bronx outside, I would blink, disoriented, almost as confused as Poe might have been if he could walk out and see Alexander's discount store where, I suppose, a pasture had been in his time. It turned out that the cottage, while from the Bronx, had not originally stood on this location. It had been moved there for the convenience of visitors. This fact, supplied by Len, who loved history, added to the cottage's fairy-tale feel. It was like a toy that could be moved, complete with its interior of dark dreams.

I was progressing in the shadowy terrain of such stories; I knew Grimms' fairy tales, too. So the woods remained, as they had been in my experience, seductive but filled with as much suspense and danger as beauty and peace. I continued to want to explore. "Laura the Explorer" became Gabe's nickname for me, and it was he who led me toward more challenging terrain.

Gabe took me upstate to Mount Beacon. What I recall about that first mountain climb was how ill-dressed we were for it—neither Gabe nor I seemed to have any idea of wearing outdoor sports clothes. I wore a dress and Mary Janes, while Gabe sported his usual costume— a business suit and polished street shoes.

We climbed rapidly at first, following a trail. I recall the season as autumn. For some reason, there seemed to be more yellow leaves that year, and I remember the day in shades of gold and gray. Gradually, the angle of the ascent became sharper, the walk became a true climb, then a rock scramble. We held on to roots and branches to tug ourselves to the top. We both were winded but exhilarated when we reached the summit. There, I saw for the first time the sweep of the glacial formation that had carved out the Hudson River Valley. From where we stood, we saw no sign of man. A wind blew; the atmosphere seemed different, thinner. We both took a deep breath: for the first time in my life—and perhaps in Gabe's—we had plenty of *Luft*.

The descent was more difficult than the climb; the angle was so steep, we slid. Gabe often reached out to hold my hand, but his shined shoes had no traction and once we both fell and tumbled a ways down the slope, caught short at the edge of what we both regarded as a cliff. Solemn at our escape, we took the rest of the mountain in silence. Our joy at the bottom was heightened by our near miss. We shared an apple and two peanut butter-and-jelly sandwiches, and in the aftermath of our adventure, they tasted like ambrosia. We rode a bus back to the Bronx in silence, a silence that we shared like the best of conversations: we were satisfied.

Len and Gabe maintained my mother's celebration of the moveable picnics, but they had their own bachelor style. They were innocent of "picquenique" flourishes. My uncles were uninfluenced by charming French films or Impressionist paintings depicting the languid pleasures of the al fresco meal. They did not think in terms of baguettes, ripe cheese, or voluptuous clusters of grapes. Even the classic red-and-white-checked cloth seemed to wave good-bye, replaced by a king-size paisley bedspread. They had what I thought of as masculine idiosyncrasies—Len believed all picnics should include hot food. He carried along a giant thermos, within which swam boiled kosher franks. They were great-hearted, but my uncles did away with the feminine niceties. Pragmatism prevailed. "Let's skip napkins and use a roll of paper towels," was an uncle suggestion.

We picnicked in the larger parks of the Bronx—Van Cortlandt was a favorite. We would always take time to eye the mansion (which I dreamed of moving into someday) then choose a grassy spot to set out our fare. We would spread out the paisley bedspread, anchor it with my uncles' size-thirteen oxblood shoes, and picnic within this fringed territory.

When I was nine, we were joined by a most enthused fourth—a cocker spaniel pup named Bonny. My uncles bought the puppy for me in an attempt to assuage what they could never quite address—a child's unconsolable grief. The little black spaniel did instantly delight and distract me. And, of course, even on her leash, she dragged me toward country, or whatever could pass for it. Having an animal put me in touch: Bonny lived in the realm of the senses, sniffing and rooting at the earth and the grass. She tugged to run free, to paw the leaves, to snort up life as she knew in her dog heart it should be.

But in the city, a dog leads a somewhat schizophrenic existence. Bonny was, like me, an apartment dweller: she lived in 7G. She wore a collar, had to be walked on a leash. My uncles went one step further and made her wear a plaid overcoat on cold or rainy days. I think she even had galoshes. Len and Gabe could not conceive of a creature that did not have to be so garbed. They said no one in their family had ever had an animal in the home before.

In 7G, it was all too easy to forget that Bonny was a dog. She had a luminous gaze, a simpatico tilt to her head. She was so gentle I could ride her back, so patient I could force socks onto her paws. She seemed to be a member of the family, even down to her preference for kosher corned beef.

"She's not a dog," Len declared. "She's a democrat." It was, therefore, a shock to take Bonny to the park and see her undergo a canine change akin to Dr. Jekyll's. In the park, her entire visage would move forward in a feral way, accentuating a prognathism that was less apparent in the junior four. Her usually soulful eyes would glow: twin red lights seemed to flare in them. And worst of all, she would bark at squirrels and give murderous chase. In a real lapse of taste, Bonny (our Bonny!) would clamp her teeth into a rotted critter carcass and return wild-eyed, reeking of carrion.

She had other instincts, too, some less alarming. One afternoon, Len and Gabe and I rented a rowboat at Van Cortlandt Park lake and set forth with Bonny, snout pointed, at the prow. It took about three seconds for her to dive overboard and demonstrate the swim-to-retrieve style that was her heritage and which had been hitherto unused in her living-room existence.

Of course, I loved that dog, who sometimes was not a dog but a friend, a sister. She led me daily for the most routine of reasons to the parks. So, each day, I was reminded of the natural world even as it was adapted to the Bronx. One day I found a demi-cave, a rock niche that just fit my back, a natural seat where I could relax while Bonny exhibited her "wild thing" behavior.

But for ten years, my visits to real country were peripatetic. For a time, I attended a day camp that accentuated the fact that it wasn't real country. I commuted each day to a suburb outside the city where the Jewish Y had a civilized camp, cyclone-fenced and well-patrolled by lifeguards and counselors. The children put in almost a workday, reversing the journey of the adult suburbanites. We spent almost as much time in the bus on the clogged city highways as we did at the camp.

One afternoon though, at even this short remove from town, I discovered a thicket, somehow left unmowed, and within it, hidden like garnet jewels, clusters of black raspberries. I picked in a blind passion: for a time, nothing mattered but that next berry. I stained my lips and fingers purple and almost missed my bus back to the Bronx.

For the finale of the season, the day camp offered a single overnight. The magical word "sleepaway" was invoked.

On the big day, I boarded the bus with a duffel bag stuffed with a sleeping bag, a pillow, a flashlight, and a change of clothes. My heart pounded in anticipation—I had been unable to sleep the night before. I could not have been more excited if I had been off to Yellowstone.

At four o'clock, the buses pulled away—without the overnight campers. We were left at our campsite to watch it undergo the transition to night. I felt an odd undertow, as if I should have left, as usual, on the bus. There was a weird sensation of being abandoned in what now should have been the deserted camp.

The pool was empty—birds darted, dipped a wing. Without all the campers—just the handful that had signed on for the overnight—a silence fell that made me aware of how much noise actually surrounded the camp: the roar of two adjacent highways, overhead jets.

That night, I lay in my sleeping bag, looking up at a sky that reflected the red glow of the city. I could not only hear but feel the hum of the highway. I could not sleep, aware of the distant diesel thunder and the deep snores of my fellow campers. I watched the dawn come up over Pearl River and waited for the bus back to the Bronx.

That sleepaway left me forever with the belief that if you are to leave the city behind, you should go as far as possible. The real danger lies in limbo, in the land neither city nor country—the aptly named suburb.

The next time I left the city, I vowed, I would really *leave* it.

f i v e

I returned to the country, briefly, when I was eleven and my uncle Gabe forty-one. Gabe was, as he put it in his song, "lookin' for an on de level lay-dee." He hoped to find one at the Pioneer Country Club, a white-stuccoed Orthodox resort in the Catskills. I have no idea why he took me with him, but I was glad to go. I packed my moccasins and a pink taffeta princess dress. Uncle Gabe bought an entire new wardrobe for himself—which isn't saying much.

Gabe seemed to own two summer outfits and two winter outfits. All his clothes were outdated, appearing vintage even when new. Uncle Len, who ordered his clothes custom made from Abercrombie & Fitch or a tailor in Hong Kong, disapproved of his kid brother's wardrobe. "You won't have any luck in that bow tie and those baggy pants," he would warn Gabe anytime he stepped out. While for summer evenings, Len might wear a white linen suit, Gabe would show up in a short-sleeved acrylic sport shirt and drooping trousers. He seemed not to own any casual shoes, so he wore those shined oxblood lace-ups wherever he went.

My uncles' costumes advertised their differing romantic styles: both were long-term bachelors, but only Gabe yearned to change his status. He was ready to propose marriage at first sight. Len was elusive and, as a result, was pursued by amorous women all his adult life. He

would not have set foot in the Pioneer Country Club, which billed itself as a place "where the single Orthodox meet."

Gabe was ardent; he wanted a wife. He had heard matches were
made up at the Pioneer, and he was determined to find a bride there.
He packed his unattractive new clothing, extra pairs of his wire-
rimmed glasses (he often dropped and broke them), and fresh note-
books in which to record his "yearning, burning" poems and songs.
Len gave Gabe a farewell lecture, advising him not to appear so eager.
"Don't show them the poems right away," was one tip; another was to
"hold off on any proposals until you're back in the city."

Then, in a reprise of our trip to Camp Ava, Gabe and I boarded a
city bus for the mountains. Again, Gabe sang of travel—"Oh, they say
you are leaving this valley"—as he retched, regularly, along the way. At
a decayed Sullivan County rest stop, we were met by the Pioneer lim-
ousine, a limping Chevy into which were crammed some eight Pioneer
guests, prospective love interests. Gabe was outnumbered: all the other
passengers were single Orthodox women, wearing incredibly red lipstick, eyeing him with fixed stares. He crumpled against the car door,
overwhelmed.

I was looking forward to the green mysteries of the mountains, a
chance to explore. By this time, I had breast buds and the beginnings
of my own tendrils of need. I hoped there would be cute boys.

From the onset, the vacation centered around Gabe's attempts to
"woo," as he put it, the most intimidating of the amorous Orthodox:
Rebbetsin Esther Finster, a formidable redhead with steel teeth, who
seemed to have marched over to America from her native Poland. She
was built like a refrigerator (I later realized this was Gabe's type) and
she seemed to have set herself squarely in position to return home
with a new husband.

What had happened to her old husband? everyone wondered.
After all, the woods were not filled with unattached rebbetsins, rabbis'

wives, on the hunt. The other women whispered around the patheti-cally small swimming pool of a scandalous divorce—a *get*. The fierce rebbetsin had caught the rabbi fooling around and would have none of it. I imagined her tossing him like a shotput. She did not wish to re-main single, however, and she advertised her cooking and homemak-ing skills.

Around the rebbetsin, Gabe, normally shy, became almost cata-tonic. His eyes misted as he gazed at her freckled face: he was in love. "Esther, Esther," he immediately wrote in his poetry notebook. "She is the best-er."

Gabe followed the rebbetsin on walks around the country club. I came along, I suppose as a chaperone. The grounds were a pathetic at-tempt to tame nature, to turn an inhospitable mountainside into a manicured Westchester-type club. The single groundsman, a tooth-less immigrant from Russia, had to groom such steep slopes that his hand mower seemed almost to get away from him. Every day, we watched this small, gnarled man, Hymie, disappear over a knoll, prac-tically dragged by the mower. The result was an eccentric herringbone pattern that zigzagged down the mountainside.

The Pioneer's buildings all were whitewashed stucco over cement block with turquoise trim. The main building and guest cottages sat on the uneven landscape like installations. Here and there, a handball court stood, cracked concrete, facing the sun. The tiny pool had cracks, and green algae clung to its sides. The effect was of a lost civilization, left in the Catskills equivalent of the Amazon.

Inside the buildings, the damp cement, the scent of mildew and the chlorine used to combat it, created an atmosphere of sanitized decay, a losing battle against nature. Mold grew everywhere in spite of the chlorine.

The guests claimed they came for the fresh air, the surroundings, and, most of all, the food. The food was as awful as it was abundant.

The dining room was an arena of pain for me: not only did I disdain *schmaltz* herring and whitefish, two staples, but I was subjected to a round table of inquisition at each repast. "So why is an uncle here with a niece? What happened to the parents?" was a typical guest interrogation.

I would look down on my plate with its hammered bronze fish and feel as dead as the carp. Uncle Gabe suffered, too. We were both unable to answer. "It's a long story," he would say in a choked voice. "Let's not go into it."

Soon I gravitated to the recreation center with its canteen and snack machines. I lived on pretzels, chocolate bars, and chips for the duration.

I was nourishing a small crush on the young man who bore the title of social director. He was distinctly cute—macho Jewish in the Israeli tradition with curling Paul Newmanesque hair and azure eyes. He was built and paraded a tanned torso by the tiny pool each day.

Meanwhile, I was being pursued by a twelve-year-old boy, Melvin, who wore a crocheted yarmulke attached to his hair with bobby pins. Melvin was pale, serious, and sweet—he had a thin, poignant visage, as if his face had been designed to accept disappointment.

His eyes were the color of water and seemed always to swim with tears. "But I like you," he would say, following me around the grounds. "I really like you. You're the only one." I often wore my pink taffeta princess dress, which showed off the beginnings of my figure, and a matching bow in my hair. "You're so pretty," Melvin would murmur. "None of the other girls are pretty like you are."

While Melvin yearned for me, Uncle Gabe yearned for the rebbetsin, and I yearned for the social director. We walked in circles all week, seeking signs of reciprocated love. Gabe courted the rebbetsin against Len's instructions: he proposed almost at first sight, showed her the love poems, and escorted her from one activity to the next.

She soon began to make a gesture with her hand, as if swatting away flies, when he came near. I played hard to get with the social director—I struck silent poses, pretending not to watch him as he led us in song fests or on nature hikes around the so-called lake. In my silence, I spun imagined conversation in which we vowed our passion. I planned an entire life while he wove baskets in the arts and crafts hall. I foresaw the wedding, our children, even a triumphant return for an anniversary at the Pioneer Country Club. My sexual knowledge at this time was incomplete—I thought intercourse occurred without penetration, a gentle nudging at the gates, so to speak. I also still believed what an older girl had told me—that boys developed permanent erections. I had seen no evidence to contradict this. In point of fact, the social director wore a brief red-and-white-striped bathing suit pulled taut by a drawstring that threatened to pop against the strain of his male part. He tilted upward at a sharp angle, to the right, the direction I assumed our future might take. I interpreted the smallest gesture—tossing me a basketball, for example—as evidence of his interest.

The main activity at the Pioneer Country Club was eating, but some sport was introduced to "work off" the leaden meals. After each meal, we walked, "stretching our legs," and on occasion (though never on shabbos), ancient horses were led in for the Orthodox guests to ride.

I was excited by the possibility of the horses, and I begged Gabe to sign up for riding. He agreed and invited the rebbetsin to join us. And so it passed that we were led to three swaybacked nags. I can still see Uncle Gabe trying to mount his retired police horse. Rebbetsin Esther climbed onto a stouter mare: she looked prepared to ride in an invasion. I had lied to Gabe and the pony guide, swearing I had experience. None of us even knew how to hold the reins or sit on the saddle. There were endless adjustments to the stirrups before we took off. And take off we did: my mistaken cry of "Giddyap!" sent all three horses into full gallop. It turned out that they were heading for the barn, where their main meal waited.

This was their single burst of energy for the day (perhaps for the summer). Our rear ends levitating, our hands clutching leather, we bounded off down the bridle path of the Pioneer Country Club. Gabe's yarmulke flew off, like a tiny silk flying saucer. We all screamed until, at last, the horses, winded, reached their feed trough. There, the three steeds abruptly lowered their muzzles into the trough, and all three riders slid over their heads and tumbled to the ground.

Sore and humiliated, we marched back to the Pioneer, but later embellished the tale at a dinner of herring and *tsimmes*, grated carrots. That night, even I enjoyed the dinner, which culminated in the comfort of a cheesecake. Danger was what we had needed, it appeared, to add relish to the vacation.

Emboldened, Gabe asked the rebbetsin to take a moonlit stroll by the lake. Lake was a misnomer—there was a shallow bog at one end of the Pioneer Country Club. A beaten footpath circled the body of water, most likely carved out by the tread of guests seeking a non-weed-clogged point of entry. Plenty of underbrush and several weeping willows provided a veil of privacy for lovers.

Again, I was invited to accompany Gabe and the rebbetsin. Perhaps it was against Orthodox rules for a man and a woman to walk alone together by moonlight. I myself was followed by Melvin, who whispered, without a hope of convincing me, of his lasting love and admiration—"The other girls aren't pretty *at all*," he said. Meanwhile, I kept my eyes peeled for my Adonis, the social director, who was known to take night swims—if an attempt to navigate the clotted pond could be called swimming.

We met with disaster. As we sat by the murky shore of Pioneer Pond, we heard a strange new noise. At first I thought it might be the lapping of low waves against the muck. But there was no movement on the surface of the water. Then I interpreted the recurrent moist sounds as the suction of frogs or other amphibians entering the mud.

Only the rebbetsin was sexually experienced enough to recognize what we heard. The social director was having intercourse with an unknown but well-lubricated female under the willow tree. In a glimpse I will never forget, I saw through the curtain of green the nude forms of the handsome young man and a girl with upraised white thighs. They were oblivious of everything but each other and never knew the three guests had observed them.

The rebbetsin snorted and led Gabe and me away, but not before that sound effect of coitus registered on us all. I felt a sharp squeeze on my ribs, the pain. Oh, why couldn't it have been me? I was only eleven, but I felt I was ready. The social director had chosen someone else. I saw our entire future vanish, replaced by the uncensored vision of the entwined limbs. In spite of the smarting disappointment, I acknowledged that what I had seen was beautiful, but Rebbetsin Esther said I must forget it. That night, she turned down Gabe's proposal, and I refused to kiss Melvin.

In the morning, we all left the Pioneer Country Club, oddly enough vowing to return.

"I feel completely refreshed," Gabe said, retching on the bus ride back home.

s i x

An "out-of-town" college. The expression lured me as "sleepaway camp" had—another pull north toward the great unknown of the country. I didn't quite grasp the distinction of an Ivy League college, but I wanted the ivy. I was determined to outdistance my fellow high school graduates, at least geographically. Most of my friends were set to attend City—City College, a short subway ride away, in Harlem.

I longed to go farther. I had read enough books, seen enough movies, to imagine a college campus in the countryside. I imagined stately buildings against a backdrop of blue mountains.

So I sent off applications to distant colleges upstate and in New England. And it came to pass, one spring day, that Uncle Len and I boarded a train from Grand Central station to check out a small state college on the Canadian border. We both wore trench coats and shades.

I can't imagine what the upstaters thought of us—I'm sure we looked quite unwholesome. My trench coat was white, and as an added touch, I wore matching white vinyl boots. With a wraparound head scarf and outsize sunglasses, I must have looked as if I were trying to visit the campus incognito. Len always appeared as if he was trying to be incognito, so I imagine we drew double takes as we stalked the campus, seeking out sylvan charm.

The campus was verdant enough, and there were purple mountains in the backdrop. But the orientation office made the mistake of showing film clips that depicted their winter season—students bundled like refugees from the siege of Leningrad, staggering through ice tunnels to reach their classrooms. It looked like a death trek. The dean also mentioned the skewed sex ratio—four girls to every boy.

I essentially said to Len, "Get me out of here." We rushed to catch the next train back to New York City. The image of those arctic, boy-less winters had cooled my heels. Instead, I compromised and chose a school not so far north, near Albany.

The best part of the college was the train ride up, a scenic tour of the Hudson River Valley. I thrilled to the vistas on both sides—the river, gleaming, reflecting the skies and the shoreline, alive with deer, quacking ducks, marshes. Here and there along the way, I glimpsed turreted Hudson River castles and cupola-topped mansions.

It was a letdown when I arrived. Albany combined the flaws of the country and the blight of the city without offering the pleasures of either. The small city turned out to be remote and dreary.

The college was set in a brick quadrangle. There was no ivy, only dried-out grass. My dorm was like a slab of Spam, divided into cubicle-like rooms. Somehow, I had not fully addressed the fact that I would have to do something I loathed—share a room with a stranger.

And what a stranger she was. Gladys was eighteen, two years my senior, a girl of prematurely middle-aged appearance—sprayed pageboy, harlequin glasses. She was all pointy angles, and her speech was adenoidal. Her response to any remark was, "That's *noice.*" She was bidding adieu to her parents as my uncles and I entered the room. "Now don't smoke, drink, or get in trouble with boys," her mother warned. The instant we were alone, Gladys whipped out a pack of smokes and a beer, and said, "And I'm not a *voigin.*" Dressed in cardigans and tweed skirts, Gladys appeared conservative. I, in my shades and white lipstick, leotards and black stockings topped by the white trench coat, looked unsavory. But it was Gladys who saw all the action. Our room reeked with her vomit as she retched up her Friday nights. She gave me nasal accounts of her sex life, which featured a boyfriend who spanked her as they parked at the Albany airport (he spanked during takeoffs but not landings). Gladys was my first upstate "intimate," and I observed her as if she were a Martian. I could not get over the fact that we had been matched by the admissions office based on a shared affinity for folk music cited on our housing questionnaires. We soon began seriously not to get along: she hated Jews and beatniks; in her book, I was both. I found myself in the odd position of having come to an out-of-town college to discover new people only to be forced to seek out my own kind. I banded together with the small group of dislocated city transplants: in the cafeteria, I ate with the lone gay guy, the only other Jewish girl, and two black girls from Harlem.

There was little to redeem that single joyless year. I found myself beset by country boys—rough-hewn fellows whose advances made me laugh. "How about a romp-out in my room?" one boy invited. Another said, "I have my grandmother's old featherbed in my room. Just about anything we'd do on that featherbed would be heaven." I stared at the country boys in disbelief. Could such approaches work?

I was at this time quite innocent. I affected an attitude and appearance of experience, but I had yet to do anything beyond fend off the advances of teen-aged boys. My fantasy life was arrested at the juvenile stage, in which, as my alter ego, the Indian maiden Deer Girl, I was pursued by great-looking braves. In my bedtime scenarios, I would mentally explore a mysterious woodland or indulge in dreams of rescue. In my favorite sequence, the handsome warrior White Eagle would appear, an arrow in his shoulderblade, and I would nurse him in secret, in a hiding place behind a waterfall, until he became well enough to try to ravish me. Then, panicked by his response to my care, I might run through the forest, following a zigzag path, half hoping to be captured.

Mores were changing in the late sixties, but not fast enough. It was still possible to be branded a tramp, something to be avoided, even if you secretly thought it might be fun to be a tramp. My sexual experiences in the Bronx were a history of thwarted encounters I called the "zipper wars." I was in the last wave of girls who did not feel quite free to do it. We were saving ourselves, if not for marriage, then for an ultimate love. The line became increasingly fine in my teens: feeling up on top but not on bottom was a credo. Boys and girls alike found frustration in heavy petting or grinding, as the engorged boys strained against their flies and tried to undress the girls, who clung to heavy-duty elastic girdles we didn't need, except as barriers to penetration.

Although I qualified as a promiscuous kisser (thirty-six boys had kissed me good night, pressed against the door of 7G), a sometime heavy petter, and a slow dancer who could navigate "I Am the Great Pretender" while dodging what seemed to be the permanent erections of seventeen-year-old boys, I was, during my first year of college, a virgin. I wasn't especially eager to remain a virgin, but I also didn't want to be labeled a slut. Even in the sixties, easy was too easy. A boy had to earn his entrance, so to speak, or you both would suffer.

So I was at once happy and confused when the first boy to fall in love with me at the upstate college was almost the man of my dreams: an actual Native American (never doubt the power of fantasy). This boy, a pure-blooded Mohawk, seemed to materialize out of my desire at my first "frosh" mixer—an event that pitted the hard-on-afflicted freshmen boys against the trussed-up good girls, or allowed them to slip away for orgiastic but not well-regarded encounters with the more available tramps like Mary the Drainer, who tended to service in quantity (she took care of all of Alpha Beta Chi, earning their ultimate derision and her poor reputation).

Into this charged atmosphere came John Runninghorse, a college freshman version of nothing less than White Eagle. He even wore a necklace with a tribal insignia inside his button-down shirts. At six feet, with black hair and almond-shaped eyes, he was unbelievably handsome with unbelievably bad teeth, which I wondered whether or not to hold against him.

John Runninghorse escorted me from my first dance to a forested nook on campus, a detour I connected to his heritage. If only he could have worn the buckskin, or at least the loincloth, of my day-to-night dreams, my history would have been written that night. But he was poorly costumed in a madras shirt and chinos and, for reasons unknown, was more inhibited than I was.

My journal reports: "J. R.H. Kissed without biting, not sloppy, just right, but *confusing.*" An elaborate code reports that although he strained fiercely against his chinos, a stricter moral code prevailed. He stepped back and said that *he* was a virgin and that he was saving himself for his wedding night.

This remark shocked me more than all the grapplings back home. He tried to explain: "Even if my wife doesn't know, I'll know." I didn't know how to react. I was speechless. All I was accustomed to saying was "Please, stop." I regret to say I let him slip away, a tall figure gliding through the pines.

No mind. I slipped into a pattern of dating the country boys upstate in the more familiar mode of my city encounters. They pushed; I resisted. Eventually, we drifted apart for lack of coital connection. The boys became involved with Mary the Drainer or a girl in B dorm who was infamous for allowing group visits while she lay back on a frayed pink bathmat. Other boys became involved with girls who got in trouble, a condition that still bounced a girl out of college in those days.

There were several sudden weddings and a few girls banished to out-of-state homes for unwed mothers. Everyone would come back to college the next year, deflated.

I was so miserable upstate, however, that before the end of my freshman year I decided to transfer. During the final days of my spring semester, I did feel some stirring of my old longings for the country. In a fit of yearning, I bought several packets of flower and quick-growing vegetable seeds. Never mind that I didn't even like the quick-growing vegetables, radishes, I was anxious for positive results, something to justify this year in exile from the city.

So on a May day, I hopped on a bicycle and pedaled as far from campus as I could, until I found a patch of earth that seemed unspoken for and possibly tillable. Remembering my city apartment gardening, I had thought to bring a soup spoon along with me, and I dug up a good-sized plot and planted my seeds. I worked with a happiness and intensity that must have been akin to some pleasant form of insanity. I forgot my woes, my social failures at the school, my upcoming finals. All that mattered was this admittedly demented endeavor. The sun beams slanted and it was near dark when I considered my work done. I regretted that I had not thought to bring along markers to label my different beds. I trusted that the flowers and radishes would provide their own identification as they popped up from my spoon-plowed earth.

I never returned to my garden. The day after I planted it, I discovered odd pink welts on my hands and knees. By evening, the welts burned with the worst itch I had ever experienced. By the next day, the welts had erupted into blisters; by nightfall, the blisters and I wept. The weeds I had yanked from my plot of earth had been the virulent runners of a spring growth of poison ivy.

My left leg swelled to science-fiction proportions. On campus, elephantiasis was a joke disease. "Heh, heh," a boy in biology class had said to me one day, shoving an illustrated text under my nose. "Look at this guy in the medical book. He has elephantiasis penis. He's pushing it in a wheelbarrow." *Heh, heh.* I hadn't thought the picture amusing (although it was arresting). Now I had the experience of hearing the word applied to myself.

Heh, heh. "She has elephantiasis leg." The taunts added to my pain. I remember limping, dragging my outsize leg as I tried to cross the campus to reach my zoology class. A few country boys sang, "Roll me over, roll me over, roll me over in the clover. Roll me over and do it again." This ultimate irony—that I had not even "rolled over in the clover" but had contracted the poison ivy during a bout of loneliness—pushed me toward the edge. I considered suicide, perhaps the first poison ivy case to do so.

"I can't go on," I moaned to my roommate, Gladys, who must have been between airport spankings. "I can't stand this awful itching."

"That's *noice*," she said.

I boomeranged back to the Bronx to our family doctor, who gave me cortisone to save my sanity. I limped back to the out-of-town college to finish the semester. I applied for a transfer to a college safe in the cemented city.

No, that spring, while my legs shone pink from the scarring caused by the rash and my face was still ballooned from the cortisone, if anyone had asked if I would even venture out to the country again, my answer would have been *"No."* As they said in those days, *"No way."*

Two years later, I found myself "on location" in Woodstock—making a small independent film. I must preface this tale of how I ended up in the most primitive of rustic settings with a disclaimer: I am not now nor have I ever been an actress. This fact becomes clear if you view the single film in which I received featured billing, a movie shot in the Woodstock of the sixties.

I had been attending college in the city, grateful in fact to be downstate, when I was tapped for stardom. The film's producer, a young man by the name of Joel, whose beret and red beard gave him an appearance of seriousness, tapped me as I ran across Washington Square Park on a June afternoon. He had to sprint after me to do the tapping; I was late for Sociology II. "Hey, you," he said. "Slow down." If the film had turned out other than it did, this would have been a classic moment of discovery—eighteen-year-old college girl, loose-leaf binder pressed to her chest, discovered on her way to an evening class.

I stopped. The hour was the most beautiful of the day—the final hour of sunlight, the "magic hour" as it is known to filmmakers for the surreal glow it casts upon faces and the intensity it adds to color. "You," said the producer, "are the one." Told that I was perfect for the role of a young girl who has survived the nuclear holocaust on a former chicken farm near Woodstock, I was escorted to the producer's office for a quick reading. I was told the audition was a mere formality. I read from Ibsen's *Ghosts*.

I didn't mention my lack of experience or the fact that I had never even had the ambition to act. It all seemed beside the point as the producer exclaimed how right I was for the role and booked me for an immediate costume fitting.

The words "costume fitting", "rehearsal," and especially "location" held magic for me. I believed that this was the beginning of the interesting adult life I had always anticipated. As is my style, I didn't want to know too much going in, as I suspected that the facts would deflate my expectations.

The costume fitting might have warned me. I had imagined an elaborate dress or perhaps a futuristic silver bodysuit. What I saw when I walked into the room labeled, in Magic Marker on a posterboard "wardrobe," was a stack of potato sacks.

My sack had laces up the sides. Each potato sack was cut to a different configuration. There were six sacks altogether. The plot of the picture began to emerge: six sisters had survived the nuclear holocaust. I would be playing the youngest, Lily.

As I was being laced into my potato sack, I was introduced to the director, Jim, an aging munchkin with a human bite mark on his right cheek (a souvenir from a former lover, I learned later). "We found her in the park," Joel said.

There was an odd pause. "I don't know about this one," Jim finally said. He pointed out that I had no background in film or stage. Joel mentioned that I had read from Ibsen's *Ghosts*.

"Oh, all right," Jim said. "It's too late to replace her."

Although these remarks augured ill, I agreed to rendezvous with the rest of the company at dawn the following Monday at Washington Square Park. From there, I was told, the movie company van would take us on location. The park was four blocks from the fifth-floor walk-up that I shared with a boy I'd met in a class entitled "The Art of Crit-icism." I'd lived with him for three months; we'd been in love for six. Our studio apartment was so narrow that we almost had to cleave to-gether to fit into it. The room didn't even have four walls—it had three, the triangular *atelier* of an old brownstone. There was no kitchen—we stored snacks on the windowsill and cooked on a hot-plate. Our life together thus far had been a series of sexual picnics con-ducted on a bedspread on the floor. We did little but make love, sleep, and eat cheese and fruit.

"I can't believe you're leaving," my boyfriend said when I broke the news.

"I can't believe I'm going," I said, heading for the door.

This was our first separation, our first disagreement. He was pout-ing as he turned to bellysmack onto the single bed we shared.

How could I leave him? I wondered. He was my first serious boyfriend. Could I be sure that he would be there when I returned? I hesitated, my hand on the doorknob. Then, trying not to think of the consequences, I opened the door and walked out, letting it shut behind me.

I ran down the four flights to the street, intent on the journey ahead, the promise of that rustic location. As I raced, my fake leather suitcase in hand, across Washington Square Park that dawn, I was sure I was headed for the wilderness I'd always wanted to explore. The city trees quivered in the early morning breeze, a skimpy chorus line fronting for the full show that awaited me upstate. As I entered the park, I could see the rest of the company gathered under a street lamp that was still lit. There was no mistaking my fellow actors. They were the only people upright in the park at that hour.

The cast of *Sisters: 2,000* A.D. huddled over takeout coffee and bagels, the instant camaraderie of the company already established. A few cast and crew members were bidding adieu to their mates. One girl, a blonde named Fran, performed a protracted farewell to her stocky, balding husband, who would be remaining at home to tend their children. She kept kissing him, crying, saying good-bye, then calling him back for yet another final embrace. "Two whole weeks," she wept. "How can I stand to be away from you two whole weeks?"

That night, we all had reason to recall Fran's protestations as the farmhouse set vibrated from her coitus with another crew member. A case of sex at first sight.

Fran's groans and thumpings were almost enough to distract me from the strangeness of my new setting. I had completely envisioned the farmhouse location in advance. The image had been detailed—a white colonial farmhouse nestled in the mountains outside Woodstock. In my projection, the house came furnished with pristine featherbeds, quilts, porcelain washstands. I'd also been sure there would be a country kitchen with a plank harvest table, where I would share robust home-cooked meals with the cast and crew.

But the reality I first saw from my window seat in the van gave new meaning to the word "derelict." The farmhouse stared, hollow-eyed, through its broken windows, half hidden by the high dead grass of a neglected meadow. "Rustic" was the single truth to the location description. The farmhouse was set miles from civilization. There was no clue that we were in the twentieth century. Later, I suspected the producer chose the spot because there would be no witnesses. The farmhouse was so abandoned, it was also possible there was no fee for using it.

The front door swung open, not in welcome but because it was off all but one of its hinges. I did not hesitate—I ran inside. This might not be the farmhouse I'd envisioned, but it was a great stand-in for those haunted houses I'd longed to explore. Inside, the house had been stripped. Faded pale green wallpaper hinted at the past decor. Pie pans had been mounted over holes in the walls and ceilings that had once been the apertures for woodstove pipes. It was summer, but winter had not been banished from these rooms. A chill had settled into the house; damp warped the woodwork, and cold raised wax to the surface of the floor, whitening the boards like a permanent frost. The smell of mildew came from the damp walls, and the open cellar door exhaled a cold breath. Wind whipped freely through the house. The corners of the ceilings were draped in cobwebs, and here and there an actual spider hung, like a lightcord. There were no furnishings save a bare mattress in each bedroom. The kitchen held a warped table and a group of mismatched chairs that had been carried in from the van. There was no heat, electricity, or running water.

I could not suppress a thrill. The farmhouse sagged with rot, but it was still a rural fantasy I could inhabit. It would be my home for the next two weeks. The other actors stalked the abraded floor and muttered about the accommodations. The single sign of summer was the mosquito swarm that began to whine and circle the heads of the actors as we learned the true name of the movie we had arrived here to film: *Sin Sisters: 2,000 A.D.* The producer and director were pressed as to why they had omitted the word "sin" from the title until after our arrival on location. "We just added the 'sin,' " explained the director with the bite mark in his cheek. "It's an art film, but we have to suggest sex to sell it." The plot was now fully revealed: a nuclear holocaust has destroyed the United States and most of the world. There is no intelligent life on the planet except on this defunct chicken farm outside Woodstock. Here, six sin sisters have survived to claw subsistence from the contaminated earth around them. They believe that they are the only humans alive until three brothers appear. The dramatic conflict is built in: how will the three brothers satisfy the six sin sisters?

The director, Jim, like Woody Allen, fed his cast only a page or two of script at a time. We found the first two pages lying beside our stained mattresses. Jim claimed that he did not want us to leak developments of the plot; I suspect he may still have been writing the script or that he feared the actors, if they could read the story in its entirety, would flee.

As I settled onto my stained pallet the first night, I was in the literal dark as to how X-rated the movie might be. I had been assured that I would not have to do anything; as Lily, the youngest sin sister, I would be called upon to interrupt sexual activity rather than participate in it. I accepted this assurance at once. The truth was, it never occurred to me to leave.

I was entranced by the farmhouse. I've always loved empty rooms, and this place was full of them. I was eager to explore the cellar, the attic, the many decaying outbuildings. Also, I liked my companions. The actors were affable and attractive, chatting away, as actors do, of past jobs and future gigs. They tended to be identified by their most illustrious former roles—one sin brother, Frank, had been the City Center Jud in the latest revival of *Oklahoma*. We were awaiting our leading lady, who had been a Shakespeare in the Park Ophelia.

Although far from the circles of power, we could still feel the centrifugal force: most of our conversation revolved around the Obie, Tony, and Oscar awards. We considered ourselves, in this wasp- and mosquito-infested farmhouse, in the business. The production of *Sin Sisters: 2,000* A.D. mimicked the structure of a bona fide film: the director and the producer had clout; we had a star. There was, therefore, a hierarchy, and the three individuals at the top of it received preferential treatment—not easy to achieve, under the circumstances.

The director and his lover, Kip, shared the large front master bedroom and a large, mostly unstained mattress. A second-floor "suite" was reserved for Briarly Lee, the Central Park Ophelia. She was given the next-largest and sunniest room, the least stained pallet, and her own private, if nonfunctioning, bathroom.

Briarly, especially, was catered to, to ensure her participation. We all knew we were lucky to get her between Shakespearean roles. Not only that, it was on the basis of Briarly's being cast that other actors had signed on to the project. As a result, Briarly had not only been assigned the best sleeping quarters but also, in deference to her position, had not been required to ride up with us in the van. Instead, a car had been dispatched to fetch her.

When the time for Briarly's arrival drew near, the other actors gathered on what had been the farmhouse's front porch. As we watched, the car, a rusted automotive equivalent of the house, pulled up, spluttering from a wounded muffler. Briarly alighted—preceded by her dogs. Briarly alone had been permitted to bring her pets, two black Scotties so overweight their wide backs could have served as end tables. Briarly herself was slim and pale blonde, her hair shaped into a helmet. She looked for all the world like St. Joan, whom she had once played.

Whenever Briarly Lee stood nearby, the other actors' conversation acquired a strained casualness. She was the star, and a force field existed around her for the duration. Briarly appeared asexual-leaning-toward-gay, but whatever her sexual preferences, she maintained a monklike celibacy during her stay. She was quiet and dignified and lent her seriousness of purpose to her role as Violet, the eldest and most controlling of the sin sisters.

Like Briarly, all the other actors had something I didn't— credentials and talent. They were, for the most part, members of the Actors Studio, the New York hotspot that had nurtured Marlon Brando and Paul Newman. The three sin brothers shared a sinewy similarity. They seemed more accustomed to expressing Tennessee Williams's exquisite torments but lent themselves with muscular grace to the conflicts of *Sin Sisters: 2,000 A.D.* The fact that several excellent actors were so employed was a sad reflection of theatrical opportunities that summer. The only good news was that, in 1966, even exploitation films didn't exploit that much; there was an innocence even to our guilt. The single nude scene featured an actress topless—her full breasts bounced. There was little sin among the sin sisters—the film soon came to resemble a demented, nihilistic version of *Seven Brides for Seven Brothers*.

As befitted my novice status, I was given the smallest room and the most stained pallet. My room was below Fran's. Every night, I lay awake, listening to her orgasmic cries and her thrashing efforts to achieve more. Her needs were so urgent and the plaster so old that at her finale a white dust sifted over me as I lay chaste and alone.

By day, the power struggle aped that of more highbrow movies. Jim of the human bite mark had earned his scars. He rode the cast with his whip hand. Kip followed, apologizing, "He doesn't mean it. He doesn't mean it the way it *sounded*." Jim achieved his "reactions" from the actors by screaming at them; later, he actually hit some of them. He had a few favorites among the cast—I was not to be one of them.

Jim adored a girl named Hope, who played my slightly older sister. Hope was an anorexic beauty who had posed for Salvador Dali. I could see why; she had the same surreal droop of so many of his famous paintings. Hope was indulged in all the "arty" sequences of the film. It was understood she would not participate in scenes of sexual activity but would wander, like Rima the Bird Girl, parting foliage and hiding behind her waist-long hair. Occasionally, she would emerge from between fern fronds to utter a faint bird call.

Another actress, Marsha, was regarded as extremely serious and given some good-sized chunks of dialogue. Marsha turned out to have a real boyfriend, who lived in a lean-to in the woods nearby. He showed up on the set one day, and I was stunned but impressed by his scratched and bitten almost-naked physique. And, of course, there was Briarly, the star, who was awarded "preparation time" and brief rehearsals before her major scenes, most of which required her to burst in on her sinning sisters and punish them for their sexual transgressions. "You whore!" Briarly had to shriek in a climactic scene as she pretended to sear one of her sister's hands on a hot stove.

It quickly became clear that *Sin Sisters: 2,000 A.D.* would not be a happy shoot. The cast, uncomfortable on their pallets, unable to bathe except in a nearby river, soon became irritable. Perhaps in retaliation, they began to mate in various combinations. Every night the house shook, the boards groaning with the actors.

I stayed out of trouble for almost the entire filming. I was intent on exploring the land. I became friendly with Kip, who was as gentle as his lover was mean. Kip led me on woodsy expeditions to find wild rhubarb and sassafras. Kip also functioned as the company chef, and he brewed everything we picked into tart stews.

The days turned hotter, and the entire cast itched and scratched. We all were decorated with insect welts and sought relief in the river. We found a rope hanging from a tree on the shoreline, and we took Tarzan-like swings into a deep swimming hole.

The director regretted casting me as soon as he had to shoot my scenes. The truth was, I was awful. As soon as I was aware that the camera was rolling, I felt strained and could hardly move my arms and legs. I remember being directed to walk across the kitchen and feeling every motion become unnatural, as if my arms had turned into salamis. I could not even feign sleep in my sleeping scene.

The director and I were united in a single emotion—dread. I had one big scene in the film, and it was too late to replace me. I had to discover another of the sin sisters, Dahlia (we all were named for flowers), sleeping with the sin brother I secretly coveted (the City Center Jud from the revival of *Oklahoma*).

In this scene, I was called upon to skip, in my innocence, to the henhouse. I held an egg basket in anticipation of gathering the only slightly radioactive eggs laid by the barely mutant chickens, an important source of protein for the sin sisters. It was a demanding scene for me—I had to throw open the door of the chicken house, see the sin brother making love to my sister, and deliver a profound reaction. The other two actors in the scene, Frank and Marsha, were forced to lie on decades' worth of chicken shit and pretend to writhe in lust. At the sight of them so engaged, I dropped my egg basket and shrieked, "Why?" The director was not pleased with my first take. Again and again, I skipped to the chicken house. Again and again, I flung open the door. Frank and Marsha rolled over and over in the chicken shit. At last, at the end of the longest day, my "Why?" seemed to have the right note of anguish, and we wrapped.

Meanwhile, I was being wooed by another actor, the most attractive of the sin brothers who had survived the nuclear holocaust. This actor, whom I shall call K, was definitely cute. He had dark curling hair and a golden complexion that extended to his well-developed pectorals. He had one of those hairless bodies that appear to be naturally polished. He was also soft-spoken and sweet, not a bad combination.

Back in the city waited my serious love, whom I believed at that time to be my one and only, but after almost two weeks on the rhubarb diet and a series of tirades from the director I could not entirely resist K's offer of physical comfort. K was married, and I had no intention of actually making love with him, but I did enjoy his company.

One afternoon when we were not needed on the set, K and I wandered down to the river. We were alone, and we walked through the water, under the overhanging branches of the trees toward a swimming hole, formed by a waterfall and some rock cliffs, and completely secluded. The sensation of being alone in nature with a handsome, nearly naked man was overpowering. The woods and the air seemed to pulsate. Birds shrieked, butterflies fluttered.

I fell under the spell of the situation. K waded toward me in the thigh-high water, and we embraced and kissed. Without warning, the weather changed; the sky darkened and a rain began, pelting the surface of the water, surrounding us with lively circlets. K pressed himself against me. The drizzle turned chilly, and we held each other, conscious of the heat of our skin between us. K caressed me for a long time, in all ways but the ultimate, and wondered why we didn't proceed. "Isn't it just a technicality now?" he whispered, his voice soft in my ear. The river ran fast between our legs.

We returned, wet, to the farmhouse to find that the mood on the set had deteriorated with the weather. Jim had slapped Briarly Lee. The other actors clustered around her. There was more drama in the kitchen than in the script. Everyone was screaming or sulking, demanding to be "let out" of the picture. Briarly's Scotties, who had been permitted on the set, had now pooped on it. K flashed me a look, half grin, half grimace, and tugged at his constricting swim trunks. He was still laughing at what under the circumstances we could call the ache in his loins, when the farmhouse door swung inward on its single hinge, and in walked a woman who introduced herself as his wife.

When I saw K's wife, I thought, *Thank God I didn't get carried away downstream.* She was an angelic-looking blonde whose pale beauty was enhanced by an aura of sadness. The marriage was in apparent trouble, and it seemed to me that she had come up from the city to salvage something. She seemed nervous and dropped her purse, which cracked open and spilled a compact of birth control pills among a scattershot of lipsticks and eyebrow pencils. She left the kitchen with K, and I sat in a chair, listening to their footsteps as they walked upstairs.

They came back down too soon. K looked stricken, wearing the hapless look of a husband who still loves his wife but knows that he will soon leave her. His wife disappeared shortly after, seeming to realize she had inadvertently violated some etiquette of the location, a world unto itself for the time the film was being shot.

Later that day, the director turned his attention to me—I had failed. He had seen the dailies, and I was more awful than he had feared. All my scenes needed to be reshot. The other actors protested, especially the City Center Jud and Marsha, knowing they would be forced, once more, to simulate sex on the chicken shit.

Again and again, we shot and reshot the scene. Again and again, I surprised the lovers cavorting on the dung. Next, we shot the finale—we were forced to run through rain, our pitchforks raised. By nightfall, I had strep throat.

In the damp of the farmhouse, my infection deepened. I shivered on my pallet, unable even to communicate my agony. "Guuuhhh," was all that I seemed able to say.

In the dark of night, K returned to my side on the decaying floorboards. He knelt and nursed me until dawn, offering me cups of tea and reading aloud from an old Hemingway novel he had found in a mildewed pile of books beside my bed. I think K's sweet solicitude cured me. The next day, I rose from my pallet, donned my potato sack, and went back to work, although I was still running a slight temperature. If fevered memory serves, at day's end several sin sisters lay slain on the field, their potato sacks pierced by pitchfork blades.

I bid K good-bye—on camera and off. He went on to divorce his wife and was known for years as the live-in lover of a hot tamale Latin singer. He later made better movies. *Sin Sisters: 2,000* A.D. premiered at Newark Airport. To my knowledge, it was never reviewed.

When I boarded the Trailways bus in Woodstock to return to New York City, I could not have known that I would return fifteen years later to buy my ultimate country place just twenty minutes' drive from where we had shot the film. And I would never have imagined that thirty-four years later I would try to find the location again, to see if the sagging farmhouse still stood. On the day I rode the bus back to the city, I was intent on returning to my boyfriend to see if he was waiting in the little pie slice of a room on a crooked street in the Village.

eight

My boyfriend had waited. In fact, his interest was piqued. We went from being students in love to becoming unofficially affianced. I was eighteen, and he was twenty-four. I regarded him as an older man, and he presented himself as such, jaded by life's experiences. "I've seen it all," he said often.

He was, in fact, quite experienced for his age. He had done his military service, lived in Asia, and spoke Japanese. I had fallen in love with a man my mother would have wanted. He was a Larry type; in fact, his name even rhymed with Larry, and the physical description was exact: he was a country boy, tall, handsome, towheaded. He even had a cowlick.

My fiancé had come to New York from Pennsylvania. He mentioned early on that his father was from a farm family and that his parents kept a weekend place in Appalachia. They owned eighty-six acres, he told me. I was as impressed as if he'd said they owned the Blue Ridge mountain range. In the world I came from, there were no acres, there were only lots.

I could hardly wait to go to his family farm. But my love was working nights as a newspaper reporter, and we had almost no free time. Then, before we could plan a trip, he received an overseas assignment to cover the war in Vietnam. As my disappearance to Woodstock had heightened his romantic interest, his dangerous job similarly upped the ante.

As soon as he went to Saigon, we began exchanging love letters, and our future was sealed—if he returned home from the war.

While my fiancé was in Vietnam, he urged me to visit the farm with his parents and his two sisters. I was thrilled to do so. I took a train to Pittsburgh, and then his parents drove me through the Pennsylvania hill country, down to where the mountains grew steeper, the valleys more shadowed. We drove through a town infamous for its coal mining, where the sun had stopped shining for an entire decade and laundry hung on a line would go black.

The farm itself filled a valley; the road cut through the valley's heart. It was autumn when I visited, and the mountains were golden with flashes of crimson. The farm turned out to be a small red farmhouse, most of its acres spread out behind it, climbing up the side of a mountain. It was as simple a house as could be—painted clapboard with a small porch. Inside, my husband-to-be had taken a pickaxe and smashed through a wallpaper-covered wall to unmask the original fireplace, an event he had described to me in detail back in our room in New York. I'd loved his account—how the wall had been papered with newspapers dating back to 1912. The house had been built sometime in the 1870s. My future in-laws had bought it from an elderly woman who had been born in the house and was still sitting in her porch rocker when it was sold. She sold the farm, rocker and all, for five thousand dollars and went to town to live with relatives. The winters were getting too hard for her.

The farm was located on the West Virginia border, near a town named Happyville. And that was what the farm came to be—a private Happyville. My fiancé's parents were not true farmers, but one of his grandparents had been. His father's father had owned an egg farm and kept goats. The family legend was that life seemed more ordinary after they sold the farm. This weekend place was meant to restore my future father-in-law's pride. And, in fact, it had become the thing he loved most. He was a tall, handsome man, silent to the point of stoicism. He showed little of his feelings, save for a big grin when he'd pull up to the porch in Happyville.

The Happyville farm offered nothing but its natural beauty, the absence of diversions other than the weather, and the chance to spot wild animals. The necessary tasks—drawing water, fetching food—took up considerable time and were, for that reason, somehow more interesting and relaxing than you would expect.

That first weekend, the family had welcomed me, and we all sensed the seriousness of my presence at the farm. I was free to explore the little house with its faded-papered rooms, bare floors, the now familiar pie plates over unused woodstove apertures. There was a barn, with a loft to climb into. I sat up there, looking out at the hills, observing my fiancé's family for signs of resemblance to the young man with whom I'd fallen in love. (The truth was, he didn't look that much like any of them—a bit like his father, but less stern; blond like his sisters, but finer featured.) It was as I sat in the barn loft, wearing, of all things, a white pantsuit, that I felt sure I would be married and that I would be a part of this for the rest of my life.

We were diverted by visits from the local mountain people—a child bride who appeared, trying to give away kittens, a boy who was hunting squirrel for dinner. My future in-laws laughed, but their laughter was a bit strained. They were not so many years or miles removed that they could afford to condescend. When they gathered around a small electric organ that my fiancé's mother played, they sang fundamentalist hymns—"Oh, there's power, power, power in the blood of the lamb"—it wasn't quite a put-on.

Later, I felt a bit alien, too Jewish, too city. My mother-in-law-to-be protested the marriage. "She's too smart," she'd hissed to my husband-to-be when he finally returned from Vietnam. "She's too smart about men." I'd had to jump up from the Thanksgiving table and run around the corner into the small kitchen to hide my tears. "Are you going to marry her?" she'd shrieked.

We'd left then, and we did marry—an elopement at the Fifth Avenue Presbyterian Church, no relatives invited. My husband's mother accepted the marriage after the fact, and we ultimately returned to Happyville. But I never again quite felt the right to be there. My mother-in-law kept pointing to my lack of experience on the farm. "She's never seen a pump before." "She's never ridden bareback." Still, it was fun on that farm. The neighbors, a mile away, had a horse that was led over for us to ride. In turn, we each sank onto her swayback for a plodding circuit of the farm. The horse was so old and so slow, it was possible to believe that she'd been there since the last century, just like everything else.

My in-laws told tales of their past, and their voices became twangier in the recitation. They still had a few relatives who lived in the hills. One, Sky Hart, was notorious for having his wife serve him his meals as he sat on the toilet. Usually, we sat around the fire and listened to country music, which I immediately loved. Again, it was pointed out that I was not even familiar with the greats—Patsy Cline, Hank Williams—but no matter, I loved them, and the bluegrass music, too.

Fortunately for me, there was another outsider in our circle, my brother-in-law Nathaniel, tall, handsome, and intriguing in his silence. Much was made of the fact that he was Russian, although he was a second-generation American. Nathaniel and I communicated our love of the farm without words, in deep glances. I knew we were sharing a reverence for the country as we discovered it.

My sister-in-law laughed and said, "On Friday nights, when it's time to go to the farm, Nat twitches like a *dawg*." I understood his excitement, understood, too, when he bolted, the first to divorce, ten years later. The family suffered a string of divorces—mine being the last—and the farm was eventually sold.

Some years later, I asked my former sister-in-law what had become of the farm, where despite our differences and ultimate separations, we'd enjoyed some near-sacred times. She said that she had wondered herself and had driven back to see, hoping to introduce herself to the new owners. Instead, she found a police barricade across the rural road. An accident had occurred—something to do with toxic fumes or a leaking nuclear reactor. As a result, the farm was cordoned off. And the house? The little red farmhouse? Sealed for a hundred years in a giant plastic bag.

n i n e

Almost the minute we were married, my husband launched a campaign to move out of the city. My old yearning toward the north reawakened.

I'll never be able to separate that first true life outside the city from the sensation of being in love. My husband seemed older than me, more experienced. In retrospect, I can see we were both hardly grown. But I looked to him to make decisions, and I was delighted to go where I had always wanted to explore, north, where the mountains rose and the trees cast their mysteries. He went for different reasons; he hated the city. He was literally kicking up a fuss—screaming at parking meters, having fits over alternate-side-of-the-street parking rules, city rents, and city rudeness.

My husband was a country boy who had had enough of the big city. He wanted grass, land, a place to park the car. He was willing to commute. He had fond memories of renting a carriage house while in college. One Sunday, he scanned the listings north of the city and came up with an ad for "an unusual place in the country: converted carriage house." Always trust fate: we arrived at a gated community, Tuxedo Park, some forty miles north of the city. I did not know its history that Sunday afternoon, but I learned it soon enough. Tuxedo Park had been created in 1885 as a sportsman's paradise for the robber barons of that era. The Lorillards, Astors, and Whitneys all built palatial cottages in a twenty-five-square-mile wilderness that soon included miles of bridle trails and lakes stocked with rainbow trout. Many of the houses resembled castles in England and Europe.

By the time I arrived, the houses were considered white elephants, and many sixty-room chateaux sat empty. A few had been razed to avoid taxes and the high cost of upkeep. Their ruins provided a scenic backdrop—charred armatures rose in the woods, and stone turrets remained where once entire castles had stood.

The carriage house was already rented, but the realtor whisked us to a former mansion known as the Castle that sat stolidly at the top of a mountain overlooking Tuxedo Lake. The Castle had been divided into nine apartments, and the largest, "the great hall wing," was for rent for four hundred dollars a month. I stepped inside the stone castle and caught my breath: *Ivanhoe.*

The apartment had soaring forty-six-foot ceilings, flying buttresses carved by immigrant Italian woodcarvers, a walk-in stone fireplace. A Juliet balcony had been incorporated under the eaves and led to a guest bath and bedroom. The details were grandiose and endless: a library paneled in walnut that opened onto a stone terrace with mountain and lake views. The kitchen alone was the size of our apartment in the city. Not only was the Castle apartment almost comically grand, it came with a baronial dining set and many European antiques (I found out later they were too large to be moved and would not fit the current owner's next home).

In a delirium, we signed the lease, gave up our rent-controlled apartment in the city, and moved to the Castle. The Castle was owned by a judge who had picked up the house when the former owner went belly-up on maintenance. The judge appeared on weekends, trading in his magisterial robes for paint-splattered overalls, as he spackled and painted the halls himself. "It's therapy," he would say from his perch high on a ladder when I passed.

The Castle was my introduction to life in the country—and what an introduction it was. This country was almost foreign. Tuxedo Park was then undergoing a transition and was composed of three social groups: the "old guard," the descendants and kindred spirits of the founding robber barons, the "new people," middle-class professionals who had picked up the white elephants for the proverbial song, and the working class, the primarily Italian-American artisans whose forefathers had cut the stones, carved the buttresses, and hacked out the bridle paths from the thorny woods.

The old guard still lived in the chateaux, but few could afford to do so in the style to which their ancestors had been accustomed. It was not uncommon to hear remarks like, "The Trentbogens can no longer go upstairs: they can heat only two rooms near the kitchen." Their pipes froze every winter, and many an aristocratic family, unable to keep up with their Victorian plumbing, simply moved on to the next commode. They could do this for quite a while; most of the mansions boasted at least eight to ten toilets. The old guard had founded the Tuxedo Club, for which dinner jackets were named and at which a lame version of the original social life still took place. Several charming features had survived—ice skating chairs for the lake, electric boats that silently glided across it, and the descendants of the original rainbow trout and big bass that seemed to have no "hook memory" and would leap to even a proletarian fishing line.

Some vestiges of the old guard were less appealing. There was a high incidence of the "Three A's": adultery, alcoholism, and antiquing. A typical old guard couple seemed to drink and commit adultery out of boredom, as often as their ill health allowed, which was pretty often. They were very involved with their ancestral manses, which had names like Casa Rosa, Morganhead, and Wisteria.

These mansions had such strong personalities that they had to be dealt with in human terms. This anthropomorphism was intensified when the old guard spoke of their homes using the houses' nicknames: "Wisty is a happy house," "I love old Rosie," or "Mo'head is a serious place."

When I got to know a few members of the old guard, I found it hard to separate them from their houses, as they spoke in the voices of their edifices: "My balustrades are crumbling," said one old-timer. "I'm missing my original sconces." Edith Wharton, a contemporary of the original Tuxedo Park crowd who because she was a perceptive observer of her society was way above it, said that people *became* their houses, even looked like them. This was especially true in Tuxedo Park, where the old guard developed a stony-faced, above-it-all condescension to those who seemed below them.

Definitely below them were the new people who had picked up mansions at giveaway prices. Upon my arrival in Tuxedo Park, a chateau belonging to the Empress Zita of Austria was for sale for less than a hundred thousand dollars. The chateau was a three-story mansion on the lake with a series of bedrooms that had accommodated the empress's private order of nuns. Eventually, a doctor bought the house and did away with the many little iron bedsteads and washbasins. Other castles had been purchased by orthodontists and periodontists who comprised what we could now consider a "dentocracy" in the Park. They were fairly well funded and spent fortunes restoring the Casas and Mo'heads to their former glory.

The blue-collar class lived, for the most part, outside the gate in the village on the literal wrong side of the tracks. Some families occupied former carriage houses or stables on "stable row." While this group did not have social cachet, they had power, as they did all the repairs on the crumbling mansions and in winter, held the jumper cables that could revive the dead cars and frozen houses in the Park.

"Who made the world?" asked Vinny, a stonemason who worked on "my" castle wing. "Did they make the world? No, stupid people made the world! With these hands!"

Vinny was one of two caretakers who kept the Castle from falling further into ruin. The other was Albin, who lived on the premises. Albin and his Scottish wife, Jeanie, occupied the ground-floor apartment under the great-hall wing. We shared an entry. In effect, they were our downstairs neighbors.

I soon learned that country places come with country people. They require the knowing services of retainers familiar with the metal guts of their cellars, the slippery scales of their roof, and the ganglia of vulnerable pipes that snake through subcutaneous layers behind plaster and stone.

In the years that followed, I would meet many caretakers who came with houses. But because he was the first, Albin has become my caretaker of record. "Is he like the super?" I asked, city girl that I was.

"Not exactly," answered the judge, who technically had hired him. "Did you ever see the movie *The Servant?*" I recalled a film in which a manservant dominates his master. I think it starred Dirk Bogarde as the malevolent power. Here, in the castle, Albin had the leading role.

Albin had been a seaman in his youth; he still wore a Navy pea coat and a woolen watch cap. Like many caretakers, Albin had a link to ships; he knew boilers. I connect his experience as a seaman with his status as master of the furnace. I would later come to know the sensation myself—of standing in the basement beside the grunting behemoth, eyeing the fire in its belly, and feeling myself the commander of something resembling a great ship. Albin was of indeterminate but advanced age. His face was as white as his thinning hair; he had a glacial stare. He seemed like a refugee from an Ingmar Bergman film, in which he would have been cast as a harbinger of death.

"That's what I don't like" was his favorite expression. I came to know the deep distaste and pessimism that remark barely hid. But my first impression of him had been wonderful. The first time I saw Albin, he was seated with Jeanie in the entry hall of the Castle. They sat together on a carved bench before a roaring fire. A giant collie, Laddie, slept across their feet. They appeared to have been toasting each other with schnapps glasses filled with an aromatic home-brew they called glog. It was a heart-warming Yuletide evening scene, save for a single detail—it was a July afternoon.

Eager to embrace every aspect of our new life in the Castle, my husband and I accepted the warm liquor and toasted Albin and Jeanie. "To life in Tuxedo Park! To the Castle! To being in the country!" My husband and I exchanged glances—wasn't this cozy? The first in a series of quaint images of our new country home.

Jeanie was as sweet as Albin, it turned out, was surly. She was pretty, with pink cheeks, blue eyes, and curling white hair. Jeanie spent her entire day cleaning their apartment, which had achieved a degree of spotlessness not usually seen outside of surgical theaters.

On the afternoon we met, Jeanie offered to show me how she had spent the entire morning polishing the rungs on her dining chairs by up-ending them on her table. I quickly learned that Jeanie had a daily "show and tell" feature. If I tried to pass through the entry hall, she flagged me down with her clean dustrag and a remark like, "Aye, I've just cleaned the rubber of my Frigidaire. You wouldn't believe the dirt hiding in the grooves. You know that black soot that can get into the creases? Well, let me show you how it looks now, so bright and clean." Jeanie executed similar displays of food. "We'll be having these two nice lamb chops tonight for our supper. Don't they sit pretty next to that mint jelly I put with them?"

Albin and Jeanie seemed to have made a miserable marriage, which was in no danger of ending. Albin had won the war for control. Jeanie could not drive, and the Castle stood three miles from the nearest food shop. Thus, she had to be driven to town for even the most minor supplies. Albin took his time about accommodating her.

Jeanie could often be seen in the entry hall, seated on a faux medieval bench, her purse at her feet. The bench, with its carved gargoyles and claws, seemed to reiterate the vulnerability of her position. She might wait an entire day. If I offered to give her a ride to town, Jeanie would say, "That's what Albin wouldn't like."

Albin seldom left the grounds of the Castle or the bowels of its basement. He spent his days seeking out damage and attempting to repair it. He would greet me with non sequiturs: "Leak in the basement"; "Got to patch the roof"; "Rats in the garbage." Albin's nemesis was the flying squirrel. "That's what I don't like," Albin would say, pointing to the damage the little critters had caused. He'd been obsessed with them for years. The flying squirrels leapt from the adjacent hemlock trees into spaces below the Castle's eaves. Once within the sanctuary of the Castle, they gnawed at the hand-carved beams.

"That's what I don't like," Albin would repeat. "They *shoo*. They *shoo* the wood." It took me a few weeks to realize that Albin was saying "chew." By then, I was on the side of the squirrels. They were adorable—I could see them spread their winglike underarms and fly. They could also be overheard chattering their excitements.

Whenever we had guests who stayed in the balcony bedroom set under the eaves, they would descend in the morning with accounts of "munching" sounds in the woodwork. Indeed, a rodent social whirl was taking place over our heads.

Albin tried every means to bring down the flying squirrels. Traps, poison, and, eventually, a shotgun. It was a miracle anyone at the Castle survived. In his blood lust, Albin could have taken us all out, and we would have ended up as one of those gory stories recapped on the local news.

Finally, Albin seemed to go around the bend. He wandered the grounds muttering, "They *shoo*, they *shoo* the wood." One night I spotted him under a full moon, in his pajamas, on a spire of the Castle. He was armed and dangerous.

His nature, always ill-tempered, worsened, and he turned his flinty gaze upon me with the same squint he used for his rifle sights. Had I left my car in the wrong part of the Castle driveway? Was that my lint in the Castle laundry machines? "That's what I don't like," he said. Cars parked downhill. Fluff in the dryer trap.

Ultimately, Albin got to me. I dreaded going out of my apartment for fear of running into him. He seemed to loom from every dark cranny. Between him and Jeanie, waiting in the wings to display her lamb chops or shiny linoleum floor, I knew I could not make a clean exit from the Castle.

The Castle itself did not wear so well over the long haul. When heating oil became more expensive, the concept of warmth in the building essentially vanished. The furnace produced only enough heat to protect the pipes and the woodwork. The Castle was maintained at a steady forty-six degrees. The walk-in fireplace became almost that. Often I stood with my backside in the fireplace. At night, I slept in two layers of long johns and under three comforters. I came to appreciate battery-operated socks. I briefly considered buying a similarly wired body bag. The advertisement for it was ominous—a person swaddled in hot-wired bunting, stuffed into a recliner, apparently for the duration.

I came to know the true meaning of being cold. Cold all the time. My first reaction was to restrict my radius of operation—I would shuffle from the couch to the stove and back for constantly bubbling soup. Any detours—to the bathroom or to actually risk a bath or change clothes—were undertaken in sudden dartings.

Eventually, I learned the secret of the Nordic peoples. Outdoor exercise. I clambered around on cross-country skis. Cross-country skiing burns eight hundred calories an hour. Unfortunately, I also had to consume eight hundred calories an hour to stay warm. Nonetheless, I did adapt. In fact, some of my most ecstatic memories of country life in Tuxedo Park revolved around trying to stay warm. I ice skated across the three-mile lake on *glace noir,* the perfect, bumpless black ice that forms under ideal conditions. I skied some fifty miles of bridle paths. I lived a life I witnessed in movies depicting survival treks, such as *Jeremiah Johnson.* I learned how to build a crude campfire in the snow and subsist on charred kosher hot dogs.

I imagined myself as a Native American scout in the original wild land *T'kucedo*—Ramapo for "lookout." Like a character in one of the Grimms' fairy tales that I had both loved and feared as a child, I fell under the dark spell of Tuxedo Park. I led a beautiful if brooding existence in the shadows of the giant hemlocks. I loved wandering alone through the woods, coming upon the ruined stone ramparts of some long-ago castle. I found flowers blooming where formal gardens had once stood. Now the walls and statuary lay broken down, but the lilacs and peonies flowered, unseen except by me. I picked the flowers and carried them home. I was the robber barons' unlikely heiress. Often, I spent entire days without seeing another human being except for Albin and Jeanie. I started at the sight of the woods creatures, the rabbits that hopped out of my way, the guinea fowl I flushed from their hidden nests. I came upon a large flock of turkey vultures skulking, black wings hunched, as they stared down from the remains of stone parapets.

Because I seldom saw anyone as I climbed the lonesome trails to the mountaintops, my thoughts turned inward, an exploration of the uncharted territory of the self. I fell into the habit of addressing my thoughts to someone else. I didn't know quite to whom I spoke, but gradually I realized that my train of thought had become an intimate revelation—*If only you were here.* I didn't know then, as I clambered along in hiking shoes or on cross-country skis, that I was gliding out of my marriage toward an unknown other. If my husband walked with me, he did so in impatience. He would keep asking, "Are we there yet?" His habits—skipping stones, slashing off tree limbs—annoyed me. I never saw the wildlife with him; he created so much noise, the animals were scared off. Ultimately, I stopped asking him to accompany me, and I wandered on alone, going farther, deeper into the woods that held me in a growing enchantment.

Tuxedo Park was conducive to such romantic, if lonesome, reveries. Its beauty was somehow sad, and even a bit threatening. The area was cast in a deep emerald shade; the pitch of the cliffs was steep. The woods were as dark as the Black Forest of Germany. There were glens that the sun seemed not to penetrate, that gave off the musty exhalations of caves and mushroom. Only the oval of the lake was unshaded, and there, the glare cut at your gaze like shards of glass.

Day after day, the woods and mountain called to me. Each time, I ventured farther than the day before. I grew stronger, the muscles in my legs delineated. I not only hiked, I climbed and swam in deep, forbidden lakes, accessible only by miles-long trails. I was silent most of the time and wrote things in my diary like "Conversation replaces thought." My joys were small moments of discovery—turtle eggs, like leather, set into a lakeside nest. My victories were private—a deer led me to her fawn, curled in a secret sleeping place, the grass flattened into bedding, fresh and green. A porcupine froze in midclimb to stare me in the eye. Sometimes, I stayed out too late, and dusk deepened the shadows among the trees. The calls of birds turned to night shrieks. Then I would quicken my pace, walk faster, faster, till I found the final trail home.

Some nights I went out deliberately to have adventures denied to me by day. The main lake was off-limits to swimmers, so I slipped amphibianlike from the shore. I would enter the water, barely cooler than the air, and take long, nervous swims, scared of being apprehended by the police or something inhuman. One night, I borrowed a canoe from the clubhouse docks and rowed silently across the lake to enter the subterranean tunnel that led into the boathouse of one of the greatest abandoned estates. Another dawn, I entered an abandoned mansion. A doe walked out the front door, passing me in the marble foyer.

My first solo hike promised the thrills that followed. On that initial walk, I set forth, as I almost always would, alone. I was twenty years old, slim but not in truly good physical condition. I carried a pack of cigarettes. The walk down the mountain from the Castle left me breathing hard. At the foot of the hill, I tossed away my cigarette, snuffed it out under my sneaker. The fresh air, yearned for since childhood, burned my tobacco-scarred lungs. I opted for *Luft* and inhaled.

Determined to make a fresh start, I marched on to the lakefront and entered an area that I later dubbed the fern forest, a low-lying marsh of delicate greenery. As I gasped at the beauty of the spot, my intake of breath turned to a scream—a six-foot-long snake slid, heavy, over my sneaker. I can still feel the weight of it, see the black tire-tread width of its body.

I screamed, and no one heard me. The snake slid past, focused on its own destination. I caught my breath, and walked on.

t e n

The Dump, famous for its discarded Victorian treasures, was set an easy half-mile behind the Castle. The walk was a former bridle path that wound through a pretty stretch of forest. I took this trail every morning. Because of my early arrival, I was often the first to pounce on the day's most valuable discards. The great mansions were continually being sold or remodeled, and whenever a change occurred, much of the old houses' contents seemed to end up at the Dump. Over the years, I found many items of historic interest—a collection of letters, dated 1789, written on board an oceangoing steamer to England ("Everyone is travelling," the author complained in his spidery hand. "The seas are overcrowded this season. There's nowhere left to go.") I found photographs belonging to famous families—the Burdens, the Harrimans— including a sepia snapshot of a young man and woman labeled "His First Proposal." My very first trip to the Dump yielded treasure—a brass bed and a steamer chest labeled "Marseille 1880." The chest was still packed with priceless linens and china plates wrapped in tea towels to prevent breakage. I felt I had discovered the equivalent of the *Titanic,* and recalled the "treasure chest" my cousin Willy and I had found at the "end of the city."

I was forty miles to the north now. From the Castle tower, I could, on a clear day, see the Empire State Building: spires from opposite cultures. I was a refugee from one, a new colonist in the other. The green woodland of Tuxedo Park became a kind of cathedral, and I worshipped nature with the reverence that had begun on those litter-strewn lots in the city. My meanderings were always meditative. The walk to the Dump was the most motivated: I loved the promise of a surprise at the end. Sometimes, I was so excited by the environs and the thrill of discovery that I ran all the way there.

One day, I found a triple-paneled hand-painted screen depicting scenes of colonial life in the Hudson Valley. Another morning, I discovered a locked chest. Inside were sealed bank envelopes containing old, folded bank notes. A black lace Victorian dress, along with stays and pantaloons, was also inside. I could not have imagined a more perfect gift.

Of course, this situation was too good to last. Enter the Phantom of Tuxedo Park, also known as Panty Man.

Panty Man. As I scored more and more marvelous objets de trash, I began to notice something strange happening in the woods surrounding the Dump. One morning, I looked up and saw that the trees were wearing underwear. High in the branches, deliberately arranged, were panties and outstretched brassieres. I let out a small squeak, but I was loath to give up my daily adventure because some unknown person dressed the branches in lingerie.

Every day, I trekked in, but I became more alarmed as the panty parade appeared to get more elaborate, closer to the Castle, more intrusive at the Dump. Did I want to meet the person responsible? Who was he? What would he do if I came upon him dressing a bush in panties? Was he dangerous? I kept on, wincing, but my heart pounded, and I found myself jumping at the snap of a twig. I began to invite friends and neighbors to walk with me, which went against my solitary nature. One neighbor surprised me by asking, "Aren't you afraid of Panty Man?" So he was known to others. "Yes," my neighbor elaborated. "I saw a maple tree wearing a Maidenform bra and panty set. I ran." But she, too, was determined not to give up the woodland jaunts out of fear of Panty Man. We theorized that he was not an underwear fetishist or a pervert but an antique dealer who wanted to scare off anyone else who might snare valuable finds. This theory fell apart when one day we saw small dolls, heads and legs twisted askew, hanging in trees that also wore panties. No antique dealer, we felt, would go that far. I began to tremble on my daily walks, and I always went with the neighbor lady, who was also scared but undaunted. We continued to find Victoriana—parasols, a Tiffany lampstand—but our fear overshadowed the joy.

One morning, my neighbor was ill. I decided to risk the hike to the Dump alone. It was a beautiful day, with more light than usual dappling the trees. The woods were alive, as always, with bounding white-tailed deer, hopping rabbits, bandit-eyed raccoons clambering up tree trunks. I saw no evidence of new panties or any sign of Panty Man himself, so I walked on to the Dump. I was deep into trash that had slid down the open hillside when I heard heavy steps approach. I froze in my efforts to extricate a wrought-iron filigree lantern.

It's him, I thought. Reflexively, I dove under more garbage. I pulled a sheet of aluminum siding over me and cowered. Then I heard a second man's steps. On the rise above me, I could hear two men speaking in gruff voices. Panty *Men?* Was it a sick team? I could not make out their words, but they seemed to be challenging each other. Then I heard the *ping* of fluid zinging off my metal shield. They were *pissing*. Possibly pissing and competing for distance.

I almost flung off my aluminum-siding shield and sprang forth to declare, "You win!" But I was too embarrassed at this late moment. How would I look, climbing out of deep garbage, muttering about piss? I was, however, relieved that they did not seem to be perverts involved in dressing trees or beheading dolls. The two appeared to be innocent salvage men, intent on recovering lumber and, I realized as they whipped off my cover, metal.

They screamed and ran.

I laughed that day but not the next, when I returned to the Dump to discover a white birch wearing a nightgown. I issued an all points bulletin in the Park and called the police chief, a man who seldom left his Gothic-style stone station.

With the word out, Panty Man became a hunted creature. Soon there were sightings of suspects in the woods. A neighbor who rode a dirt bike said she "scared up" a thin man with a dark moustache hanging high in a maple tree. She had not spotted panties in his hand, but who else could he be? Hikers also reported a moustached man, walking oddly or lurking behind trees. One neighbor said she yelled "Go 'way!" at him and he fled. She then found a silver chest still filled with sterling and a set of ivory-handled steak knives. I cursed Panty Man for depriving me of my personal treasure hunts. But I was, by now, too scared to enjoy them. I never did find out who Panty Man was or why he strung up panties and dolls in the woods. But the stories of his behavior became cautionary tales—the woods could hide weirdness previously unimagined.

On my last walk to the Dump, a year later, I was accompanied by a city friend. I told her the tale of Panty Man as we strolled. We reached the Dump and had almost exited the woods when we became aware of a man behind us. He walked oddly—almost on tiptoe, silent as a snake.

"He's behind us," my friend whispered. I was afraid to turn, but I did. The man was unreasonably close—within two feet of us. I felt the hair on the nape of my neck rise, cartoon-style. The man was thin, dark, with a pencil-like moustache. His expression did not change in the instant that I regarded him. He did not smile or nod.

"Hurry," I instructed my friend. We were only yards from the entry to a more traveled road. The road appeared as a sunlit gap—as open as a door—ahead of us. We ran toward it. By the time our feet hit the paved road, the man had vanished, slipped back into the woods or behind a tree: I turned to look, and there was nothing but the forest, the green shade, and the motion of leaves in the spring breeze.

Soon after, the Dump was closed. As if an outdoor place could be shut down. But it was—heavy bars and chains blocked the entry to the trail. Warning signs were posted. All of this had nothing to do with Panty Man but was part of a political war over garbage collection. There were rumors of a Mob struggle. One day, a corpse was found at the Dump. Soon after, the area was bulldozed, declared off limits. Trespassers or violators would be prosecuted.

e l e v e n

Soon after I moved to the Castle, my family, the *mispucha*, followed, visiting the gated community that had so long excluded Jews. My uncles arrived, even my aunt Tessa and my cousin Willy. I rowed the entire family in a dinghy around the borders of Tuxedo Lake.

It was summer, the first summer I lived in Tuxedo Park. All was beautiful, languid. The trees were great, heavy-headed like broccoli. The sky was bluer than any city sky. The weight of my family made the boat ride low in the water, but it also gave it momentum as I paddled along.

My uncles reminisced about another boat ride—my grandmother Etka's immigrant voyage. Etka from Minsk had sailed here on the *Carmonia*, passed through the chaos of Ellis Island. She had arrived, as had so many Jews, fleeing the pogroms of Russia with little more than the clothes on her back. But what clothes! She wore her best—a frilled white "waist," a fitted black Victorian coat and full skirts, high buttoned boots, and a large plumed hat. She was in her twenties, a beauty who disdained marriage. She also brought her books—Plato and Socrates—some sepia-colored photographs, and her memories.

"America is a wonderful country," my uncle Gabe said as I dipped the oars in and out of the once-forbidden waters. We edged closer to the shore, to the great estates that sat empty, museums of past wealth.

Like me, my uncles admired the smaller houses, the outbuildings. The greenhouses, the gardeners' shacks. The long, slow boat ride allowed them time to recall Etka from Minsk's stories of her own country place—the dacha. The dacha had been a small but charming wooden building, not at all like the grand stone home they had owned in the city of Minsk. It was the contrast that my grandmother had enjoyed—the washed wooden floor in lieu of the plush carpet in the city; the intimacy of the few sunlit rooms as opposed to the formality of the many draperied chambers back in the winter house.

Etka had described both homes in detail. Even as a child, I knew about the decor: the parlor was wine-colored, "my bedroom was white." In the city house, the daughters had their own rooms, and the servants lived in a separate wing. In the country, everyone was thrown together—all the boys shared a large room while the five daughters had their "girls room." The three maids—Rashka, Mashka, and Kashka—had slept diagonally on a single bed, laid out, my grandmother recalled "like sardines." But the tight squeeze inside had not mattered, for outside the door the world waited. The sky pressed the earth, which pushed back with a bursting harvest of plums, cherries. Everyone sat outside to take the air, the original *Luft* of the old country. And they drank the fiery fermented juices of their own fruit.

I could sense the ecstasy, secondhand, in these reminiscences. And then the bitter aftertaste of my grandmother's family losing everything but their lives and enough money for a "ship carte," a ticket to America. The sons were drafted into the czar's army, a death sentence. Instead, they fled, smuggled out of Russia under assumed names, in steerage. One brother had not been as fortunate—he was whipped by Cossacks, crippled, and forced to remain. A neighbor's daughter had lost her parents and her face—branded with a poker hot from the fire. No wonder they fled.

98

My grandmother's family took very little with them, but somehow the photographs—posed studies of the family in Russia—made the journey. And a single photograph of what was perhaps the final picnic at the dacha—a sunwashed cottage, almost hidden behind a blur of blossoming trees. The sun was so bright in that photograph, it nearly extinguished the delineations of the dacha, but preserved forever its euphoric mood.

It was not until my family walked the paths of Tuxedo Park that I heard all about the lost forest back home, the woods, the mushrooms, the cottage. It had taken more than fifty years for this family to be more than transient visitors to the countryside, for the day trip to extend into a true visit.

My uncles came to Tuxedo Park often. Len loved its mystery and history. He recited what he knew of the robber barons who had developed the area. He knew even of Spencer Trask, who had built the Castle (and who later built a near-duplicate manor that I would also inhabit, the Main House at Yaddo). It was Len who told me, as we sat in the baronial hall that was now mine, stories of the Great Depression, the crash that destroyed the fortunes of the families who had built this place.

Gabe enjoyed Tuxedo Park on another level. He truly loved the poet's "ramble"; he claimed inspiration at every grove. He also managed to get a hernia almost every time he visited. I never did understand Gabe's hernias. I'd grown up thinking a hernia was an organ, that every man had one. Gabe seemed to strain himself rather easily. The first hike to Eagle Mountain, which the Ramapos had named Point Lookout, did the trick. Gabe ended up having minor surgery and spending the rest of the summer in the bedroom under the eaves, where he could hear the squirrels *shoo* the wood.

My aunt Tessa was calm now that not as many relatives lived in 5R (she may have seemed shrill to me as a child, but later, as an adult, I regarded her as a near saint—imagine, seven people in three rooms). Tessa looked around Tuxedo Park with an appreciation that bordered on disbelief. "It's so *beaudy-ful,*" she said over and over again. My cousin Willy, who had first taken me to the "end of the city" and who still lived in 5R, walked with solemn enjoyment through the woods. Perhaps because he had some birth defect that would forever set him apart and slow his speech and his walk, Willy proceeded at a measured pace that gave him a natural dignity. He wore a three-piece suit, shined shoes, and a fedora. He never wore anything less formal on his visits to me in the country. A trip to the country was an occasion—and he dressed for it.

I stayed in the Castle some thirteen years, and my home, rented though it was, became a destination for my family. I was the one, now, with a place in the country. We hiked, we sailed, we picked flowers and berries. To complete the dacha experience, I put in a vegetable garden, a garden as remote and mysterious as Tuxedo Park itself—a sanctuary I cherished as I had the childhood tales of such secret gardens. The area surrounding the Castle was filled with abandoned estate property. The ruined gardens were still so beautiful that I found it hard to believe that they could have looked better when maintained. I loved the overrun of vines, the rampant wildflowers mixed in with the cultivated blooms.

Closest to the Castle, down the steep side of the mountain upon which the building sat, was an old flower garden, long untended. Whoever had planned the garden in the 1880s had loved lilacs. Dozens of lilac bushes had been planted as a border, squaring off several acres. The lilacs came in all hues, from white to dark purple, their blossoms triple- or at least double-budded, and extra fragrant. Just to walk the aisle of lilacs in May was to become intoxicated. One afternoon, under their influence, my husband and I sank to the earth and held each other.

The garden was a magical place, and private. It was adjacent to a forgotten tennis court, now fenced in with wild grapevines, its surface cracked as if by earthquakes. Grass and flowers burst through the court's softening surface. Nature was reclaiming this place—until I stepped in, five-dollar spade in hand, to pull it back toward cultivation.

For the privilege of toiling in the soil of this now Guam-like jungle, I had to request permission from an order of nuns who owned the land. I went uphill to the convent, housed in a former mansion, and waited in the marble lobby for a woman known as Sister Rita.

I can still remember how cool that anteroom felt after the hot sun of the garden. Sister Rita swept in to see me, black habit swishing, rosary clicking. We were far, far back in time here. I made my request, feeling a bit the peasant. Sister Rita bowed her head and nodded. Yes, I could have a garden.

Downhill I ran and explored the terrain more thoroughly now that it was "mine." There was not just the garden—the perfect plot in full sun—but also a spring house in a rock wall set into the mountainside. I yanked the door, and it gave way. Inside, all was dark and sweetly chill. A bona fide root cellar—jars from another century and stacks of miniature terra cotta pots remained. I walked uphill to the Castle cradling a tower of the tiny pots under my shirt. How cool they felt against my skin, retaining the temperature of their decades within the root cellar. I had a plan—and a few hundred seed packets. I imagined the picture on every packet springing to buoyant life in my borrowed secret garden.

I was twenty-one years old and completely happy. I was in love with my husband, who rushed home each evening to get to the garden before dark. He dug with me—we had two spades and the rich black earth gave up its stones, its weeds, its old secrets: the occasional rusted Victorian key, a coin, an ivory button.

My husband claimed to know about growing vegetables, but I soon suspected he knew as little as I did. He put in sixty tomato plants, enough for a commercial sauce operation. Each plant bore at least half a dozen fruit. We were soon inundated with tomatoes.

In retrospect, I wonder at our success, for it would never be repeated. Perhaps the animals did not see us plant the garden or were so bemused by our activity that they chose to wait for the next year's harvest. Whatever the reason, no animals ate that year, giving us the incentive to replant the garden every year for the next seven years, although after that first unique crop, almost everything was devoured by critters.

We started planting vegetables that deer and groundhogs might not like. It turned out that we and they had similar tastes; if we liked it, so did the animals. So we ended up planting vegetables we hated—zucchini and cauliflower. The animals spared these, but so what? We were left holding bat-sized zucchini, impressive as weapons but tasting like wood.

Finally, the animals developed a taste even for the cauliflower, eating it roots and all. Perhaps cauliflower roots are tastier than the head. My seed-packet markers were trampled. Hoofprints were everywhere—the little Vs that marked deer victories.

Why didn't I give up? Eventually, my husband did abandon the failed garden, but I didn't. Year after year, I planted, only to be annihilated. I would come upon scenes of Armageddon in the garden—bitten tomatoes lying everywhere. But I continued to plow, plant, hope. Even failed gardens yield—surprises.

One morning, digging with my spade I unearthed a lizard. He was as big as the spade, black with orange polka dots. He had a marvelous soft skin, and he breathed gently, his eyes fastened on mine. I felt honored to see a lizard of this caliber. I was a bit less pleased to dig up white-kid-leatherish snake eggs—interesting to behold, but I didn't want to see them hatch.

Another day as I was crouched weeding, I heard the sudden thunder of hooves. A doe leaped the garden fence. She landed right beside me, then almost levitated in shock: it was hard to say who was more surprised. She pounded her front hoof hard on the ground, stamping out an alarm or perhaps simply expressing her anger. *Thump, thump, thump.* Then she leaped out again, leaving me stunned, sitting up on my knees. She probably ran back to the thicket to tell the other deer, "That fool is back, planting our salad bar."

The most exciting animal to appear, or reappear, in the woods was the mysterious black bear. I never saw him (or her), but I did see the bear tracks and the berry-studded bear spoor. I felt no fear, knowing that black bears are said to be timid.

I almost saw the bear one day when I went raspberry picking. If anyone loved berries more than the bear it was me. Tuxedo Park was blessed with acres of wild raspberry canes. No one knew if they had escaped from someone's berry patch or they were indigenous to the area. Whatever their origin, these berries were superior to any raspberries I have ever tasted. They were clear as rubies, many-clustered. The raspberries grew in thorn-studded thickets around the lake and in and around the ruins of several mansions. With diligence, it was possible to pick a bushel in a day.

Every August I went into raspberry overdrive: picking, then preserving what I could not eat. I had feasts of fresh raspberries in sweet cream, sour cream, au naturel. Then I moved along to frozen raspberries, canned raspberries, and prepared raspberry pies, tarts, and muffins.

I was completely compulsive and left no berry unplucked. One morning, I woke early to get to the berries before the birds, the bugs, and the heat. I was half-asleep, a bucket dangling from my elbow. As I entered my favorite thicket, I heard a powerful *smash*. I looked up to see the bushes part and the shadow of a wide black furry rump. The bear! He never turned around, but his claw prints in the mud were a signature.

My other association with raspberries was romantic. One August day, my husband picked berries with me. We nibbled as we picked. I refreshed myself with frequent dips into the clear lake beside the berry patch.

My husband was overcome and said, "Remember this date. The hour. I want you to know that I will always love you, and if we are ever apart, each year I will come to this raspberry patch at exactly this time." I was stunned—this declaration was so atypical, and he had had to be cajoled down to the berry patch. We kissed and swore to remember the hour, the date, the time when the berries were perfect. "Remember the raspberries," he whispered.

I do remember them, but I've forgotten the date, the hour—and, besides, the raspberry patch no longer exists. A pseudo mansion, glorified tract housing, was erected on the spot. The thousands of jewel-like berries were cleared along with the underbrush. My marriage soured and went bad to a point past recovery, but I do still taste the sweet with the bitter when I remember the raspberries.

t w e l v e

In a sense, I didn't leave Tuxedo Park—Tuxedo Park left me. Gradually, the place changed. The abandoned mansions were sold, renovated. Their doors were no longer left open for predawn explorations. The boathouses were locked. The ruined gardens were rehabilitated. Acres were sold. The trees began to wear red ribbons, reminding me of animals at a pound marked for execution. Yellow bulldozers bit into the earth. Old houses were "razed." New houses were built. At one edge of the Park, where I had roamed through meadows and woods, the trees were chopped down, the ground leveled. Dirt roads were paved. Even in the backwoods, violent change began to occur. There was the sound of blasting. There was talk of secret mining for uranium. The terrible energies of destruction were at work in the Park.

One winter day, I skied to a favorite secret place and found the white birch tagged, red-ribboned—they were next. I sank to the earth and was surprised to see my tears melt holes in the snow. Tuxedo Park was on its way to becoming like other places: it would not be completely destroyed; it would become more ordinary.

The number and size of the old mansions would keep Tuxedo Park from disappearing altogether. It would always be extravagant and, because of the stone gatehouse, private. But the privacy now seemed more for the sake of security ("twenty-four-hour police gate," the real estate advertisements bragged). The estates, so charming as ruins or poorly maintained homes, became once more lavish monuments to consumerism. In the Eighties, house lust ran rampant.

The Park seemed filled with real estate brokers. If you stayed long enough, it seemed possible you would become a broker, or at least a buyer. A tribe of women real estate brokers worked the Park in a roundelay of musical mansions. Fueled on alcohol and fired by divorce, the brokers sometimes sold houses to each other.

"Do you want an important house?" was the lead question asked of me by the Queen of the Realtors.

Did I want an important house? My husband and I had looked at the houses, but in a desultory manner. We walked through sixty-room mansions, then underpriced, but despite the bargains, we didn't seriously think of buying. I still truly liked only the outbuildings—the gardeners' cottages, the gatehouses, a former aviary, even a renovated chicken house.

But I wasn't entirely immune to house lust in the Park. I fell for the most romantic property in Tuxedo—the Ballroom, a turn-of-the-century reproduction of the Petit Trianon, the "playhouse" built for Marie Antoinette. It was owned by a count and countess who always seemed to be abroad. It seemed like a house built for a single occasion, a coming-out party for a turn-of-the-century debutante. It shimmered in the moonlight like a distant memory. For decades, it was an exotic rental. Even though I never bought it, rented it, or even entered it for more than the occasional lunch or dinner, the Ballroom played a significant role in my life. I mentally inhabited the house for my second novel, *Third Parties*, and it occupies a permanent place in my imagination.

As the publication of *Third Parties*, which lampooned the society of Tuxedo Park, approached, I became increasingly eager to leave. I felt the old guard, the new people, and perhaps even the Italian-American artisans would be offended and storm the Castle. I imagined a finale straight out of Frankenstein, with the torch-bearing villagers coming to get the monster—me.

It was time to move on. The house lust was infectious. I didn't want to succumb and end up like some of the new people, who lived to serve their houses, subordinating all other interests to the expensive upkeep of the beloved mansion. The new people looked like Lilliputians moving through the great halls. I knew one woman who pushed a floor buffer for what seemed like half a mile of marble flooring, tethered to a hundred-foot extension cord.

So many of the formerly normal people who had bought into the grandiose dream eventually seemed to succumb to house psychosis. The disease, emotionally and physically debilitating, left its victims wasted. Money ran like rain from the faulty leaders and gutters. The end was all too often personal tragedy: husbands and wives finally fled, often in different directions, to start life anew in rented apartments or perhaps a hotel room or, in some cases, even the YMCA.

After years of stripping and sanding, these new people seemed to end up numbed, sitting on a motel bed flipping through albums of snapshots—Wisty or Mo'head going through the change of seasons. "Wisty: Winter 1989." Important houses scared me. They also seemed to prove the rule: architecture is destiny. I feared if I bought a house with such dominant needs, it would subvert my own.

I had a feeling I should avoid ancestral manses. Descendants had a way of descending. If you bought the old Van Bruyck place, could you really expect to be free of latter-day Van Bruycks? Might they not return to visit or check on the house's façade? I imagined them swaying nostalgically on the doorstep.

So when I began to search for my own house, I remained wary. When I inspected a house, I tried to discern the true reason it was on the market. What had happened to the former owners? Had they left in midrepair? In midmeal? There were always clues: Zipstrip coagulating on a banister, an unfinished playroom. In most houses, I felt I was touring the marital equivalent of Waterloo—signs of the battle and the losses were everywhere.

In Tuxedo Park, most of the houses were just too big. Now, how big is too big? What can it hurt to have a few extra rooms? Even an extra floor? Isn't it nice for storage? Couldn't one forget that third floor is up there? I could not deal with the idea of vacant chambers, except in Freudian terms. No matter how hard I might try, I could never forget a third floor was up there. I could feel a psychic draft whistle through the unused rooms. Not only that, from what I saw of such extra floors, they were not that unused. Third floors were never truly unlived in— they were simply lived in by other species. On my first house hunts, before I acknowledged that I could never handle a mansion, I was forever finding elaborate hornet nests, powder pyramids, the remains of great insect civilizations.

I was also alarmed at the presence of so many unconscious or dead birds in the attics. They must have flown in and knocked themselves out. I wondered what the bird mortality rate was in some of the great houses; more than three birds a year, I bet. I looked at a house where a couple had dealt with the problem of the extra floor by having it removed. The decapitated house seemed strange, sawed off, and the couple themselves had a disconnected look.

The last house I looked at in Tuxedo Park was what I call a "schizo": it had been moved. The realtor confided that the house had originally been up on the mountain and a previous owner had wanted it to sit beside the lake. So the house had been dragged downhill and was now chained in position. I felt the house groan as I toured it, I could feel it listing, trying to return to its original foundation.

I benefitted from my house search in Tuxedo Park—at least I knew what I didn't want: a house that would possess me. I made up a list of what I truly wanted. At the top of the list was a house without ego. I did not want a pretentious house. I did not want a house with a mistaken identity—a Mediterranean villa or an adobe house. I wanted a house that sprang naturally from its roots; a native place, a home farm.

If there was a word I kept in mind, it was "humble." I thought in terms of cross-stitch samplers: "Be it ever so humble, there's no place like home." I wanted a place where I could have and bring up children without feeling the moldings and floorboards were more precious than the kids. I wanted a pretty but rough-and-tumble family house. I imagined something like Rebecca of Sunnybrook Farm's house, or, from my own history, that little leftover farmhouse on the city street in the Bronx. That was what I wanted: a farmhouse, not a mansion. A farm. Not a gated community.

So I fled those gates, just as my novel was published. The Tuxedo Park natives never did turn on me. They actually had a farewell book party, and the library stocked up on copies. But I was history there, and I looked farther north, to the apple country, to find my ultimate dream place.

thirteen

The search for the perfect house went on for ten years. Every weekend, I scoured the Sunday *New York Times* real estate section. Certain phrases lured me—"fenced for horses"; "former grist mill." The *Times* functioned as mulch for my imagination. (Later, the newspaper, buried between layers of soil, would serve as the real thing.) For a decade, I read the advertisements, visualizing myself in every write-up. Mentally, I traveled as far north as Maine and as far south as Maryland.

But when I ventured forth to investigate the properties, the shocks multiplied faster than the listings. No place lived up to its description. Every perfect house had an unforeseen flaw. The perfect dairy barn "on the Delaware" wasn't on it, it had been under it.

"Well," said the realtor as she tried to explain the water marks that ran around the room where wall met ceiling, like a border motif, "this is the flood plain." The water had not risen that high in more than a decade, the owner insisted. But the scent of mildew filled the house, the floors felt soggy underfoot. A sump pump sat in the cellar, wheezing and sucking up the moisture that seeped into the house. The structure, for all its colonial charm, seemed to be weeping: fluid streaked the walls. "We call this 'internal rain,' " the realtor told us.

Next, my husband and I saw a pre–Civil War homestead in Putnam County that boasted a personal footbridge over its private moat.

We were smitten, but I grew suspicious when the broker drove us to and from the property by a circuitous route. On my own, I walked to the back acres and spotted what she had tried to hide: a small nuclear facility, derby-shaped, with red-and-white carnival-striped stacks. Ground zero. Who cared about the original cooking hearth, the "random" floors, the sewing nook? Radioactivity seemed to float, iridescent among the dust motes, through the spring sunshine.

The search became a raison d'être. I toured three states, seven counties. I was looking for something that was, the brokers insisted, impossible to buy. An old house, set off the road, with several acres and complete privacy.

"Complete privacy no longer exists," I was told. "Not in your price range." Only Wall Street billionaires, rock stars, movie moguls, or prizefighters could buy seclusion. The most I could hope to attain would be "some privacy," advised the Queen of the Realtors, a lady in Orange County who wore outsize sunglasses and kept her hair in a lacquered flip.

"There is no such thing as 'some' privacy," I argued. "A place is private or it isn't." She fought back, citing "privacy on the side" or "privacy to the back." I vetoed these definitions, foreseeing a future in which I would have to slink from my home in only a single direction. My privacy criterion was strict—I must know that I could walk outside my front door in a nightgown or less without being in plain view of my neighbors. It's not that I expected to be walking out naked very often— I just needed to know that it was possible.

This idiosyncrasy of mine ruled out ninety-nine point nine percent of the properties for sale. My need also required that I find a most simpatico realtor, one who would not lead me astray or deceive me.

The realtor-buyer relationship is an odd one. At best, the relationship is a marriage of need and profit motive. Traveling with a realtor day after day, perhaps over a period of years, guarantees an enforced familiarity. I can think of no other situation in which I have been alone in cars and empty homes with an individual with whom I might otherwise never have chosen to spend time.

Therefore, before I could find a house, I had to find a compatible realtor. The first realtors I knew seemed formed in a mold. They had fixed flips and sunglasses and carried designer purses that snapped shut. They wore perfume and drove late-model American cars. Each conveyed a mood of false enthusiasm mingled with pragmatic despair—they drove around with prospects like me every day, but seldom won the commission. Whenever I explored new territory, I would pair up with a new realtor. It was a succession of blind dates with unlikely women. I recall one male realtor and the odd tension that accompanied us on our tours of bedrooms and baths. In the hush of empty homes, I could imagine how sometimes realtors might have sex with would-be buyers: opportunity was everywhere, and also a desire to please.

The male realtor was a former model who posed in each room he showed me—I suppose to give me an image of the future life I might lead there with my husband. *Here I am,* he seemed to say, *coming in from work, heading for the wet bar; here I am, helping you in the kitchen.* He was married, but unhappily. I became used to absorbing personal bits of information like that from realtors—we spent so much time together it was inevitable that we would chat and occasionally even stop for snacks or to use a bathroom.

The realtor I spent the most time with was a diligent woman nicknamed Pippy, who dominated the listings in a county an hour from New York. She looked like a human magnification of the terrier she sometimes took along with us. Pippy wore her hair in a topknot that matched her pet's, and her hairline moved forward in excitement whenever we sniffed out a new listing. She usually wore fur and wafted

Joy. Like many others, Pippy was a former showgirl and the veteran of two divorce wars.

Pippy's style was to show me houses beyond my economic reach. She was a voyeur of the lives of the rich and selling. She took me to houses that she loved, would have liked to buy for herself and her terrier. They were slicked-over colonials with Subzero freezers and bidets. I repeated that I could not afford these homes, that I was looking for something less polished anyway—a pristine farmhouse. I could care less for anything new, even in old houses.

"You're going to have to add a couple of zeroes" is all she would say. My dream of finding that unspoiled house for under two hundred thousand dollars was unrealistic. "I got that for an unrenovated dog kennel," she remarked toward the end of our relationship.

"Was it private?" I heard myself ask.

Next I met a gamine named Tina who ruled another county, across the river. Tina admitted that she couldn't help in my price range, but she took me around anyway, saying, "You can always make an offer . . ." She tipped me off that the best time to look was during ice-and-mud season, when no one else wanted to drive backcountry roads.

"It's ideal," Tina told me. "The leaves are off, so you see where you really are." This was a brilliant point, as I learned over the years. Leaves hide a lot—telephone company installations, access roads, rusted trailers, distant prisons, ugly neighbors.

"Also," Tina added, "the sellers are desperate—they have to heat a house they no longer want to live in. The meter is running. They know most people look in the spring. It's so stupid—the minute the leaves come out, so do the buyers. And they drop off when the leaves fall. *That's* when they should *start*." Indeed, Tina gave me a tour of frozen-looking sellers who winced every time their furnaces fired up. Other homes had been deserted and sat there, maintained just above freezing, offering up their chilled selves at discounted rates. I could not afford even the frozen, desperate-to-sell homes, but I did enjoy Tina. She looked a bit like Natalie Wood and chatted about her new lover, a cop. Her story of how they made love the first time—he threw off his uniform but retained the holster—stays with me as one of the weirder sexual tales I have heard.

Next, I met a former actress (the woods are filled with them), Nancy, a peppy redhead who would stop at roadkills and skin raccoons for their fur. I was farther north, and this seemed a part of the friskier frontier setting. Nancy showed me fanciful abodes with colorful pasts. We saw Isadora Duncan's dance colony in the woods above the Hudson near Croton. Nancy twirled a bit as we stood in the surprisingly small wooden barnlike structure. It was awfully cute, but there was no privacy. Isadora Duncan had lived rather communally, and clusters of other artists' homes nudged her own.

I moved on, my journey taking me farther and farther north, where it seemed every ten miles meant a drop in price and an increase in acreage. "Within weekend driving of the city" was a definition that stretched like the elastic of old panties: I looked at counties so distant they had signs in French. There *were* great places up there at the French-Canadian border, but the thought of getting there for a weekend was daunting.

I asked Nancy not to take me past Albany, where I had formed such miserable memories of the state college. She agreed and continued to call me with "exciting listings."

What I liked about Nancy was that she was one of the few realtors who didn't fool around with me on the privacy issue. In fact, a few of the places she took me were *too* private. The standout in this department was the "estate of Gunther Mueller," a deceased former Nazi who had built a house that could be cleaned by a central hose. The floors slanted toward a main drain, as the floors of some shower rooms and slaughterhouses do. The estate of Gunther Mueller *was* private; he had built it bunkerlike into the side of the mountain. The acreage was well defended by chain-link fencing. The Rottweilers who had once occupied the barbed wire–enclosed dog runs were now gone, as was Gunther, but the aura of militaristic madness remained.

"You could plant morning glories over the chain link," was Nancy's suggestion. "More flowers in the yard would do wonders."

Her next selection was a Cotswold-style stone cottage with a private waterfall. The cottage was set far, far back, at the end of a dirt road. The owners sat in catatonic quiet at their kitchen table with a giant Akita named Bo. I could see an alarm system had just been installed; floodlights were aimed at the house. What had happened here? "It won't affect you" was all Nancy would say.

As we went into reverse, backing out of the driveway and the deal, Nancy, in an unanticipated turn, began to quote from the Book of Revelation. I had not guessed, until that moment, that she was a born-again broker. I gathered from her singsong incantations that even as she tried to sell plots of earth, she felt we were doomed.

My relationships with brokers waxed and waned. I was not faithful to one. After a few fruitless months, I went out with several women in a few counties, sometimes in separate states.

Over the course of a year, my husband and I tried to buy three compromise dream houses. The first was a converted dairy barn in Sergeantsville, New Jersey. We had been taken there by an aging male realtor who drove us in circles, reciting the history of the barn. It had been "José Limón's Dance Factory." It was a pleasant enough place, but the true reason that we agreed to purchase the property was its location. My husband and I were then embarking on what turned out to be an eight-year stint of "commuter marriage." He would be based in Washington, D.C., during the work week while I would be professionally based in New York. The compromise was that a weekend place in

Sergeantsville, New Jersey, would be equally inconvenient for both of us. The problem was that it was so inconvenient we could never find it again. Just as well—we also failed to qualify for the mortgage.

The next dream house we found was a true heart-breaker—a Revolutionary War–era farmstead near Rhinebeck, New York. The house, a beautiful telescoping colonial with a pond and a dozen outbuildings, was being sold by a divorcing Brooklyn couple, a pair of headhunters.

The kitchen was the most stunning I had ever seen—it was a separate building, linked to the main house by a charming passage. The summer kitchen featured a wall-sized brick hearth and a long harvest table. A dreamy scene of blue-and-white shepherdesses decorated the walls and induced in me an immediate revery that was sustained by the view out the window—a shimmering pond, complete with weathered wooden dock.

On the day we stood in that kitchen and offered to buy the "Old Hudson Place," the warring couples' final meal was still in evidence on the pine kitchen table—a fossilized exhibit of half-eaten bagels and shriveled cream cheese. Their Sunday *Times* lay yellowing beside this still life, giving mute testimony to the date of the breakup, in midbrunch. *How could anyone fight in such idyllic surroundings?* I wondered.

The caretaker, Old Dan, was still on the premises. He gave the classic city-people-in-the-country post mortem, gesturing in explanation to the pond, the sheep runs, the sagging huts and barns. He said, "Yah, they tried to do too much." Nothing was as it appeared. The sparkle in the pond was the result of a chemical concoction that had to be injected regularly to kill voracious algae. The house itself, so beautiful, was in midrenovation. It needed new toilets.

Yet we marched toward the closing. We surveyed the property, got rid of its powder post beetles, and formed a relationship with Old Dan. We did all this even though the signs for a happy outcome were poor. The sellers continued to snipe at each other, and on one visit to the house, the mother introduced us to her weeping daughter as the "couple who are buying your house." The little girl, a swim tube still around her waist, burst into more dramatic sobbing and fled up the stairs.

"See," the mother said to me.

Meanwhile, Old Dan muttered of uranium under the barn and clicked his tongue to simulate a Geiger counter. The water failed a coliform test. The sellers drank it before our eyes and said again, "See." Yet we had a crush on this house and went through all the motions but the last: at the closing, the sellers failed to show. Stood up at the real estate altar, my husband and I decided it was pointless to sue. How could we prevail against the battling duo? The realtor wept as we walked away. This broker, a descendant of Huguenot settlers, immediately led us to another house. "Get back on dat horse," she said in her strange accent. "Yah, I will get you another house."

Tinkle Bell Farm was the property of a former actress and her husband who were devoted to raising Nubian goats. The actress, a Celeste Holm lookalike, led my husband and me into her large, immaculate barn. She rang a tinkle bell, and thirty baby goats ran toward her. They all wore tinkle bells. Outside on the grass, her pet donkey took the tinkle bell as a cue to roll on his back, kick his hooves up, and bray in apparent delight.

I saw a new joy in my husband; his features contorted with pleasure.

The former actress led us into her country kitchen, where a blueberry crumble was bubbling in her oven. There we sat, having coffee while my husband read *American Goat* magazine. He read aloud from a column titled "Bleatings." This was what he needed, he told me, to save him from the psychic toxins of working in the city. If we could not afford two places, he would be happy to commute the five hours a day. "It would be worth it to come home to these adorable goats," he said. I thought it over, the tinkle bells, the happy donkey. I liked seeing my husband this way. I agreed, and we three celebrated. But not for long. The actress's husband came home (he commuted the five hours to the city) and informed us that his wife had accepted our offer without his approval and that it was far below the asking price.

"But they love the goats," she bleated.

He was unmoved. I was secretly relieved. I had worried about all those goats and the five-hour commute. I had also picked up on the actress's plan to move—only a half-acre away, into an identical house that she was building. This turned out to be a phenomenon: sellers not truly leaving their properties. When I would ask, "And where will you go?" the answer was often, "Right over there." Sellers were cunning creatures, devising ways to reap a profit while still staying on the property. They sliced off sections for themselves and stayed in easy eye- and earshot.

So I did not jump for my car keys, when, almost a year after fiasco number three, another realtor called to tell us about the perfect house. We had, in fact, almost given up looking when this broker called in real estate heat. "You must come up here right away," she said. "This one's going to go."

My husband and I resisted. It was raining, we had colds. We were preparing our income tax returns. The last house I'd seen had made the estate of Gunther Mueller, the dead Nazi, look charming. But her voice burbled on in my ear, "Don't you remember? Two years ago? That driveway that we passed and I said, 'Doesn't it look like England down there? That's an English estate.' And you said, 'Thomas Hardy! *Far From the Madding Crowd*'?"

I felt a wave of telepathy through the phone, as if the line could conduct not only the broker's voice but also her sincerity. "I kid you not," she said. "This is the one you have spent ten years looking for. . . . This is . . ." she paused. "A house that Eleanor Roosevelt would have bought."

She had spoken the magic name. Eleanor Roosevelt. Eleanor Roosevelt had long been accorded sainthood in my family. Not only was she revered for her politics, her active role as First Lady, but she had once driven my grandmother home from a lecture in the Bronx.

I grabbed the car keys and my umbrella. My husband wrapped himself in a blanket and said, "You're driving."

A hundred miles later, in a downpour, we saw that the realtor had spoken the truth. I felt my heart beat against my raincoat as we entered the maple-lined driveway.

Here, even the rain seemed cosmetic, a silver scrim through which we could see a series of buildings that composed a classic English-style country estate. A white fog floated before the main house, the Manor, and drifted past a smaller building, the Casino, a Victorian "playhouse," and the carriage house. Far down the driveway, peeking over a knoll, was the farmhouse we had come to see.

Deer appeared in the fog and stepped daintily out of our way. The animals regarded us, luminous-eyed: *Who are you?* they seemed to ask. *What are you doing here?*

What was I doing here? I thought of my birthplace, the tenement on East Twenty-seventh Street, the series of small apartments I'd inhabited through my childhood. We had been seven people in three rooms. And those rooms themselves had been squeezed into a project with narrow entries and steep-pitched stairs, across from a firehouse that wailed, night and day, of urban distress. What was I doing here? The private driveway wound down for half a mile, then circled the house known as The Inn.

The Inn was a squared-off colonial painted pale yellow. It seemed to wink welcome to me from behind its many shuttered windows. The realtor had not lied. This was a house that Eleanor Roosevelt would have liked. It was beautiful, with its gray-and-white porches, but not too fancy. The Inn was set on thirteen acres, most of the property given over to a sloping pasture to the west. The pasture was in use—a herd of Holsteins could be seen, heads lowered to munch the first shoots of spring onion. Beyond my imaginings and almost past comprehension were the outbuildings—a matching barn and the stone foundation of another structure, into which had been set a tennis court. *I would have settled for much less,* I thought as I stepped from the car, already saying yes, as the broker had predicted.

The realtors—they were a pair from the same office, one blonde, the other brunette—waited on the front porch. They beamed. My husband followed, wrapped squaw-like in his blanket. In spite of his flu, he croaked his approval. "This is it."

We told the brokers that we would be happy to give the sellers, an English lord and lady who still lived in the Manor, their asking price. But was it truly possible to buy this place? Orphans from the Bronx didn't end up in houses like this. Or did they? I walked into the center hall and looked straight up the steps to my yearned-for warren of rooms. The realtor said there were eight bedrooms. This was so far beyond my childhood wish for a room of my own that I hesitated to look at the second floor. I remembered the dream house I'd spotted when I was seven—the little farmhouse squeezed between two high-rises that had somehow been left behind in the building boom in the Bronx. How I had coveted that tiny colonial, envied the little girl who had lived there, with her own garden and her countless brothers and sisters and their tantalizing unseen world of an upstairs.

Downstairs, The Inn was divided into a front parlor, a country kitchen, and a formal dining room. I ran up the steps, straight to the front bedroom. *This is my room,* I thought, reprising the house-hunting game played so long ago, when my mother and I had toured every open house we could find. If only she could be here with me now, to see this bedroom, papered with the flower that bore her name. Roses were everywhere—in bouquets on the old wallpaper, in the small hand-painted designs on the wooden bedstead, and in the pattern of a chintz-slipcovered chaise lounge. The chaise, plumped with down cushions, was set close to the fireplace. A stack of white birch logs had been placed in the grate.

I saw the house in a trance of desire. I walked from room to room—there were at least eighteen, more if you counted the third-floor servants' quarters with its nooks tucked under the eaves. Toward the back of the second floor, I stepped across a seam in the wide board floors, the dividing line between the original house and the 1899 addition, a second house, called The Innlet. I walked through a Victorian linen closet to reach the three back guest bedrooms. I was charmed. Everything—from the long silver keys to the stacks of starched monogrammed linens—struck me as perfect. There were, of course, flaws, but I saw these defects only as endearing traits. The bathrooms seemed weird, added in 1840, with gravity-flow running water. At the front of the house, there were twin toilets that looked as if they had been sliced in half: I had to ease in sideways to view them. But no matter, these odd bathrooms were set into the prettiest house I'd ever seen. Could we really buy it?

"The lord is pretty choosy," the realtor told us. "You will have to have an interview."

The next weekend, we appeared at the Manor. The lord was the grandson of the founder of the estate, which was called Willowby. His grandfather had been an American businessman named Edmund Talbot.

The current lord's mother, Hilary Talbot, had married a prominent Englishman, Lord Edmund Hodgson, who had been close to Queen Elizabeth II. After 1942, Lord Edmund and Hilary had divorced, and Hilary had returned to America, to Willowby. Her son, the present Lord Hodgson and the inheritor of her estate, had been selling off chunks of the property over the past few years. He'd already parted with the dairy farm that had made up the eastern side of the property and a historic stone house that was set at the north end. As he "simplified" his life, he also sold off some smaller parcels of land and a few cottages. But the realtor warned me that The Inn was dear to the family, and His Lordship would be particular as to whom they sold the place, if they sold it at all. They had already declined the offer of one would-be buyer. The house was not quite officially on the market. My husband and I dressed for the interview. I wore a 1940s plaid coat with a Harrod's label that I'd found in a vintage clothing store on Columbus Avenue.

"What an excellent tweed," were the lord's first words to me as we stepped inside the Manor. It was early spring, but inside, the house retained the chill of the past winter. The thermostat was kept low, just above the temperature at which veneer can crack.

I wonder if the lord would have sold me the house if I had not been a writer. His mother had been a writer, he told me at once. She had published a book, *A Sordid Boon*. He showed me a copy and explained that the title was from Wordsworth. "The world is too much with us/ Late and soon, getting and spending, we lay waste our power/Little we see in Nature is ours. / We have given our hearts away—a sordid boon!"

The lord and lady led us past a Della Robbia in the marble main hall to a sitting room where we took our places on an antique sofa. A small fire crackled in the grate. My husband caught my eye, and we both almost laughed in relief. We were surrounded by objects and furnishings assembled by the lord and his antecedents. Much of the carpet and all the golden silk upholstery and wall coverings were frayed, but this wear added a gloss of beauty and authenticity. A set designer could not have conjured up a more perfect English country house.

I felt as if I might have stepped into a hybrid play—a cross between *Hay Fever* and *The Bald Soprano*, half drawing-room comedy, half inspired farce. The lord and lady were perfectly cast as themselves. You could not find a better type than Lord Edmund Hodgson—fine aquiline features, parchment-white skin, a tall, bony build. Lady Marguerite was a bit more offbeat. Dutch by birth, she had acquired her husband's English accent and manner. Her eyes, slightly slanted above high cheekbones, flashed with the merry beauty she must have had when she first attracted the lord's attention. I felt I could see the girl she had been peeking out from the woman she had become.

His Lordship was fifty-nine; Her Ladyship, nine years younger. They had raised four children, ranging in age from fifteen to twenty-one. The Hodgsons were not old, in fact they were slim and attractive, yet they seemed to belong to another period. Their faces looked blanched, as if they had just come into the glare of the current year and been a bit taken aback. They seemed like out-of-season flowers that had been nipped by a frost.

Lord and lady were drinking Cutty Sark. "Our antifreeze," Lady Marguerite said, cupping her hands around her tumbler. They offered us drinks and cheese and crackers. We chatted, the Hodgsons warning us off a famous local restaurant known for its strained creativity (etched glass menus viewed through candle-holders, that sort of thing). "We like blueberries," Lady Marguerite said, elongating the vowels (*"bleuuberries"*), "but we don't care for *bleuuberry* soup."

Lord Hodgson continued to be intrigued by the fact that I wrote novels and plays. "That's so interesting. The house has a history of women writers." Not just his mother, who had written her autobiography, but also an Indian woman, Nivedita, who lived in The Inn at the turn of the century and wrote a spiritual text, *Kali, the Mother*. The lord touched on the religious connection between The Inn and a famous Hindu monk, Swami Vivekenanda, who visited in 1895 and again in 1899. "He blessed two women in the house," he said. "The Inn *still* has a special aura. You'll see."

"We lived there for a time ourselves," Lady Marguerite added.

"When the children were small. It was bliss." They both sighed, re-calling how much cheaper to heat The Inn had been.

"The Inn is snug," they said together.

The lord escorted us on a tour of the grounds. He donned gloves and carried a walking stick. As he led us down a hidden path behind the Manor, he flicked away a poison ivy vine that might otherwise have grazed him. "You brute," he said to the offending vine.

Lord Hodgson led us down a winding path, over a small plank footbridge to a secluded swimming pond concealed by weeping wil-lows. The pond followed a cleft in the landscape and emptied into a stream that in turn ran into a meadow, where more cows could be seen. A maintained lawn led to a handmade dock, and then, the water. As we approached, a gray heron started and took flight. I oohed and aahed; my husband shushed me, fearful I would jinx the sale or raise the price. But the lord and lady accepted our offer of the asking price, which was modest, even then. In return, we vowed to honor the lord's restrictive covenants, which would be revealed later, in full detail, in our deed. He gave us the gist: "No subdivision, noxious smells, sounds, or lights that could glare into the windows of the Manor. . . . No mo-torcycles, no snowmobiles, no salting the road for winter ice," and so on.

I noticed that the word "noxious" was frequently repeated, along with "objectionable." Sometimes, Lord Hodgson used both words in the same sentence. When he showed us "our" *Rosa rugosa* bushes, he said, "In summer, you'll be subjected to the Japanese beetles mating two and three at a time on your rosebuds. It's so objectionable. And then, if you kill them in a Bag-a-Bug, you must dispose of their nox-ious remains."

As we walked the property line, Lord Hodgson remarked, "Your boundary goes on the diagonal here." He indicated a triangular patch of mowed grass in front of the house. I wondered why the line was cut in such an odd way, but I was afraid to appear critical, and so didn't say anything.

Seventeen years would pass before I knew the reason for that diagonal cut. By then, the property line would be of crucial interest to me, and I would spend thousands in legal fees to determine my right to prevent a threat posed from the "other side." But, of course, I knew nothing of the future on this spring day, and I chose not to give the triangular design of my front lawn any further thought. After all, my husband and I had started our life together in that three-sided garret in Greenwich Village; perhaps we were destined to inhabit pie-slice-shaped spaces. Yes, the shape was fine with us. We also promised to pay our share of the care for dozens of old sugar maples that lined the Avenue, as His Lordship called the driveway.

We almost skipped up the winding path to the Manor. I could smell the soil as the sun warmed it. Robins tugged at worms. Bona fide Eastern bluebirds flew past in azure pairs and perched on branches, twittering at us.

We and the house were sold. The lord would hold the mortgage at twelve and a half percent. I envisioned him actually holding it, as a yellowed parchment scroll, in his fine-boned white hands.

Three months later, my husband and I drove up at sunset to take possession. It was July 2, and the grounds were almost violently verdant, the sugar maples heavy, in full leaf. Across the pasture, the cows walked single-file, the lead cow's bell clanging melodically. The air was still with the moist heat of dusk, and a shocking pink streaked across the western sky. For a moment, everything we saw was rose-tinted, even the cows. The roses themselves were in bloom, a thousand flowers on the old *rugosa* hedge that grew in front of the house.

My husband picked me up and carried me across the threshold. We'd been married for fifteen years, but we were still in our thirties, and this was our first real home. We laughed as we kissed.

Inside The Inn, we found a welcome note from the lord and lady and a chilled bottle of good champagne. My husband had no sooner set me down to pop the cork when we heard a car pull into our circular gravel drive. A couple—strangers to us—hopped out. They carried suitcases and were waving a key ring. They said that they'd rented the Innlet from the previous tenants.

My husband and I had been vaguely aware that there had been British "renters" on weekends, but we'd been told that they had returned to England. In any case, according to our deed, their lease would be up in ninety days—then they would be gone forever. But without telling us, the outgoing tenant had sublet The Innlet to this new couple, who were now demanding that we turn on the hot water heater so that they could shower. And so my dream of privacy ended, and my true role of homeowner, that of custodian, began.

As the light faded, I stood looking at the hedge roses, and the lawn beside them seemed to come alive. The Japanese beetles, as predicted by His Lordship, emerged from their winter's hibernation and whirred through the air before alighting on the rose petals and eating them.

As I watched in horror, I also became aware of a strange glow in the sky. The sun had set, but a blood-red aura appeared across the fields, emanating from a site half a mile away. I knew that there was a commuter college somewhere over there, known as "UCK" or "Ugly College" (officially, Ulster County Community College), and as the evening descended, the school's system of anticrime lights flared into phosphorescence. Atmospheric conditions stained the light red, and the college glowed like a Martian heliport.

Later, I learned that Lord Hodgson's mother had donated forty of the acres on which Ugly College squatted. Miss Talbot had envisioned something more like Harvard being constructed, and she had been horrified at the uninspired brick buildings that followed.

Lord Hodgson himself had tried to "plant out" the college. Half the year, UCK did indeed disappear behind the greenery, but when the leaves fell, there it was—with less charm than the local prison. Not only that, I was soon to discover, UCK was not silent. UCK would emit what Lord Hodgson called "noxious noises," rock concerts, football rallies. Whenever such an event became too "noxiously noisy," Lord Hodgson phoned the college and asked them to please be silent. More often than not, UCK obeyed. The land, after all, had come from "Mother."

So on my first night in residence at The Inn, I tried to absorb this triple shock—the tenants' demanding hot water, the Japanese beetles eating the roses, and the warlike skies over UCK. My husband looked at me and asked, "Are you crying?" I denied that I was. I was sure His Lordship had left instruction as to how to deal with problems, and so he had. Next to the bottle of champagne was a note extolling the abilities of the seventy-eight-year-old British caretaker, Cecil Green. He would solve everything. "Cecil," said the note, "is the Brain." I looked up the hill toward the south, to the carriage house, where Cecil still lived, where he had lived since he arrived by ship from England more than sixty years before. "Follow Cecil's every advice," Lord Hodgson instructed. "You shan't regret it."

I phoned the carriage house and begged Cecil to come down. Cecil appeared, driving a '78 Chevy, his new car; he had recently retired his Model-T. Following a style that had fallen by the wayside elsewhere, Cecil Green still wore a uniform—a green suit. In summer, the outfit was cotton. In winter, it was padded and sported a fur-trimmed collar. Cecil always wore a green cap and kept a pipe clenched between his teeth.

He was indeed the "Brain." He knew everything about The Inn; he understood the basement, the grunting furnace, the reset button on the hot water heater. He knew the map to the "zones"—the maze of pipes that sent heat and hot water through the different sections of The Inn. He could remember the gravity-flow water system, and showed me the ten-thousand-gallon tanks that still rested in the attic.

The single drawback to Cecil was that he was deaf. So when I screamed, "How do you turn on the hot water heater?" he answered, "The flowers need water, no rain for a week." Which was why we also had to retain Stewart Lee, who always wore an orange cap, and his own version of a vintage uniform—a 1940s brown jacket. Stewart moved close to Cecil and bellowed in his better ear, "Hot water heater."

"He had a hearing aid," said Stewart. "Yes, yes, but he lost it in Forty-nine, trimming vines behind the tennis court."

The men soon had the hot water heater burning, but Cecil warned us to get rid of it. "It costs a hundred dollars a night to run," he said. In spite of his long history as a family retainer, Cecil seemed excited by the change in ownership of The Inn. In a style I would become accustomed to, he stood stock still, breathing hard for several moments, then took a deep draw on his pipe and made a pronouncement. "Electric water heater costs too much. Get an oil-fired one." A few more inhalations and he added, "And I'd reroute the furnace pipe. Miss Talbot had it that way because she said it made a rude noise up the chimney. Fuel company always said it could blow up." We agreed at once to do as Cecil suggested. This was the first in what was to become a series of basement consultations. In what became a tradition, every autumn for the next decade, Cecil would show me how to adjust the heat pipe zones and bleed them if they got air bubbles or "froze up." As the years passed, this event became more emotionally charged, as Cecil always began with "In case I'm not here next winter," which, toward the end of our association, brought tears to my eyes because I had come to care for him as everyone at Willowby did.

"The amazing thing about Cecil," Lord Hodgson said to me once, "is that, deaf as he is, he can hear perfectly in an emergency." And so he could. When, months later, on our first winter weekend, we felt a suspicious warmth spread through the upstairs (The Inn was snug, but it wasn't toasty), we phoned Cecil and he arrived at two A.M., in his uniform, with a flashlight, and found the problem: a burst pipe in The Innlet. There, the walls streamed with a cascade of steaming water, pouring gallons a minute from an unseen break. Cecil hatcheted through to the problem, stemmed the flood, and left.

fourteen

On our first morning in residence, we woke to several surprises. The workmen began to arrive, an invading army of pickup trucks and vans, their services emblazoned in script on their sides. First to appear was the "tree man," Arthur Woodcock.

While the sugar maples that lined the Avenue looked lush and healthy, Woodcock informed me that their appearance was deceptive. He led me from tree to tree, informing me that we were actually touring an outdoor hospice for the terminally ill trees.

"They all have crotch or butt rot," he diagnosed. I laughed, but not at the proposed cure and the projected medical bill—ten thousand dollars to treat their distress and chain their sick limbs together.

A cast of dozens followed. The house came with a master plumber, a man to service the fire extinguishers, women who did landscaping, and a water-conditioning expert who promised to rid us of the sulfur in the system, which he referred to with the first in his series of rustic asides, as our "fart water." The sulfur gas would permeate our home, blacken our silverware, and corrode the pipes. Whenever we showered, we were told, fumes would fill the house like an exploded stink bomb. We signed on, and on.

Then we met our neighbors. I had been aware, of course, of the dairy farm in my peripheral vision—it rested downhill to the east, at an esthetic distance of a quarter-mile. I could see it from the kitchen window and the upstairs bedrooms on the eastern side of the house. From that distance, I saw a Tinker Toy image of a red barn, silver silos, the domino pattern of the cows, the tiny yellow tractor pouffing blue smoke. I was aware, too, of the farmer's deeded right to graze the herd on our pasture. I was less cognizant of the complications of operating a dairy farm—the tractors and manure spreader soon began chugging up our hill. It turned out that our "private" location, half a mile off the road, was in fact on a manure and hay route, traversed, in season, many times a day by rumbling John Deeres and backfiring Farm-alls.

"You can suggest they drive round," Lady Helena advised, "and then you could plant out the back driveway, turn it into a charming flower garden." My husband and I went to see the dairy farm to get a better understanding of the situation.

I soon saw that this place was to become my husband's personal Happyville. He was returning to his genotype, which I suppose could be called Celtic chicken farmer. We walked down the lane that connected The Inn to the farm. The farm was a compound, a series of barns, animal enclosures, and two houses. It was named for, owned, and operated by a father-son team, Abner Bowers and his son Nate. Approaching on foot, we came upon the barns and the resident Holstein herd before we saw the people and their habitations. Even a city girl like me could see that this farm was superior to most. From where I looked down upon it, the farm was framed by the forever green Shawangunk mountain range, part of a former Quaker preserve now belonging to Mohonk Mountain House, the area's most historic resort hotel. The Mountain House itself was visible ten miles away, a wooden castle high above our valley. By night, the hotel glittered like a brooch set on the chest of the mountain. For a time, the Bowerses renamed their place Mohonk View Farm, but the name didn't stick. Their own, Bowers Willowby, did.

The barnyard seemed like a resort for cows. The Holsteins were lounging by a babbling brook when I first visited; a few were wading, up to their black-and-white ankles. Other cows were licking a molasses wheel and looked up from their dessert as we passed.

The farm road led directly past the main barn, between the father's and the son's houses. The father's house, a clapboard cottage, was set into the earth. The cows and fields were more than visible from the windows—they seemed almost as if they would spill into the rooms within, where Betty Bowers, Abner's wife, was perpetually baking.

On the day we met them, Abner and Betty were walking across the barnyard to their house. Betty held a wire egg basket, and Abner was saying, "How many eggs, today, Mother?"

"Twenty-four, Father," she answered. I was stunned that they called each other Mother and Father. I had never heard of such a thing. Abner was slight and seemed permanently tanned. He wore mud-caked overalls and a seersucker milking cap, a hat sewn from an agricultural store pattern. The cap sits flat on the head as the farmer presses himself against the cow's flank while he milks. Betty wore a simple shirt and skirt. She was smaller and rounder, with fair skin and sensibly cut graying hair. Abner was around fifty-two then, Betty somewhat younger. They'd been married since she was eighteen. Betty had kind blue eyes and a matter-of-fact friendliness. She managed to be sweet but not cloying, even while delivering lines like, "Well, come on in. I'm taking my pies out of the oven."

"Sorry if the house smells like old wet dog," Betty said as we entered the house, in what I would soon realize was her characteristic way. "But we have an old wet dog." And indeed they did—Dixie, an Australian blue heeler, lay, paws crossed, under the table, pups sucking from her elongated nipples.

"Good cow dog," Abner said. "Part dingo."

We shared a pie, hot-baked cherry, made from fresh-picked fruit, and washed it down with the rich, grass-scented milk. I wondered aloud if they didn't worry about cholesterol. "Oh, we used to drink straight cream," Betty said.

Abner invited us to watch the milking. We walked back across the yard. I noticed my husband had acquired a rustic gait to match his increasingly twangy way of speaking. We went into the great barn, where hay was stacked, two stories high, in aromatic bales. Light filtered down from a cupola. Doves in the rafters started, cooing, and exited at our entrance. I could hear music coming from the milking parlor. "They milk better to music," Abner said.

We followed him along a zigzag corridor, packed in hay, into the area where the milkers stood, listening to taped Patsy Cline. *I'm crazy, crazy for loving you. . . .* The cows turned to gaze at us with the benevolent interest I soon learned was typical of them. Milking was not what I imagined: any fantasy I had of milkmaids or rustic lads on bended knee, tugging rhythmically on pink teats, went straight down the manure chute. The milking was done mechanically, each udder plugged into a ganglion of suction tubes that gripped the cow's teats like so many metallic fingers. The tubes, in turn, connected to clear pipes that pumped the milk above our heads.

When Abner flipped the switch, the barn began to pulse with milk. The clear pipes ran white, along complicated conduits to their ultimate destination: the milk room, the metal vat where the milk would wait, cooling, until siphoned the next morning into the tank of the milk cooperative's truck.

The cows stood wearing neutral expressions; they seemed like barely animate adjuncts to this hydraulic system that drew on their insides. Abner, Nate, and Nate's daughters, two blonde girls in jeans, ran up and down the aisles to prepare each cow. They worked fast, to the music, swabbing every nipple with Bovadine Teat Dip.

The milk machines looked heavy, like metal and rubber octopi, and had to be carried from cow to cow, as each got her turn, hooked up to the suction. As Abner explained the process, he was, for a moment, framed between two cow rear ends as both gave way. "It's not all glory," he said, grinning between the twin flumes, a Niagara of cow piss.

He would milk now, and again at two thirty A.M. In the "in between times," he would clean the barns, tend the crops, sort the feed, and follow such "to do" chores as listed on the barn blackboard: "Breed #124." The breeding was more and more these days done by "A.I.," artificial insemination with a syringe. Nate, a quiet man of twenty-five with intense blue eyes and a square face that resembled his mother's, was getting good at it. "When he's as good as the bull, the bull will go," Abner said.

We walked outside to the bull pen, to see Astro before it was too late. Astro was a presence. A black behemoth, big as a building, he cast a giant shadow in the barnyard. Astro wore an actual brass ring through his nose, and, a farmhand explained as he fed him, led a constricted if sensual existence. The young cows ready to be served were led into his bull pen, two at a time. It took two heifers to satisfy Astro, and everyone wanted to see him satisfied. If he wasn't, it was understood, he could trash his pen and do away with all of us.

Astro bore little resemblance to the cows. His eyes were narrow, red. He had forehead fur that hung like bad bangs over his sullen expression. He snorted and looked as if he would like to trample us. I could see why the farmers were trying to perfect their technique with the syringe.

Life on the farm appeared hard enough without Astro's mischief. We watched as they ran a steel machine called the barn cleaner and maneuvered tractors with buckets of silage feed and scoopers of manure. The work was never-ending—and dangerous. Abner had almost lost his arm to the barn cleaner—"If I'd had on a good shirt, my arm would have gone. My shirt was so old, the cloth ripped right off." Soon enough, I met other farmers who had been less fortunate. The man down the road at the stand was missing three fingers; the fellow across the river had only one arm. Then there were the farmers we never met at all because they had been killed.

It was instantly apparent that it would be unthinkable to interfere in any way with the workings of Bowers Willowby. There would be no question that they could continue to use the back road. In fact, I was thrilled when I heard my now-twangy husband offer to forgive the sixty-dollar lease on our pasture. *Why, shucks,* he practically said. *I wouldn't dream of taking your money.* We walked back up our hill. My husband kicked dried cow manure ahead of him, as earthy Frisbees. I could still hear the Patsy Cline song in my head, *Crazy for loving you.*

At our house, the motorcade of repair men was pulling out for the day. We went inside The Inn to discover that the lord and lady had been back. They left a note apologizing for the intrusion and giving detailed explanations of why they had had to move some of the furniture in and some of it out.

The *"fuuurniture,"* pronounced by the Hodgsons with the elongated initial vowel, seemed to be a part of the moveable feast here at Willowby. The Hodgsons were emotionally involved with certain pieces that had been left in our house "on loan." They were forever shifting them to other locations on the property. One morning, early on, Lady Marguerite phoned to say, "Contain yourself. Don't get too excited, but I believe I have located the missing finial to the settee in your entry. But don't get too excited, I'm not absolutely certain."

The next day, Lady Marguerite phoned again, near tears. I was afraid that something had happened to His Lordship or that she had injured herself.

"Lady Marguerite, are you all right?" I asked.

"You may dispense with our titles," she answered. "That nonsense. Something dreadful has happened," she said, her voice cracking.

"Teapot. Been with us from before the Blitz. It slipped from my hands as I was emptying tea leaves in the toilet. It just slid and broke into a thousand pieces." She took a deep pause. "Edmund's been awfully good about it." I realized then, by the close of my first weekend, that I had not merely acquired a place in the country—I had entered another culture.

Within days, the original British tenants "in the back" returned and took up residence in The Innlet. They arrived with two children, two hairy dachshunds, and a parrot that spoke with an English accent. They had lots of friends on or around the estate, and when I arrived for my next weekend, I saw them playing tennis on "my" court, while eleven guests (I counted them) lounged on the Adirondack furniture and drank gin.

I ran upstairs to the rose-papered room, threw myself on Miss Talbot's chintz-covered chaise lounge, and thought, *What am I to do?* I looked, possibly for an answer, to the life-size portrait of Miss Talbot that stood, somewhat askew, against the wall by my bed. Miss Talbot, regal in full-length gown, stern of lip and brow, seemed to narrow her varnished gaze at me as if to say, *My dear, you should have known.*

As I sank into the down cushions of Miss Talbot's chaise lounge, I took comfort in a retreat into the past. I felt fortunate to have Miss Talbot herself as my guide. Not only was she looking down at me from her portrait, I had in hand her memoir, *A Sordid Boon.*

I was struck at once by the photograph of the author on the back of the dust jacket, because it was not what I might have expected—a photo of Hilary Talbot the time she wrote her book. She would have been seventy-two years old in 1968, the year of publication. Instead, the portrait she chose for her book cover is one of herself as a child, an eight-year-old, in 1904.

She looked out at me—a beautiful dark-blonde little girl, with the same thin face and pallor as her son, the current Lord Hodgson. She wears a white lace dress and is not smiling. Her expression is poignant, almost tragic, as if she somehow anticipated the fate that awaited her in four years. Her father died, without warning, when she was twelve years old.

Hilary Talbot and I could not have had more different backgrounds. "Little Hilary," as she was known, was born into privilege, the child of a late-in-life marriage of two prosperous parents, while I was the out-of-wedlock daughter of a single mother who began life without any means at all.

But in truth, we had much in common. For me, in a sense, time stopped when I was eight—for years afterward I would, if I did not check myself, write the wrong date, automatically scrawling 1955, the year of my mother's death, before realizing my mistake. So the eight-year-old girl who still somehow lived inside me recognized the eight-year-old on the back cover of A Sordid Boon. We were both only children, daughters, born at the last biological moment to women who had been prepared to go on alone for the rest of their lives and seemed surprised and delighted to have a daughter, almost by default.

I could read in Hilary Talbot's eyes the days spent alone, the wait for a father's return. Like me, she was to devote many of her adult years to trying to decipher what had happened between her mother and father. For as my parents had not stayed together, neither had Hilary's.

Her book is a curious volume, as it tells the story of her mother, Sara Jenson, and her father, Edmund Talbot, from a backward perspective. Even as I enjoyed her narrative, I found it oblique and hard to follow. She seemed to withhold herself—never resorting to the first person, instead referring to herself as "Hilary" or "the child of that marriage." In keeping with this approach, the single photograph of herself as an adult shows Hilary with her back to the camera.

This may have been a most accurate portrait, for the more I read of Hilary Talbot's life story, the more I could see she had turned her back to the world. So it is appropriate that she is shown this way, her spine as stiff as the wrought-iron garden chair upon which she sits. She faces away, contemplating the view from Willowby, looking at the "blue mountains," as they were known in that time. Hilary Talbot appears slim, taut, her hair upswept, her face and expression forever unknowable but her pride and defiance of custom unmistakable.

As I lay back on her chaise, sipping English breakfast tea from what must have been her own Spode cup with its pattern of roses and thorns, I lost myself in her life. I could not know, that first summer day in 1981, that I was also reading a blueprint for my own life. There was no way to forecast that I would reprise her pattern. I was aware, of course, that like me, she had married at nineteen, a childhood sweetheart. But I couldn't guess that I, too, would divorce after twenty-seven years of marriage, at the exact age at which she had, forty-six.

I was absorbed anyway—I wanted to know what drew her back here, alone, in midlife, to start over again. I was impressed, too, that she had refused to maintain a façade when her marriage failed. She was not one to go through the motions; she had abdicated.

The book held more clues than I could ever count. It would take almost twenty years for the events of Hilary Talbot's story to come full circle and affect the course of my own life. At the moment that I read, the sun streaming through the lace curtains, I was grateful for the details I could glean. Here was the beginning of Willowby—the "bachelor project" of Hilary's father, Edmund Talbot, built before he married Hilary's mother. Edmund Talbot is described as a serious, middle aged, "conservative businessman," fifty-five at the time of his marriage. Her mother, Sara Jenson, was forty-two, a widow.

Hilary Talbot's telling of the tale is genteel and leaves a bit to the imagination. Reading in the more racy present, I wonder at the speed of Sara Jenson's remarriage. She should be in widow's weeds, when she is suddenly appearing on the doorstep of her new suitor's mansion, chaperoned only by her eccentric spinster sister Mab.

The *deus ex machina* of the romance is none other than a figure who would come to haunt my own life—the Hindu monk Swami Vivekenanda. The Swami appears in a photograph in the book—he is young, in his early thirties, with butterscotch-colored skin and soulful eyes. He wears a turban and poses with one hand over his heart. It is easy to see how he became a romantic figure in the 1890s, when he roamed the United States as a charismatic speaker.

Edmund Talbot and Sara Jenson began to court by attending the swami's lectures in New York, in a salon near Sara's city home on West Thirty-third Street. They were always accompanied by Mab, who turned into the swami's most fervent admirer. The trio of Edmund, Hilary, and Mab seemed to have fallen under the spell cast by the young monk, whose speeches were by all accounts "eloquent." Did Hilary Talbot also idolize the swami, follow his teachings? Though she quotes his messages—"God made finite by my love, the intensifying of love brings resemblance"—she does not go on record as a devotee. Her overall persona seems so astringent that I doubted, even as I read her account of her parents' devotion to the swami, that Hilary Talbot shared their passion.

Hilary Talbot remains her own most mysterious character. She sidesteps all but the most discreet expressions of emotion. She never explains why her marriage failed, but gives only her solution—to return to Willowby, the estate she recalls from her earliest childhood, from the time when her parents were still in love and the house was decorated for celebrations and entertainment.

Hilary is more forthcoming on the subject of her parents' marriage. "He had tired of his wife," she writes of her father. During that final summer of 1909, her parents had decided to stay apart. Even seventy years later, the statement by Edmund that Sara and Hilary "may as well" remain abroad—mother and daughter in England while he, alone, commuted between New York and Willowby—retains a palpable sadness. Sara's love of the place had waned—"All dressed up and nowhere to go" was how she viewed the country estate. She had wanted the social excitement found in England and France. Edmund Talbot had craved only the serenity of nature and the country. The estrangement became final when Edmund Talbot died, suddenly, on a train platform, on August 29, 1909. He was returning from a solitary weekend at Willowby, en route to New York for the business week. The trip in that time was arduous and indirect; he had to go by horse and carriage down the long winding drives of Willowby to a train station at Binnewater, then by train to New Jersey and across the Hudson by ferry to Manhattan.

As I read the account of Edmund Talbot's death, I realized that he had spent his last night alive in the very room in which I reclined on his daughter's chaise lounge. The Manor was "closed up," his daughter reports, "covered in dust sheets." So Edmund Talbot had stayed in The Inn, alone. Did the estrangement, the heat, the long journey contribute to Edmund Talbot's death? No one can know. What is certain is that the end, so brutal and abrupt, brought a sharp new demarcation to his daughter's life. She awoke the next day as the "orphaned daughter," his sole heir. Ironically, she was bequeathed Willowby at the exact moment that her mother chose never to return to the estate.

Sara and Hilary Talbot became expatriates, spending most of their time in England. When Hilary married her childhood sweetheart, she forced him to return with her to Willowby for occasional visits. In the Manor, the dust sheets stayed on more years than they were lifted. For three decades, the mansion waited, a ghost house, for Hilary's return as a mature woman.

She came back to Willowby in 1942, at the start of World War II. When she returned, leaving her marriage and the war in Europe, she reports it was "the soil that saved" her. She describes its loamy scent, the feel of the earth in her fingers. She was a successful transplant. She dropped her title, resumed her maiden name and, to an extent, her old life. She walked the pastures of Willowby accompanied by her great white poodle, Belle.

Every reader forms some emotional attachment to a narrator. I could not help but like Hilary, even though I am sure, from descriptions of those who knew her, that she was somewhat intimidating. To me, she seemed to have great feeling, as opposed to sentimentality. I could respect her desire to keep her pain private, buttoned up. I am not a believer in phantoms, but I enjoyed the idea of her presence here, and, certainly, I benefited from her taste. She was flowery without being frilly, no-nonsense without being mean.

What I knew of Hilary, I liked: that she walked down to the dairy barn to buy a cow and ended up buying the entire farm. One day, I would wish I could do the same. We undertook similar projects. As I would in later years, Hilary Talbot craved a private swimming place, so she created one—the hidden pond I had seen behind the Manor. In so doing, she had diverted an underground river. Cecil told me that a plentiful well, reliable until the day of Hilary Talbot's blasting of the pond, failed, never to recover.

Hilary Talbot's portrait remained in my house for two years. Her son and daughter-in-law seemed in no hurry to reclaim it. Perhaps it was the imperious stare. One day, she did disappear—her likeness, anyway—and all that remained of her in The Inn was the floral wallpapers, the polished pieces of Victorian furniture, a gleaming mahogany dresser or two, and the chaise lounge.

As I settled into what had been Hilary's world, walked the paths she had first trod, I began to take an unexpected pleasure in the pastoral English-style life that she had, indirectly, bequeathed to me.

My love affair with cows began almost at once. It was only my second or third weekend in The Inn when I awoke one dawn to feel the house and my bed shaking. Without my contact lenses, I couldn't see the cause. When I looked out the bedroom window, all I could make out was a field of black-and-white polka dots. It took a few seconds for me to realize what I saw was the Bowers' entire herd, 168 Holsteins, on the hoof. They had escaped en masse and were galloping toward The Manor. What had felt like an earthquake was the thunder of all those hooves as they hotfooted past The Inn.

The rotary phone beside my bed rang. It was Miss Talbot's son, Lord Hodgson phoning down from the Manor: "Have you seen them, running, with their ungainly rumps, leaving their noxious patties?"

I was charmed by His Lordship's description, the cows' getaway, and, most of all, by the roundup that followed. The father-son team of farmers, Abner and Nate, raced up in separate vehicles—the father in a pickup truck, the son in his car—to block the access roads. An auxiliary force of wives and children leaped out to halt the escape.

"Head 'em off!" Abner Bowers yelled. I raced out in my nightgown and joined the tightening circle: every man, woman and child walked, arms outstretched, toward the cows. It wasn't simple to redirect the herd. The lead cow, flashing her ear tag, clanging her bell, kept taking off on her own, heading toward the open fields and the possibility of the highway and town beyond. She was a source of inspiration to the other 167 cows who, snorting fore and aft, tried to follow. At last, we forced all 168 Holsteins to trot down the farm road. They took off. As they picked up speed, their domino pattern blurred into a true-life animation, a black-and-white river that flowed downhill into the sunrise. As I watched, daybreak tinted the sky apricot, illuminated the green of the grass.

From that dawn on, I was smitten by the cows and the life of the farm that revolved around them. I was ready to know more.

f i f t e e n

If I had ever thought of cows in my previous life, it had been with negative connotations. In the Bronx, when I attended high school, cow references were always derogatory. To be a cow was to be sexually available and worse: overweight. I had never heard a single positive thing about cows.

But if I searched far into my own background, I could find a connection. My second cousins owned the "last dairy farm in the city." When they sold to a massive developer, photos of my relatives and their cows were in all the city newspapers. I even had a vague memory of visiting the "Canarsie cousins" when I was a child. I recalled a tiny barn, the land at a slant, cows crammed in, the shadow of high rises and pressure of concrete already felt at the barn door.

I remember *kugel* on an oilcloth-covered kitchen table, Holsteins gathered at the window. I know I laughed in delight, but I could not say that these cows inspired the deep feelings I would know later.

The cousins themselves were unlike most members of my extended family—they were true farmers, while my other relatives prided themselves on being members of the intelligentsia, scholars, writers.

The farm cousins were friendly. The mother, Judy, was a brunette with literal flash—her black kohl-lined eyes sparkled; her gold jewelry caught the light. She seemed like a gypsy princess who had made a rustic marriage to a husky Jewish peasant. When they sold the farm, they made "millions." They moved, with many cow knickknacks but no real cows, to a house in the Catskills, not so far in miles from The Inn, but a vast distance in country style.

The first cow I grew to love, on an individual basis, was Brightie, a Brown Swiss, one of only two in the otherwise Holstein herd. Brightie appeared one morning—looking in my kitchen window at The Inn. Who could resist? She had broken down the rustic fence that had separated us and walked straight up to the porch.

I went outside to greet her. She backed away; she was, I suppose, "cowed." We performed a kind of tango—if I stepped forward, Brightie stepped backward. This dance lasted for an hour and ended with my offering her a ninety-nine-cent bunch of watercress.

Brightie was the most senior cow on the farm; she wore a bell that clanged as she marched across the meadow. She wanted to be known. In return, she offered her warm bulk, her yeasty aroma and constant, secret regurgitations.

She was old for a cow—twelve. She'd given birth to twelve calves, and at the time I met her, she was expecting another. In her pregnancy, she looked as if she had swallowed a spinet. After her initial hesitation, she ran to me and rubbed her forehead against my back. From that time on, whenever she greeted me, it was with a back rub. I don't know whether she was expressing affection or scratching her head, but I liked it, whatever it was.

Brightie represented the past. She was not just old but old-fashioned, the kind of cow that would soon be outmoded. She could never comprehend what I would soon learn, the ironies of the cow condition. For on the dairy farm of the end of the twentieth century, we stood closer to science fiction than to nature. Every detail of cow life was now engineered by man and machine, a regimen established to keep the "girls" set on the path of lifetime lactation. For it is milk, after all, that is the motive.

I had begun to get the message on that first day that I trotted down to the barn and witnessed the actual milking. And I had learned more from the Bowerses, when they described artificial insemination. But there was still more—the Bowerses soon graduated, as other dairy farmers had, to embryo transplants, the process by which fertilized embryos are implanted into cows who are not their biological mothers.

The cows are watched closely for their receptive phase. When ready to be so served, they wear what look like inflamed thermometers taped to their rumps. The "thermometers" turn red when the cow is likely to successfully carry. There is another indicator of a cow's fertile period—she will stand while another cow attempts to mount her. Which gives rise to the question, Are cows gay? Were the 168 Holsteins and two Brown Swiss hanging out in my pasture a troop of animal lesbians? Not really. Apparently, their Sapphic routines are the result of life in a sex-segregated society; the cows are behaving the way prisoners in a cellblock do; playing the only game in town.

The more I knew, the more I enjoyed the cows, whatever their sexual orientation or biological origin. The embryo transplants (the Bowerses called them "ETs,") were as cute as the other calves, although they did appear incongruous. Most of Abner Bowers' mothers were Holsteins; the babies, Brown Swiss.

I grew used to seeing Mac, the big-animal vet, arrive to administer the transplants. Mac was a tall, handsome man with a single physical anomaly. His right arm was much larger than his left; the muscles bulged from pulling calves. It gave him an odd, asymmetrical look. He would arrive, lopsided, at any hour of the day or night to assist a cow in trouble. Most often, the problem births occurred to first-time mothers, the heifers. The older cows, like Brightie, gave birth easily and where they were supposed to—in the barn. But occasionally, a heifer would break loose, and sometimes nature took over what science had started.

During my first summer on the farm, I was fortunate to witness that rarity—a natural calf birth in the wild. I was sitting at my desk working when I heard human and animal cries coming from the pasture behind The Inn. The urgency of the cries drew me at once. I ran to the thicket at the back of the field.

Abner, Nate, and a farmhand had found the heifer, who had escaped from the barn and run to hide for the finale of her labor. Her labor was protracted and difficult. Lowing, lowing, the cow strained in the shadows of a maple tree.

There was no time to get the official equipment—the obstetrical chains—or to summon the vet. Abner Bowers whipped off his belt, and when the calf's tiny, soft hooves poked forth from the mother's orifice, he tied the belt around them and yanked. He pulled so hard, the belt broke. There was no more time: the calf had to emerge to breathe, or die in the birth canal. Abner pulled, pulled. He braced himself, one foot against the mother's flank. At last, the calf, black, white, and limp, swung into view. Abner held it upside down, to no effect.

Apparently stillborn, the calf hung lifeless, neck askew, eyes rolled back in their sockets. Abner threw the calf to the ground, broke twigs from the nearby tree, then poked the sticks up the calf's nostrils to stimulate the breathing reflex. There was no response. The calf's tiny rib cage did not move. Then, while everyone held their breath, Abner Bowers knelt and pressed his own mouth to the calf's. Exchanging human for animal breath, the farmer rose and lowered his head to the baby calf.

Within a minute, the calf's rib cage rose. Its first breath was visible; a shiver through the shining body. Then the brown eyes swiveled into their proper position, and the tension that signals life corrected the angle of the neck. The calf's limbs jerked, the spasm of animation. Instantly, it tried to rise up, looking for the great black-and-white bulk that was its mother.

The finale was anticlimactic. The mother cow was chased with yet another hypodermic—this time an injection to contract her uterus and prevent her udder from overfilling. The calf, too weak to walk, had to be carried to the farmer's Chevrolet and transported to the barn in its open trunk. But miracles cannot be negated, only slightly diminished. It is impossible to believe that an event of such suspense can be totally concerned with commerce and have nothing to do with life.

Position, I know, is everything. At Willowby, I found myself in a most interesting location—the exact center of what had once been a great estate. When I looked out from my window or sat rocking on the porch, I could see the topography of my future.

While all my neighbors were distant enough—no house was closer than a quarter of a mile—I could see all of them. To the south was The Manor, with the resident lord and lady. To the west was Ugly College, to the east, the dairy farm, and to the north, an historic farmstead dating back to 1690 that also had once belonged to the lord and lady but had been sold only shortly before The Inn to another couple from the city who also cherished their privacy.

This couple, whom I shall call the Smithsons, were youngish (our age) and, except for their wealth, shared many similarities with my husband and me. Our marriages were both mixed, theirs the reverse of ours: she was a country girl married to a city boy; he was Jewish, she was not. They joined Indiana to Brooklyn, while we united the Bronx with West Virginia. They also had no children and, oddly, lived on our street in New York City. Once I paced off the distance between our apartments in Manhattan and found it measured, almost to the foot, the space between our country homes. What this meant, I don't know, other than there is some weird fatefulness to place, and perhaps the Smithsons and my husband and I shared a trajectory.

What we didn't share were the funds to maintain the properties, and The Inn always looked like a happy if unkempt sister to The Stone Farm, which was groomed for hundreds of thousands of dollars per decade, growing more dignified and decorous by the minute. Motorcades of gardeners and stonemasons came and went, far more frequently than the Smithsons, who, as their business flourished, came less and less to oversee their perfect garden.

It became my avocation, as the more present neighbor, to observe the comings and goings at the Stone Farm, and to note if anything seemed amiss. This grew more urgent with time, as Lad Smithson guarded his privacy, even when he wasn't there. He was famous for greeting intruders with a large dog, a gun, and a polite inquiry: "May I help you?"

So for years, stonemasons hung, almost like permanent salamanders, to the sides of the Stone Farm, and Arthur Woodcock manicured the lawn. A pond was dug and stocked with costly koi fish. Once, on a rare visit, I came upon a gray heron with a ten-thousand-dollar fish in his craw. He seemed to haw before taking flight. The deer, the bear, and the coyote enjoyed the Stone Farm along with its attendants. The place maintained the quiet of a wildlife conservancy, uninterrupted save for the occasional beeps of the alarm system, which was more and more frequently set off by the only constant inhabitants—the mice.

Someday, the Smithsons promised themselves, they would have time to come and stay in their perfect place. Until then, it would live its pampered life without them, even expanding in its silence— acquiring a Zen waterfall, a charming stone-edged addition, a potting shed. The Smithsons, the lord and lady, and my husband and I made up an economic troika—we split the cost of the Avenue's upkeep three ways. My arrival had apparently been inadvertently well timed. Lad Smithson had a city kid's sense of humor, and he laughed when he greeted us: "You picked a good time to come down the Avenue. I just spent thousands on gravel and replacement saplings." Not to mention tree surgery. The Smithsons also participated in the roundelay of the *fuuurniture*—they had chintz-covered chairs and even a refrigerator that the Hodgsons "left" in the house but periodically visited or even whisked away. No one but the Smithsons would ever appreciate as much as we did His Lordship's continued sense of responsibility for the property. His Lordship called us both that first autumn to say, "I apologize for the poor color of the foliage this year. We shall hope to do better for you next fall."

Just how far-reaching was his power, I had to wonder, and how wide the radius of proprietorship? Meanwhile, Lady Marguerite phoned to say she had found a tester bed in the basement. "We want you to have it," she said. We came to the Manor to see the tester bed, agreed to buy it for a nominal sum, and the lord and lady ordered a custom-made mattress for it. Then, at the last moment before the transfer of the bed could occur, they called in the late evening to say, with emotion, that they were sorry to have mentioned the tester bed. "It *must* remain in the Manor," they said, as if engaged in an argument.

"Gee," my husband said, "we didn't even know you had a tester bed until you offered it to us." "Well, now you shan't have it," His Lordship said. "It really must remain in the Manor. We have given it a great deal of thought."

We continued to rent pieces of *fuuurniture* until it could be determined where they truly belonged. I had no problem with this; everything the Hodgsons had left behind was lovely, authentic, like them—and also like them a bit precious and with potentially vulnerable fissures. We knew we were fortunate—the tenants who had rented

The Innlet had reported that they had been charged for "wear on the sheets."

An immediate standoff occurred over the swimming pond and the tennis court. As the sale of The Inn went through, all four of us—the lord, the lady, my spouse, and I—stood on the court and discussed, with grim set of jaw, the recreational future open to all of us.

"What about that lovely pond?" I asked.

"We want you to swim," they said. "Will it be possible for us to play tennis?"

"We want you to play," we said, with the same degree of lockjaw.

And so I took tentative, amphibious swims at furtive hours in their pond. And His Lordship would appear with his youngest daughter, tennis rackets in hand.

Hmm. "I want you to play," I said, "but could you please call first?"

The Naked Test, you know. It all worked out fine: His Lordship gave up the game, and it turned out his pretty fifteen-year-old daughter Zoe was my perfect partner. She was entirely fresh and adorable, with an English schoolgirl complexion, and she chased down tennis balls like a pup. We played not by the hour but by the day, whenever we could, that first summer, and from then on, whenever Zoe came home from boarding school for visits. She, too, had the quality of being from another, perhaps better, time—a darling daughter from Jane Austen, perhaps. When I think of her, as I often do, it is in terms that predate me: we became chums. We laughed so much on the tennis court that we were dubbed by my husband the "giggle twins."

Zoe enjoyed my games of make-believe, and we spent entire days restoring Victorian white linens, drying them on the tennis net, then staging elaborate picnics. We also shared a regimen of running to work off the calories, and we were soon running seven-minute miles up and down the Avenue, ending with great splashes in her family pond, or with more daring, under the waterfall in the neighboring town.

One August evening, we ran all the way home from the waterfall, a distance of some three miles, and jogged up a shortcut through the dairy farm. The cows lowed their hellos, and our path, in the sunset, became lit by thousands of fireflies. I gasped for breath at the beauty as we wound our way up a phosphorescent tunnel, the green leaves illuminated above our heads. The air was heavy with humidity and honeysuckle. Heat lightning cracked.

I maintained cordial, and sometimes more than cordial, relations with all my neighbors. But I also knew from my experience in Tuxedo Park, where feudal law prevailed, that a key element to country life would be defending my borders. I knew ownership was most likely evil. Wasn't territorial dispute the heart of war? Who didn't feel a primal swell of rage at the trespass of a stranger? Who didn't view an unknown walker or a strange vehicle as the potential enemy? As soon as you buy land, you become aware of the lines. The primitive force asserts itself: *This is my land.* I don't know anyone who has bought property who hasn't, at some time, chased someone off it.

To the trained eye, even on an ordinary day, the scene at Willowby and its environs was not what it appeared to be. That woman watering her flowers? Not as neutral as she appears—she is engaged in a dispute over water rights with the lord and lady. They fight over her right to pump, their need to receive. The innocent trees being planted are my own Maginot Line, installed against the inevitable invasion.

At this time, my view to the south took in only the Manor and the carriage house where the caretaker, Cecil, and his wife, Ida, a curly white-haired pretty woman in her eighties lived. But someday, I sensed, there would be others, and I had best put a literal hedge on all future possibilities. God help me, I planted the lord out. "I didn't think to put 'forbidden foliage' on the restrictions," His Lordship remarked.

Ha ha, too late. In the same prophylactic spirit, I nailed "Private" signs to my points of entry. I did this early on, so that all could see it was nothing personal. I was simply private and still am.

From my first night at The Inn, I have had a recurring nightmare that my privacy is being invaded. In the dream, I look out my bedroom window and see "them," the trespassers, hundreds, thousands of them. They all are walking toward me, to The Inn. They come over a knoll, and as they clear the rise, they appear distorted; an optical illusion gives them superhuman size as they make their descent toward me. They are dressed for a large outdoor event, in tee-shirts and shorts, and they carry boom boxes blasting, at full volume, songs I don't like. They settle on my front lawn, a sea of human heads, bobbing to the music. The air is thick with them and the flies they attract as they spill sodas.

So perhaps I overreacted when the first actual trespassers appeared, looming on the horizon. They came not in huge numbers but in small bands, couples or the occasional individual. The trespassers were for the most part local people, accustomed to walking this route to my house, on the charming path that cut behind the Manor. A walk into the nineteenth century was what they called it, and they had been enjoying it every weekend for years.

Too civil to yell "Get out!," I would walk outside and glare. Sometimes, I might slam my door. I trusted these signs would be discouraging enough.

What would Eleanor Roosevelt have done? Probably organized them and passed around a petition. But would she have invited them in for tea? Encouraged future visits? Fair-minded as she was, I'd bet that good lady didn't welcome trespassers into Val-Kill, the retreat she maintained in Hyde Park. Therefore, I felt entitled to challenge the strangers with a polite "Are you looking for someone?" And when they could give no satisfactory answer, I would smile and request. "Please note, the sign says 'private'." It didn't always work. Some trespassers are like groundhogs—they won't go away unless shot. One winter, a group came on skis and clambered onto the porch, the better to see me sitting in my living room. My Naked Test certainly applies to the indoors as well as the exterior. Couldn't I relax on my own sofa without being seen? I lost it and ran outside, grabbing a ski pole and flinging it like a lance, spearing a "Keep Out" sign.

No matter what I did—posting yellow signs, like cummerbunds, on the trees or adding more strenuous language ("Trespassers will be prosecuted")—a certain number of people will not be discouraged. I understood when the lord and lady related the tale of how an ancestor had rolled a large boulder onto the Avenue to block all access.

Privacy still seemed the most elusive commodity of all, as even paid invaders, the groundskeepers, cleaning women, appliance repairmen, paraded through my day. Sometimes I felt like the hostess to visiting crews.

Then at last, one day, it seemed to be over. Even my husband left, for work in another city. A silence settled on the house. I could hear electricity sing in the walls, a fly buzz at the window.

I wandered in a trance of solitude from empty room to empty room. Especially as I explored the back part of the house, the Innlet, I felt I was walking into the past. Very little had changed: the claw-footed tub still squatted, the window glass gave the same wavy, as-though-through-water, view. My heart began to beat as it had when I was a child discovering the Indian cave. I went, as if by treasure-hunt map, to the farthest little room in the downstairs of The Innlet. And there it was, as I had sensed it would be—the trap door.

Barely discernable, a square had been cut into the linoleum-covered floor. I used a butter knife to pry up one corner. I lifted the edge, and the coolness of the earth wafted up to greet me. I grabbed a flashlight and lowered myself, feet first, down the chute-like entry to I knew not what, the netherworld of my new home.

In the cool darkness below, I cast the single beam. I caught my breath—there was a sharp drop into a cave-like declivity. I eased myself down into a rock-lined hole some eight feet in diameter. It had been clearly dug out and constructed by man. At its very center lay a bottle, opaque, the color of the Mediterranean Sea. I picked it up, and sniffed: wine from another century.

I savored such moments of aloneness. As I imagined Hilary Talbot, another only child, had been, I was at home in solitude, sometimes craving it more than company. As I sat in that dark center of my new world, I thought about where I was and lost myself in time.

When I emerged and sat on the porch, I would be, unintentionally, a witness to the next part of the history of Willowby. I was the central person—with a view of all my neighbors.

For the present, however, I chose to let my time overlap not so much with my human neighbors but with the congenial queens of the animal world—the cows that grazed my pasture. They seemed not to intrude on my privacy but to enter it. I began, frankly, to hang out with them, weather permitting. To stand among cows in a blizzard or even a drizzle is to overdo it and is no way to ward off depression. But in great weather, cows are good company, extremely consoling. They will listen to your problems with what strikes me as a sympathetic silence punctuated by the occasional thoughtful belch. I cannot say they contribute to a conversation, although you would be surprised how sustained a moo can be. Some moos last more than a minute.

What cows are not is witty. Even I, learning to love them, will not claim they are witty. But they are sweet-natured, warm, and welcoming. I have never had the feeling that they are not glad to see me.

I will confess that I have walked into the pasture and stood still among them and let them lick my arms and delicately nibble on my sleeves. They gather, six at a time, for this purpose. Cows love to do things in groups. I draw the line at them nipping at my bangs, the ultimate critique of my hairstyle, but I have let them suck off my gloves.

.=====

My feeling for cows was so new that I have mostly kept quiet, till now, about how much we socialize. I still do not like to eat a salad too near them—it just seems too familiar. I may still, city girl that I am, fear that if I come too near the cows, I will become one. So I won't go into detail about the great New Year's Eve I spent with them in a snowy pasture, preferring their company to my neighbors' parties. For the most part, I have kept our relationship a sweet secret, like the love affair that it is.

Location is indeed destiny, and mine has placed me in the heart of a lovely herd.

Sometimes I walk with them to the highest point on my pasture. There, on a fair day, I can see three hundred and sixty degrees. Without my human neighbors being aware, we *know* everything that happens here. We would be witness to everything. That was the lay of the land.

seventeen

It wasn't long before my husband tried to persuade me that we should acquire our own livestock. He had dreamed of a barnyard all his life. I was touched; I had always loved the country boy in him. Without realizing what I was getting myself into, I went along with his dream to acquire some animals.

The goats arrived first, inspired by the goat lady across the river, the former actress who had seduced my husband with her Nubian kids. I had thought vaguely, *Oh, goats, they're cute little animals*. It had seemed all right to buy a few.

I had always loved goat cheese, and I imagined a few dainty dairy goats would supply us with chevre, while cavorting as adorable pets. Thus, I accepted the delivery of two demented goat half-sisters, Lulu and Lulubelle.

I should be accurate and admit that I did not really buy these two goats. I traded a round oak table for them. The goats belonged to another new character in my life—Jill the goat girl, who was also nominally my cleaning person. She was about twenty, with buttocks that seemed as if they would pop from her cutoffs. She had a penchant for arranging still lifes as she cleaned The Inn.

After a Jill cleanup, I would find my gloves crossed on a lace throw, a nightie draped over the bedpost. She was staging a romantic life I never could quite enact, but I appreciated her efforts. She was not, however, reliable about coming in to clean.

"Yup, the ram rammed me in the thigh," she'd say on the phone the day she was expected to appear on the job. "My leg's black and blue. Guess I won't be doing any cleaning this week." All her excuses seemed legitimate. When she finally appeared, her long legs would be bruised or encased in Ace bandages. She kept a menagerie at her house. Eventually, I accepted her invitation to come see the animals and found her property fenced and landscaped like a professional zoo. Dozens of animals—peacocks, pigs, goats, and chickens—strolled the property against a backdrop of granite outcroppings. The Bronx Wildlife Conservancy had nothing on Jill.

Her goats were reproducing rapidly, however, and she kept showing my husband baby pictures of the littlest one, Lulubelle. Of course he wanted her. And of course, we learned, you can't keep a solitary goat. "Goats are herd animals," Jill told us. "You'll have to take at least her sister for company."

She delivered the goats one summer afternoon, and they were an instant disaster. Instead of filing into the paddock we had prepared at great expense and labor, the goats leaped over our fencing and bounded toward The Manor. It took all afternoon, in hundred-degree heat, to recapture the baby, Lulubelle.

Lulubelle was an adorable black-and-brown "mostly Nubian" dairy goat kid. She was small enough to carry in your arms, like a puppy. She had tiny hooves and pointy little horns. She could look like an angel— or the devil, if her yellow slitted eyes gazed at you the wrong way. I understood in about five minutes why goats are often sacrificed during satanic rites. We could not catch her big sister, who was leaping and snorting all around the property.

Jill assured us that if we tied Lulubelle inside the barn, her sister would not be able to stay away. "They're herd animals," she reminded us. "Nothing worse for a goat than to be alone." She spoke the truth. Little Lulubelle bleated piteously all night within the barn. In the morning, we found her sister pressed against the door, hoping to be let inside. It was still no easy task to confine them. Our original estimate of the height of the fence had been short; we needed something like a two-story building to keep them in the paddock. Even so, once the fence was raised, they discovered that the single stone post that anchored one corner could be scrambled, mountainside-like. I drove home one afternoon to see Lulu standing tall, like a living weathervane, high on the cornice.

The goats cost a fortune to keep fenced. Then they started eating and eating; fifty-pound sacks of goat chow went down like bags of chips. They ate and eliminated continually, chow going in one end and beebies shooting rapid-fire out the other.

Lulubelle was irresistible, however. She loved to trot up onto the porch. She watched TV through the living-room window. A few times she tiptoed into the house and tried to go upstairs. She was awfully cute.

Lulu was less cute. She had a temper. If annoyed, she would butt you with her horns. She could look lethal, thundering at you at twenty miles per hour. She often escaped, and I would find her standing on top of my car. Many a trip to the city was delayed because of goat-on-the-roof problems. But we couldn't keep one without the other, and deep in my heart, I had a place for Lulu, too.

Then Jill told me that I had to mate the goats to get the milk to make cheese. I don't know what I had thought. I must have realized that goats didn't simply extrude neat white logs of Montrachet, but I was innocent of the complex processes that led to cheese. The goat person must become involved with milking platforms and teat problems. Most significantly, the goat person must orchestrate the sexual liaisons of goats. Goats won't give milk unless they've been mated. In Rock Ridge, that meant a date with Bucky.

Bucky was the only male goat around, horned and whiskered, with an odor that seemed visible. On his first and only conjugal visit, he and the girls kicked up such a fuss that they did two thousand dollars' worth of damage to the barn before eating the windowsills. The romance had to be canceled.

My mistake. My penance: the lifelong care of Lulu and Lulubelle. In exchange for room and (literal) board, Lulu and Lulubelle occasionally entertained us with a goat frolic on the lawn. They would bang heads and execute a few choreographed moves that recalled some Dionysian rite as we watched in a stupor from the porch. Most of the time, the girls simply munched and relieved themselves.

Next came the chickens, inspired by the dream of fresh eggs gathered warm in the mornings, a dream that gave way to the reality of thirty-eight irritable Rhode Island Reds sulking in their expensively maintained nests. After several hundred dollars' worth of chicken feed (who ever first misused that word as a synonym for cheap?) there was, one day, an egg—brown, silky, and warm—under a hen who almost pecked my hand off when I reached in to grab it. Thinking scrambled, I headed back with a heavy glove.

Hens, I soon learned, are cranky creatures who suffer some form of poultry PMS. They have frequent layoffs. Even the rooster, Mr. Chicken, let us down.

Mr. Chicken was our first chicken. He was a test chicken, hand-selected by my husband from a massive poultry farm far down the road. Mr. Chicken was slated for the chicken industry; he was lost among thousands of lookalikes in a Perdue-style operation. Perhaps he had been bred without a brain. He seemed stupid, even for a chicken.

I had expected a rooster to wake us with his proud crow. But for the first month on the farm, Mr. Chicken slept late. He snoozed in the barn until lunchtime, when he would irritably rise and peck at the earth—and our legs, if we came too close.

You idiot, I wanted to say, but that would have made me a person who talks to chickens. *You idiot. Don't you know we saved your life? You would have cost three ninety-five, tops, as a fryer. You would be under plastic wrap now if it weren't for us.* But Mr. Chicken had no appreciation of the singular fate that had spared him while millions of his kind went on to be broilers or fryers. He would never have made it as a roaster. Mr. Chicken was lean and mean, white as a Klansman in sheets, with ugly red wattles. I had wanted to make him into a pet, but he hated us.

The day we drove home with Mr. Chicken, we were so ill prepared to care for our own chicken that we stopped to buy birdseed to feed him. He ate the Hartz Mountain parakeet treat in about an hour, then snapped at us for more.

Thus began long schleps to the animal feed store with its massive fifty-pound sacks of various kinds of chows. It was dangerous to venture in there, because my husband usually spotted ads for local livestock and giddily snatched the phone numbers. I caught him with the phone numbers for lop-eared rabbits, guinea hens, Hampshire hogs, and a series of championship chicks. I confiscated the numbers, but he committed a few to memory and covertly dialed them. Which is how we ended up with more chickens.

At our chicken peak, we (and I use the term loosely) had forty-five chickens. My husband started off with two dozen "normal" chickens: Rhode Island Reds, Barred Rocks (the cute black-and-white striped ones that are often the inspiration for pot-holder designs). He then branched out into what I called the punk chicks—Polish, Japanese, Spanish; they had freaked-out feather 'dos and walked around goonily strutting their stuff and poking out their necks. In a macho phase, he also ordered a straight run of roosters—all competitive, all mean. They were pretty, though—feathers black and forest green, dappled with gold.

Suddenly, Mr. Chicken began to crow. And crow. Farmer Bowers said, "Well, whad'ya expect? Before, he had nothing to crow about!" Now he was mating promiscuously with dozens of the young females, competing with the baby roosters. I guess it was chicken heaven. He ate about a hundred dollars' worth of chicken feed a day and ballooned to logo size; he looked like an ad for a chicken, or a person in a chicken suit. He was a major chicken when he was killed.

We never found out who did it. Mr. Chicken had never looked better, had never been happier. But one day I found him on the lawn, upside down, his scaly yellow feet in a death curl, his chicken face twisted in what I imagined to be a rooster's last look of horror in recognition of the predator who had slain him—*It was you, Mr. Coyote.* But he had no marks on him. His death remains a mystery. Unsolved.

Sometimes I wonder if I did it. In a fugue state. And repressed the chicken murder. In any case, my husband and I both felt we should not roast, fry, or broil Mr. Chicken. His lack of personality had become a trait. We had come to know and love him in spite of his lack of charm. He was given a chicken burial with full honors.

The death of Mr. Chicken gave rise to fear for his fellow chickens. The girls were now laying eggs daily, sitting pretty on their nests. I wanted to be sure they stayed safe. The result: the erection of a stockade we called Fort McChicken, double reinforced to prevent predators like coons, fox, coyotes, and such from entering and killing the chickens. Stewart Lee and Cecil were excited by the project. "Yes, yes, we had a chicken house here once with an outdoor fence enclosure, yes, yes, it worked good," Stewart recalled. Stewart, Cecil, and my husband pounded away with two-by-fours and, yes, chicken wire was strung. The result—a world-class secure chicken fort. A cute ladder was built connecting the outdoor yard to the indoor lay area. For days after, our main diversion was watching hens scamper up and down the ladder as they went about their chicken business.

By now I had caught the chicken love and named my favorite hen, a Barred Rock, Henrietta. Henrietta was the nicest (meaning the least mean) of the hens and would actually cluck in only minor grumpiness when I removed her eggs. She once laid an egg in the palm of my hand, which was an exciting development for me.

We were gathering so many eggs we didn't know what to do with them. We had soufflés every day, prizefighter breakfasts of multiple scrambled eggs. We excised the word "cholesterol" from our fat-clogged minds. Everything I cooked had eggs in it; I whipped the rest into homemade mayonnaise. Finally, we were giving them away by the dozens.

I just could not keep up with forty-five eggs a day. Meanwhile, we were paying thousands of dollars a year to keep the eggs rolling in. I don't know why, other than it seemed to make us happy. If I factor in the cost of the henhouse, Fort McChicken, the price per egg escalates. I think I was paying at least twenty-five dollars a dozen, but I suppose they were worth it.

Which is what possibly allowed me to let my guard down regarding the geese. The geese made the least sense of all. But we were at the hardware store, where we might as well have waved our arms to indicate the entire contents of the place and told the clerk, "We'll take it," when I caught my husband thumbing through a poultry catalogue.

This poultry catalogue was to chicken people what *Victoria's Secret* is to underwear fetishists. My husband got a strange look on his face as he stared at the listings. He wanted them all. I caught him ordering.

"What? What!" I nearly screamed. But the clerk had already written down his order: a half-dozen Toulouse goslings.

Goslings. Even the word has a nursery-rhyme sound. But what were they for? I mean, what is their purpose? In Toulouse, France, goslings are raised as meat birds. Their livers go into fatty pâtés.

Of course, that would not happen to *our* geese. It was a done deal. My husband ordered the half-dozen, and we were instructed by the hardware store clerk that we would get a call when they came in. "Better pick 'em up quick," the clerk said. "If you don't claim 'em in twenty-four hours, we destroy 'em."

Gee. That sounded rather severe. I was on pins and needles, afraid that I might miss the phone call when the goslings arrived and they would die for my sins. As it happened, I was in New York and I picked up a message. *Omigod*. If I drove eighty miles an hour to the farm from New York, I might make it in time to save them. I fairly flew and broke all records, risking my own life to get to the hardware store before closing time.

And there they were, the six of them, so cute, with eggshell still on their heads. I opened the box and it was love at first sight—for them. It's always love at first sight for goslings; they imprint on the first form they see—forever. Packaged as hatchlings, they saw me when I opened their box, so, for all time, I am Mother Goose.

They were absolutely adorable, with chartreuse fuzz, splayed orange feet, and peeping voices. Their infancy lasted an unbelievably short time. But it was lucky for them that they had a grace period in which they could be viewed as attractive.

I whisked the goslings home and set them up in the barn, but it was a cold evening and I feared for them. In fact, one gosling began to droop and shiver and didn't last an hour. Panicked, I packed up the other five and carried them into the kitchen, where they instantly perked up, listening to public radio and enjoying the warmth of human surroundings.

By dawn, an unbearable stench filled the house. Goslings *reek*.

They seemed to grow before my eyes, and as they grew, they extruded gooey gobs of goose turds. They still looked cute, but they stank. I raced them back to The Innlet and set them up in the pantry.

Within days, it seemed, they thrived to the point where they lost their baby looks. They ballooned into twenty-pound fatties with narrow, goon heads and raucous voices. Their corona of fuzz was gone, their voices changed. They were . . . *geese*.

We were still in the honeymoon phase, though. When I led the geese to the barn, they demonstrated their loyalty to me by following single-file. They clearly loved me. They even groomed me: if I lay down on my garden chaise, the five geese gathered to smooth my jeans by working the denim through their bills. They would smooth out all the creases and cover the length of my legs. If I had picked up a burr or a bit of hay, I didn't have to worry about it. They kept me well groomed, by goose standards.

They also enjoyed a walk with me, and we walked everywhere. The goats liked to come, too, so I led quite a procession as I took what had once been solitary sunset strolls. The goats were lively walkers, sometimes prancing ahead and doubling back or executing a mock ramming. The geese always followed me. I hiked as far as a mile with this crowd, and then we would settle down at a scenic overlook and view the farm from above. The heat of the sun warmed our faces. The goats were especially companionable, sometimes settling down so close their warm bellies pressed against my legs. They occasionally passed gas, but otherwise they were charming. They would eat every flower that I picked, however, so I had to keep an eye on any wildflower bouquet I had gathered. More than once, I returned home only to discover I held a bouquet of stems.

This idyll suffered somewhat as the geese came of age. Geese have an equivalent of adolescence and once they hit it they are impossible. The raucous voices become even screechier, and the honks are soon unmanageable. Say "Shut up" to a goose and it will only honk back, "Nonk." Again and again. The only male, Arnold (named for Schwarzenegger) turned mean in his sexual season, hissing and honking. If I ever turned my back on him, he goosed me.

Snacking and quacking, the geese grew obese. My gaggle, as I now refer to them, are too fat to fly and have settled in for the duration. For a time, I labored under the illusion that they would fly south for the winter, giving me a break. I had seen a documentary, *Flight of the Snow Geese*, and thought of taping it for my gaggle. Instead, I tried teaching them to fly, with the result that they flew about as well as I do, skidding a few feet down to their aqua plastic kiddie pool.

I became resigned to running a no-weight-loss pleasure spa for Toulouse geese, but my husband had other ideas. With a Jack Nicholson glint in his eye he hissed, "Christmas is coming and the goose is getting fat." I was appalled. How could he consider roasting an animal that had imprinted on me as its mother?

"It's not murder," he said, "it's agriculture." But of course I would not hear of it. They had come to me as innocents—remember the eggshell yarmulkes on their little heads? They waddled determinedly in my actual footsteps. I was touched. For life.

And then I learned the really bad news: geese live to be forty. With good care, a goose can reach the age of sixty.

Some afternoons I watch Arnold having incestuous sex with his sisters in the kiddie pool, and I feel defeated. Sixty. When he's sixty, I'll be dead. And he, like a California movie star, will be fornicating in turquoise water, without a thought of the consequences.

Great. The only smart course I've taken with the geese is to oversee their birth control. I made the mistake of letting the first two giant eggs hatch: of course, more of *them* popped out, just as deceptively cute as their parents. I quickly gave them away to another couple from the city with a weekend place. Now I pounce on that nest the minute an egg is laid. I get that egg before anything can develop, and I crack that egg and make a goose-egg omelette or a goose-egg soufflé. Goose eggs are truly extraordinary: the yolk is deep gold. They make a hilarious sight gag as poached eggs. And I'm told that they can be mixed with pigments to create tempera paints.

Terrific: let those eggs turn into anything but geese.

eighteen

As unsuccessful as we were with the livestock, my husband and I seemed even more ill-fated in the garden. From the first, all we reaped was a harvest of pain.

"No wonder they call it Rock Ridge," is a local saying. When we tilled the soil we found more stone than earth. It became a process of rock excavation—small pebbles, big stones, and then, finally, boulders. I spent most of my time preparing the alleged garden, jumping on the end of a pickaxe, trying to tilt the tip of what might be a glacial formation that extends to the core of the earth.

When at last there was a thin strip of what we could call soil, we stuck in seeds, which were instantly lost and unidentifiable except to the birds that snacked on them. We graduated immediately to seedlings that cost as much as the finished vegetables. In this way, we worked our way up, with credit cards, to the six-hundred-dollar tomato.

There was a hallucinatory moment in the commercial greenhouse when we selected flats of tomato varieties, deluding ourselves that we would someday see the fruit they advertised—beefsteak heirloom, golden, cherry. We went for the traditionals and the exotics; we got nothing.

After months of caring for the plants, of supporting their spastic branches with all manner of vegetable crutches, we were rewarded with . . . vines. The vines were luxuriant, fragrant. I crawled on all fours between the braces supporting the weak plants to sniff their essence. Good that I inhaled the aroma that had tantalized me from my rooftop past, for it would take herculean efforts to get a taste.

Oh, they grew, all right. Some tomatoes even became tinged with color. But before they could reach the texture appropriate for picking, the animals struck. The deer. The groundhogs. They all loved tomatoes. They didn't like the zucchini, but neither did we.

The garden became their outdoor Shop-Rite. They marched in by moonlight and munched. In the morning, I would run to the garden to find their chewed leftovers—the pale pulp and spit-out seeds. Their hoofprints were everywhere, marking the gazpacho orgy they had enjoyed, combining our fresh peppers with the tomatoes, leaving us only the woody discards, the dental impressions, their beebies.

In desperation, I searched out antianimal remedies. *Just let me have one tomato*, I prayed, *so I can taste it, hot from the sun, feel its juice spurt in my mouth.*

I got it, but only after heavy fencing, all-night stakeouts, and an expenditure in batteries to keep the boom box playing the rock music deer dislike. I briefly considered the nursery's other suggestion: gallon jugs of human urine hung from the trees, hair balls, sweaty gym shorts and socks. My garden was dispiriting enough without seeing these items. As it was, I decided to cut my losses and share with the herd. They could have 398 tomatoes if I could have one.

And so I tiptoed out before dawn one day to catch the critters in the act, their eyes red in the beam of my flashlight, enjoying their early brunch.

I made an animal sound that startled even myself—*Eeeeyah!*—and I charged the garden. I got it: the single, semisoft, unblemished tomato. I grabbed it and looked—no teeth marks. I bit into it—how sweet it was!—and the cost of the fence, the fertilizer, the stakes, the extended hose line system, all could be amortized. What mattered was this, the taste of my own fresh homegrown tomato.

I savored it along with a bit of extra good news. Deer do not like basil. So I had a garnish.

n i n e t e e n

Every country homeowner sooner or later creates his own existential labor—the project that somehow symbolizes his or her life struggle. This is the do-it-yourselfer that can do yourself in. The project that may or may not break the human spirit.

For one neighbor, it was stones. He started with a few stones, set them in the ground. Twenty years later, his forty acres are covered in fieldstone—and he's dead. He rode his tractor in reverse off a quarry cliff while he was gathering more stones. Today, his property is a local tourist attraction, a stone amphitheater where New Age concerts and Stonehenge-type ceremonies are staged. It is also a monument to going too far, although it has been said that the stone man died doing what he wanted to do—heave stones.

For me, the ultimate project was the pool. I had to have one. My house sits squarely in an area famed for its sparkling lakes and ponds but, alas, my property did not have water on it. What it did have was a stone cistern, set in the ground behind the house.

The cistern, which had been boarded over for more than a century, was fifteen by twenty-three feet, respectable dimensions for a pool. It had been built in the 1800s to hold rainwater, and it was still doing that. An ingenious system of conduits conveyed rainwater from the roof gutters underground and from there into the cistern. It seemed like a logical leap to imagine the cistern holding water as a unique swimming pool au naturel.

By late June of the second year, I had fallen into the "have to" mindset of the obsessive country-place revisionist: "I *have to* swim by July." *I have to, I have to.* In previous years, I had been a frustrated swimmer on other peoples' properties.

By the time I bought The Inn, I had thrown in the towel with the illicit swimming. The watery trespassing had not been entirely pleasurable; I was always crawling or darting during the buggiest hours. I was forever fearful of being apprehended. I would jump at the snap of a twig. Adding to the panic factor was the fact that I tempted fate by diving in nude, so I was doubly afraid of exposure. Sometimes my secret swimming took a manic twist—I danced a naked mazurka on the grounds of the Tuxedo Club one midnight while a charity auction was held inside.

At Willowby, I had been given swimming privileges to the lord's pond, but those rights were murkier than the water, which was said to harbor snapping turtles. Was it all right to swim there anytime? Or just when it wasn't being used? I am a lone swimmer. When I swim, it is in the same solitary spirit in which I walk. I want a dip, my private thoughts, and that's it. I don't want to chat with someone simply because that person is there getting wet, too.

Also, I may not be a pond person. I have seen snapping turtles. They are fearsome indeed, with horned prehistoric tails and hard-looking mouths. "They'll snap yer tits off," a farmhand said to me one day as we watched a particularly large snapper (he was the size of a small end table) plod across the driveway en route, no doubt, to the lord's pond. There is also the enthusiastic wasp and hornet population that often summers under pond rafts or docks. I have suffered several horror-movie-style encounters with these aggressive insects. Once I was stung on the foot—didn't realize it, imagined I had stepped on a needle, and so sat down—directly on another wasp. There is a look to pond swimmers, and it often includes a swollen body part—at least a puffy eyelid—from such encounters. Add to this the usual presence of snakes and you can have most ponds.

I wanted a pool with just the right bracing trace of chlorine. Critter-free and aqua-clear. Was it too much to dream of an azure rectangle in my backyard, a place for safe and sanitary solitary splashes? I was determined. I was going to convert the cistern—and fast. And so I began the most Sisyphean of my tasks.

Step one was investigation, and that meant lifting the lid. Like Dracula's grave, the cistern had been covered for a long, long time. The lid itself had rotted, giving rationalization to the project: those boards had to come off, anyway. As the boards were pried off, the pit exhaled its first fetid breath in more than a century.

Instead of recoiling, I rejoiced that the level of the black murk inside was high, almost to the brim. "This pit *wants* to be a pool!" I cried, although no one was listening. (During most stages of my pit-to-pool conversion I found myself alone.) The pit would divulge its secrets later, when it was too late and too costly to stop. What I did not suspect was its depth. I threw in a rock lashed to a line and watched as it glugged and sank. The line slipped from my hands. I should have known then that I was in over my head, but I went on with the project. I hired four Acadian wallpaper hangers to assist me with the conversion. In mid-July, they were the only workmen I could hire. All the bona fide pool contractors had been, like movie stars, booked months or even years in advance. I began to appreciate the grave tone in which I'd heard people say, "We're putting in a pool." Creating a pool is not something to undertake lightly or quickly. Which, of course, is exactly what I did.

I did need a pool contractor to help with the installation of the filter. Without a filter, the water would stand stagnant, a breeding place for mosquitoes and their larvae. The system is simple—a few inlets and outlets, so the water can gush in and out of the filter, which is usually hidden a discreet distance from the pool. The pipes are also hidden, underground, and the entire illusion is that the pool water stays crystalline without one's constant efforts.

I approached ten pool contractors in regard to helping install the filter. Nine rejected me. The tenth, a born-again pool contractor, seemed to feel a moral obligation to help me. He said he would give instruction, deliver the filter, and then the rest would be up to me. Enter the LeFevre brothers, whom I snared as they were making their getaway after papering my powder room. Surely they could help empty, clean, and prepare a stone pit as easily as they had plastered and papered walls. To their credit, the LeFevre brothers leaped to the challenge in exchange for my promise to do any digging that might be required. How much digging could there be?

Step two was to empty it. The volunteer fire department arrived, sirens wailing, an early omen of disaster. "We'll suck up your muck," the firefighters offered, except for the final two feet that might be so loaded with debris that it would damage their hoses. "After all," said the fire chief, "we don't really know what's down there."

"Heh, heh," said the eldest of the LeFevre brothers, a gamin of a guy with waist-long hair and a permanent grin. "Heh, heh," he repeated. "You know you got quite a few rat skulls down there? What do you want us to do with them?"

By now, I was deep in the fantasy of my pool-to-be, mentally adding Zen touches—a thin, trickling waterfall and natural fieldstone coping. I could almost read the *Architectural Digest* copy: *She integrated the ancient existing structure into the bucolic setting, adding only a few minimalist touches to enhance the symphony of natural stone and azure water.*

I was not going to let a few rat skulls detract from this image. I did end up with a rat-skull-to-volume ratio that would give any pit-to-pool converter pause—five dozen rat skulls per five thousand gallons.

The skulls removed, I obtained the first accurate measurement of the pit's depth—at twelve feet, it was deeper than I had expected, deeper than the deep end of a conventional commercial pool, generous at nine feet. There was also the problem of the uniformity of its depth—there was no shallow end. There would never be any tiptoeing in to get used to the water. For those who could not swim, this would be a drowning pool. No one, not even a New York Knick, would ever stand and touch bottom. This image of bottomlessness opened a small pit in my stomach. I felt a queasy premonition: something *bad* might happen. I did what second-home obsessives do—I redoubled my efforts.

Work proceeded, hauling buckets of muck out of the cistern by means of a system of rope and pulley that I devised. The men referred to this as the "Go Down, Moses" section of the detail. Not wanting to ask the men to do anything I wouldn't, I went into the pit with them, loading bucket after bucket, singing, "let my people go." We all sang to keep up our spirits. At last the cistern was empty, and we could clean it with brushes and hose it down, its first taste of new water in a century. I should have been alarmed at how the now buff-colored walls soaked up the spray. They'd been thirsting for this.

Then one afternoon, when we thought we had finished the cleaning and preparation, a sudden summer rain pelted the pit. Mysteriously, it began to fill—fast. The LeFevre brothers and I scrambled up the ladder. The old inlets had apparently not been sealed. It was time to learn of a new product, Waterplug, and its sister, Thoroseal.

Swinging from an improvised scaffold, armed with a spatula, I smeared cake-like gray batter into every aperture. As summer showers repeatedly interrupted my efforts, three little frogs bobbed past me on bits of wood, croaking encouragement.

I found myself alone when it came time to dig. The pool contractor, head shaved like an overseer in *The Ten Commandments*, outlined the task: "There must be eight- and ten-foot trenches, four feet deep, to carry the underground pipes to and from the filter." The filter, a bubble-headed squat R2-D2 lookalike, sat waiting in a corner of the yard. It was waiting for hookup; it was waiting for me.

Soon I found myself swinging a pickaxe and ramming a spade into the resistant earth. I became too engrossed to swat at the mosquitoes and flies that feasted on my salty wet flesh. I now understood those scenes of numbed labor in films such as *Papillon*. My body burned and hardened under the sun. I suffered and sweated but secretly enjoyed it, knowing this was a quick, albeit painful, way to get in bathing-suit shape.

At the eleventh hour, the pool almost complete, I had an attack of "aestheticitis." I would not be content with cement coping on the edges; I wanted decorative fieldstone. The only problem with fieldstone is that it comes from fields. As the wallpaper men would only make one last visit to finish the coping, I was on a fieldstone deadline, set as it would be in cement. I had to gather the stones by dawn or forget about them. Which explains why I went out to the cow pasture at midnight, with a wheelbarrow that sank at two A.M., so loaded I could no longer push it. Curious cows edged closer, viewing my predicament. I solved the problem by carrying out one or two stones at a time, staggering in the mud, then squeezing through the cow door, a narrow opening in the pasture fence, suitable for people but not bovines. It reminded me of a test an actress friend of mine was once subjected to. The director of a small feature film wanted slim women, so he had everyone walk through a narrow frame. My friend knew she wouldn't make it, but still, she said, she kept on a-coming. Like her, I could not stop.

The next day, the stones were set in cement, and I felt all the effort was worth it. By night, the pool contractor said, "You're ready for water." I was, but I wasn't quite ready to pay for it. Pool water cost $150 a tankerload. My pit would consume four loads before it was sated. The water was drawn from underground caves nearby. It was often sold as a beverage. So we would swim in the equivalent of San Pellegrino.

The tankers arrived by moonlight on a Saturday night. They, too, were overbooked in summer, and this was the one time that they could squeeze me in. There was an almost sexual rush to the filling as the mighty canvas hose humped and spurted, sending great gushes of liquid into the empty pit. By one A.M., the pit was full. The water shimmered in the moonlight, the moon and stars were reflected; a sequined stripe across its center.

I flipped the filter switch. A wavelike action began. The pool was so narrow that the force of the filter had a whirlpool effect. It was a hot, clear night. I threw off my clothes and dove in, took a delirious swim around my pool's small circumference, relished the thrill of performing two dozen laps with ease. I pulled myself, wet and spent, from the water and tottered to bed, satisfied.

At dawn I awoke—to disaster. Even from my bedroom window, I could see something had gone horribly wrong. At least ten thousand gallons of the Pellegrino-priced water had vanished, leaving the pit half full.

"Dry as a bone," the LeFevre brothers kept saying as they examined the borders of the pool later that day. We stalked its perimeters, seeking out leaks. We could see nothing.

Dry as a bone. Where could so much water have disappeared to? There wasn't even a damp spot, let alone a puddle, in our vicinity. But there had to be a leak. The pool contractor recommended a vinyl liner.

A vinyl liner. Sacrilege. Would I accept silicone in my breasts? Collagen in my lips? "No," I insisted. "We must stay natural." I crouched by my pit (I would always be the one to read it best). The bottom of the pool was watertight, but not the top half. I reasoned that the upper wall might have become porous as the rainwater level had fluctuated over the century. The walls were even more vulnerable where we had drilled to install the pipes. It was time for more Waterplug.

I set sail in a small rubber boat, armed with the Waterplug. The product promised to harden underwater. It had some dynamic action—it felt hot in my hand. I worked fast, wearing rubber gloves, feeling the tingle as I smeared the product into vulnerable areas. Then I applied a new coat of Thoroseal over the top half of the pool walls. At some point during this process, I realized that I could not get out of my pool. The ladder was gone, and now the water level had dropped so far that I could not clamber over the sides.

I called for the nearly deaf caretaker, Cecil, whom I could hear nearby riding a mower. Of course, he could not hear me. I thought too, of the farmer, who would pass, also on a loud tractor. *So this is it*, I thought—*a casualty of my own pit and my monomania.*

But I was not the same weakling who had begun the cistern conversion. The process itself had forged new flesh, muscles that popped when I flexed. I began to scale the walls in a manner I had witnessed only in Marine training films. I didn't make it the first time, or the second, or the third—my fingers left long wet stripes on the upper walls. It *was* a drowning pool. I thought of the night temperatures dropping, myself in a bathing suit in a wet stone pit. Hypothermia.

I tried harder. I scrambled up the wall and with a momentary foothold on the drainpipe, I launched myself and vaulted over the side. I lay gasping on my back.

And the pit did hold water, almost. There are still summer nights when it can be heard gurgling as the water level drops. Then the pit nurses from a hose until sated. This pit/pool will always have a bit of a thirst. But I can swim in it.

No one warned me, however, that a pool would be so much work. In movies and television shows, we see people lounging, kissing, or having drinks at poolside, but do we ever see anyone do any of the many maintenance duties associated with daily pool care? No. I don't see lovers pause to check the pH. There's no sign of the skimmer. Or a host who casts an anxious look in its direction—Is the pool level lowering? We don't even see algae—brown or yellow—or the cloudiness that is the true bane of pool life. Summer becomes about water clarity and chlorine or bacquil levels.

It's not for frolicking, but for chemistry.

And how to clean the bottom? Of course, the depth of my pit presents an extreme problem. Ordinary pool vacuums have a hard time reaching the pool floor, where sediment and leaves can and of course do accumulate. So when a friend suggested scuba gear, I leaped into a suit. Now, I regularly descend as a frogwoman (my alter-ego, "Aqua Frau") so that I can push the vacuum around the bottom. I can also casually walk around and pick up debris and lost goggles in an unhurried manner.

The truth is that I spend more time servicing my pool than swimming in it. I have almost forgotten that its original purpose was a form of relaxation. Sometimes I do get wet—by accident—while performing some maintenance task. But it's all worth it. My pool is a hit with teenage boys. "Cool," they say upon first sighting, "twelve feet deep!" They then propose tower dives from my chimney. Now, that's the spirit.

As I lug the next jug of chemicals, I try to dwell on the pool's azure beauty in the sunshine, how it will quickly lower my body temperature on hot days, and how many rodents I have deterred from suicide with my stone border. And as I offer towels to my guests, I say what every homemade-pool owner says on a sweltering day—"Oh, boy, I sure feel better when I take a dip. Doesn't it make all the difference?" (You know, *it does*.)

t w e n t y

For every cottage, there is a possible cottage industry. All around me, women were twisting grapevine into wreaths, crocheting tissue-box covers, "putting up" flavored vinegars, and pouring beeswax into candle molds. What could I do? I felt an irresistible tug to have a homemade business enterprise. I loved the idea of survivalist economics: to depend on no one but myself, fashion some homespun product, and make a small fortune without often having to leave the farm.

Inspiration struck at the dinner table. I was blotting my lips with a fine antique table napkin when the napkin suddenly presented itself in a new incarnation. With a simple fold and three narrow seams along the sides, the napkin could be transformed into a lovely ornate linen case. If I added a filler of lavender, that case would become the product I immediately dubbed potpourri pillow—*More than a sachet, these lavender-filled antique pillows scent the bedroom and the bureau.*

Zing, zing—the napkin went into my Singer Featherweight sewing machine. Three narrow seams later, the first potpourri pillow was assembled. I was thrilled. When sewn into a case, the cutwork and embroidery were shown off in a way that the original napkin form had failed to highlight. I enhanced the idea by using an antique handkerchief as an inner bag to hold the lavender. This way, the lavender packet could be removed if the lavender needed to be replaced or the outer linen required laundering. I gave a few pillows to friends who raved, "You could *sell* these."

Could I sell them? For a frenzied month, I did. With my best friend, Suzanne, I created an overnight business that grossed several thousand dollars in a few days. Within a week, the pillows were displayed at Henri Bendel and E. Braun, two of the priciest New York City emporia.

How did we do it? I should qualify my history from the start: I am not a businesswoman. I have never run a business, unless you call doing what I do—daydreaming and spinning out plays and books—a business. The only real job I ever held was my first position. For a single year, immediately after college, I worked as an editor of *Official* and *Master Detective* magazines. At nineteen, I wrote copy and edited manuscripts for both. The magazines featured true accounts of crime, mostly murders. My assignment was to make the victims seem attractive enough to warrant the attention of "our readers." I never did know who "our readers" were—I suspected that they were serial killers. Officially, they were "crime buffs." Every morning for a year, I arrived at my desk to find a large stat of a "slaying victim," alongside a cup of coffee and half a blueberry muffin provided by a dejected coworker who edited *True Detective*, a third true-crime magazine, indistinguishable from the two that I edited. Part of my job was to caption the "slay scene art." "The body of pert stewardess Polly Peters was found in this ditch *(far right)*" is a sample of my work. I quit soon after editing "Topless Killer's Texas Chainsaw Spree." No wonder I never went to an office again. So, in a sense, I already had a cottage industry: my writing.

But the truth is, I love to work with my hands; I find sewing tranquilizing, if it does not challenge me. I cannot, for example, "run up" anything requiring more than a straight seam. My single attempt at sewing a dress ended with a zipper that made me look like Quasimodo. But I quickly became addicted to sewing up the napkins. Soon, everything in sight—placemats, doilies, existing pillowcases, cut-down sheets, curtain remnants, dresser scarves—turned into a potpourri pillow. I could not go out to dinner without reflexively folding the napkin into my trademark shape.

And the business combined my country passions—linen and laundry. While I hate doing ordinary wash, I do love restoring Victorian whites. I learned from several elderly women in Rock Ridge—boil stains away in a white porcelain pot with "a goodly amount of sodium perborate" (the active ingredient in Snowy Bleach), wash by hand, then starch with old-fashioned cooked starch, *not* spray starch. And believe it or not, I like ironing, I like smoothing out creases, I like inhaling steam. I have a definite laundry fetish.

I also have a thing for lavender. Interestingly, "lave" is the root of both "launder" and "lavender." From medieval times onward, it was customary in France, source of the world's finest lavender, to store freshly washed and ironed linen with lavender to keep the scent. Lavender is also a powerful insect repellent—an effective deterrent of moths, lice, all manner of vermin. Lavender, of course, is also a lovely pale purple flower, a flowering bush that thrives on the French Riviera.

So, my cottage industry combining love of laundering, antique linens, and lavender was just the ticket—occupational therapy and a source of income unrelated to my serious and more ego-involving work. I was almost too accustomed to working in solitude, and the idea of sharing the business with a partner, my favorite friend from college days, was another inducement. Suzanne is a graphic artist, and her design sense is lovely. She, too, wanted an independent business.

We divvied up the duties. I was the front person and solicited the orders. Not knowing the poor odds for landing in a major store like Henri Bendel, I simply called and asked for an appointment. Later, other "craftspeople" were stunned when they learned that I was given an immediate interview with a buyer in Linens. One woman, marketing silk-screened scarves, had been trying for years.

Not knowing I should be rejected, I called Bendel's and asked for a buyer in Linens. I was connected to a Frenchwoman, Christine DuVal, who said, "Ooooh, I like dem," when I described the antique cases. "Bring me your samples," she invited.

What samples? I rooted through my linen closet, turned up four more napkins and two peach-colored placemats with some delicate embroidery. Overnight, I starched and sewed them into pillows, stuffed with a supply of lavender purchased by the ounce at my local natural food store. On the way to Bendel's, I ran into a home decorating store, grabbed a fabric-covered box, and set the "samples" inside. I had a typed list of possible prices and a product description: "More than a sachet . . . A decorative way to enjoy aromatherapy in your bed or bureau." I added, "one-of-a-kind heirloom linen cases, 100% hypoallergenic pure French lavender." I had always liked the word "hypoallergenic" on products. I also was reacting to the revolting gusts of chemical scent and the dye that pollute most potpourri products. Mine would be pristine.

I did not expect the success that followed. I even thought I might be sniffed out as a novice. So I was not nervous but curious when I rode the elevator up to the top floor of Henri Bendel's inner sales sanctum. There, Christine DuVal was exactly as I'd envisioned her—petite, pretty, and polite. "Oh, but dese are exquisite," she said, plucking two from my sample box. "I will buy dese two for myself." *Sold.* She handed me seventy dollars, thirty-five per pillow. "What are your price points?" she asked. *What were price points?* The small pillows, she said, could sell for seventy-five dollars each, the large, or "outsize boudoir" pillows as I instantly dubbed them, for a hundred and seventy-six. The buyer tipped me off to a secret of the trade: "You can't fill dese with one hundred percent lavender—it will be too expensive. You'll cut it with rose petals." *Lavender and roses.* "Yes, that's what I thought," I said.

She shocked me by ordering two thousand dollars' worth of merchandise "Can you deliver before Thanksgiving?" she asked.

"Yes," I said, although the holiday was only a week away.

"So you have dem in stock?" she said.

"Yes," I lied.

I tottered out onto Fifty-seventh Street and called Suzanne from a pay phone. We both shrieked with laughter—the beginning of the hysteria that would hold us in its grip for the next few weeks. What samples? What price points? What stock? Suzanne began working the Nynex directory as I walked, flying, with my sample case up Madison Avenue. Blown on a breeze of confidence, I sailed straight into E. Braun, a linen store so exclusive it sells thirty-six-thousand-dollar tablecloths handsewn by Belgian nuns who apparently sacrifice their sight for the intricate fretting. Inside E. Braun, still on my manic tear, I told the proprietor that I had a special product, sold exclusively at Bendel's.

The sales manager, an Italian gentleman of some affectation, studied the samples, said, "Appropriate for the store," and ordered five hundred dollars' worth, also "in time for Thanksgiving." By the time I reached Suzanne's studio, she had scouted out some lavender and rose-petal sources. The wholesale flower and spice trade seemed to operate out of desolate neighborhoods in Brooklyn and Queens, with a few outposts in New Jersey.

Suzanne priced the lavender—prices varied wildly—and we soon found ourselves driving out to a remote dock in Brooklyn, to a buff-colored stucco compound that could have been transported from Algiers. We stepped out at a loading dock littered with curry and dried flowers. Pungent scents filled the air, and foreign-looking men with great abs were hauling burlap sacks of spices.

"Did ya bring ya own hooks?" the gruff woman at the register window asked.

Hooks? We didn't know what she meant until we saw one of the men had a huge metal hook with which he slung the spice sacks onto the backs of trucks. Rather sheepish, I backed my old car up to the ramp and murmured, "Just put it in the trunk, please." There was something wild, sexual in the spice-tossing atmosphere. Suzanne and I exchanged looks as a handsome spice-sack tosser came toward us, lugging a hundred pounds of lavender and a fifty-pound bag of "Pakistani Petals." The sacks would not fit in the trunk, so we wedged them, like inert, obese passengers, into the rear seats.

The minute we began the long drive to the farm, we were struck by an anesthetizing gust of lavender. The aroma was overpowering. We began to giggle. Never doubt the euphoria-inducing effect of lavender. We were delirious by the time we reached the New York Thruway. We had three hundred dollars' worth of "Bleu Superieure" in the backseat, and we were as high as drug peddlers.

Back up at the farm we faced our first technical problem: getting the lavender out of the car. It took both of us to carry the sack, like a fat body, into the kitchen of the Innlet. We staggered in, collapsed with laughter. We were still stoned on lavender. Which helped, as we had to turn the kitchen into an overnight factory for the manufacture of potpourri pillows.

Good we were sedated, or we would have panicked: we were short on linen stock. I used every napkin in the house (future dinner parties be damned—we were in business). We made a mad dash to the local antique and junk stores, even the church rummage sale—anywhere a shred of linen, lace, cutwork, or an antique hankie could be found.

Meanwhile, Suzanne cut the lavender with the Pakistani petals. Together, we tried to mix a blend. The kitchen filled with lavender fumes and Pakistani petal dust.

We began to cough and considered the possibility that we could die from "purple lung," a condition that afflicted lavender workers. Gasping in the flower dust particles, we swiftly converted a pleasant country kitchen into a Victorian sweat shop and laundry. We worked through the night to wash and restore the linens; then, punchy, we tried to assemble the pillows.

It was much harder to make successful pillows in volume than as individual samples. We kept finding tiny flaws in the old linen, or creating new flaws by scorching or ripping or wrongly sewing them. By dawn, we were ready to strike or quit the business, except that we *were* the business. We had successfully replicated the kind of conditions that had brought about union labor and reform. We had turned ourselves into wretched Dickensian drudges. We did, however, end up with a lovely shipment, which we delivered on time to Bendel's and E. Braun.

A lesson in marketing followed. The day after Thanksgiving is known as Black Friday, the most significant shopping day of the calendar year. More people shop on this day than on any other. On this particular Black Friday, Suzanne and I ran into Bendel's to see our wares on display. *We could not find them.*

Omigod, I thought. *This is too much like publishing.* I was hurt, puzzled. Where were the potpourri pillows? At last, in a back corner of a semihidden boutique, I spotted some wrinkled, raggy-looking items, stuffed into a laundry basket. This was the display! Suzanne and I had envisioned the pretty pillows shown off to perfection perhaps mounted in the window or on top of a display case. The villainess soon appeared: a French saleswoman whose name tag read Veronique, had relegated the pillows to this poor position. "Too expensive for the floor," she explained. "Look at dese." She held up some polyester-lace-trimmed sachets, filled with what I could tell were dyed cedar chips and chemical potpourri.

Their artificial scent nauseated me as did the explanation for their success: "Dese are cheaper. Dese will *sell*." Alas, Veronique was right. But Suzanne and I felt she had created a self-fulfilling sales prophecy by her poor placement of the pillows. Whatever the reason, the potpourri pillows did not sell, or sell fast enough. There was no reorder. E. Braun, where the Italian gentleman had prominently positioned the pillows, was able to sell them, and he did re-order, a few weeks later.

By that time, Suzanne and I were literally winded, woozy from inhaling lavender, exhausted from combing the area around The Inn for linens and boiling and starching them. We realized we had not factored in our time and energy. If we did, we could figure that we were supplying the world with a product at cost. Perhaps it was a calling, and we would one day resume, simply to keep discerning sachet consumers in touch with a truly perfect product. Until then, we decided to retire at the break-even mark. I still had ninety pounds of lavender in a bag in the back kitchen, perhaps the largest sachet ever left in place. Any trip to that part of the house is highly aromatic. So, that may be why, when I go near it, I tend to giggle. So much for the business. I'll be making Christmas and wedding presents for years.

twenty · one

Perhaps the first new hobby, or "useful household art," as it might be called, that I acquired in the country was the time-honored activity of "putting up" preserves. This was not something I would have done in my apartment. The idea suggested itself along with the abundance of produce either cheap or free—literally falling at my feet—that occurs each harvest season.

I had started in Tuxedo Park, with the raspberries. Those raspberries were too delicious, too beautiful, and too valuable to let rot on the cane or drop to the earth and deteriorate into a moldy, sticky mass. Once you've seen fruit sell for $7.99 for a tiny pint box, you eye it differently when it presents itself gratis for the plucking. Of course, I attached no value to my time—the hours, days, weeks I spent picking the raspberries—or to the posttraumatic stress syndrome I suffered after the snake sightings and wasp stings. I didn't even factor in the medical bills for poison ivy treatment. The raspberries were free, goddamit, and I was going to pick every last one. And I did. Never mind that I staggered out of the raspberry patch scratched and bitten, covered with welts and mysterious swellings. Picking the raspberries was good preparation for canning them. This was a stations-of-the-cross project.

Every fruit has a particular insect or worm that will try to destroy it. Raspberries have raspberry bugs—delicate fern-green critters that cling to the hairs of each berry. The home preserver's first task is to pull them off and commit insect mass murder. The art of home canning includes killing the critters, then cutting off the rotted, semi-devoured segments. At last, bug- and worm-free, the fruit is ready for your technique of preservation.

My fate has been to fall for every fruit that is free for the picking. If I come upon a peach tree growing wild, I must pick all the peaches and preserve them. It's been my fortune, or misfortune, to luck into many such harvests.

I say misfortune because entire vacations have been lost to this endeavor. I spend whole nights clawing away at peach skins, pitting cherries. I have discovered new levels of viscosity, given new definition to the term "sticky." Try pitting mangoes—the stone is embedded in the fibrous fruit. It would take Dr. Debakey to extract it.

Every summer, I lug in bushels of fruit and sentence myself to all-night sessions with home canners. I fuss with the apparatus—the canner, the jars, the lids, the seals, the funnels. As I hover over my boiling cauldrons like one of Macbeth's weird sisters, I brood on the possibility of botulism, the "big B." Even *The Joy of Cooking*, a tome that waxes poetic over preserves, sounds a tad grim when it notes *Clostridium botulinum* is a germ so deadly that one ounce can kill a million people.

If I send out my gift jars this Christmas, do I risk wiping out my entire social circle? What could really be worth the work, the worry, the risk? Is my cranberry ketchup really to "die for"? The debate rages within my steamed brain. On the distaff side: here is my chance to bestow immortality upon on all my fruits and vegetables. But immortality has a short shelf life at my house. The "winter supplies" intended to last through the year are slurped up in a few weeks after canning. No matter how many jars I "put up," they are soon scraped bare in an orgy of jam eating. I shudder to think what would have become of my family in pioneer days. Then I remember: the pioneers had a life expectancy of thirty-five.

So, each year, I decide to risk the lives of everyone I know and keep on canning. I am not content to do it at home. Whenever I travel, I keep an eye peeled for free fruit. One winter, on vacation in Palm Beach, I found kumquats growing in the garden of the house my uncle Len rented. The kumquat tree itself was adorable: plump and polka-dotted with hundreds of orange kumquats. I put up thirty quarts and never saw the beach.

Why does canning inspire in me this hair-shirt state of mind? It seems to be a calling, a series of actions that culminate in a kind of culinary religion. I must be preserving more than the fruit.

I suppose I am inspired by my neighbor the farmer's wife, Betty Bowers. She puts up hundreds of quarts of tomatoes, peas, fruits. Her cellar is the edible equivalent of a visit to Tiffany's: jewel-like, the jars gleam from the racks. The coolness of the earth permeates her basement, helps preserve what she has wrought: nothing less than a display of Nature's fecundity.

twenty-two

It is inevitable when you spend as much time in nature as I have, that the life cycle takes hold and you cannot escape applying its rules and rhythms to yourself. This means accepting even mortality. On the farm and in the woods, death is as unavoidable and readily visible as life. There are discoveries—as many fossilized critters as blooming flowers. In spring, baby birds may fall from their nests like acorns, to be devoured by the cat that sits beneath the tree. There are freakish, unexplained events: the chipmunk that falls like a stone when I shake out a blanket left on the screened porch. He is cold, hard, in a state of perfect chipmunk preservation. What caused his death? Thirst? Was he trapped in the screened porch at the last slam of the door this past summer? In 1989, I was forced to face both the possibility of my own death and the hope of giving new life. It was a serious year that began with the decision between my husband and me to have a child. Where that decision would lead us, we could not have foreseen. I had vaguely dreamed of a child someday. Yet something, I didn't know what, stopped me from very actively going about having that child. I wasn't aware of being afraid or reluctant. At a certain point, I had decided to let nature take its course. There appeared to be nothing standing in the way of my conceiving. And yet I remained passive, a curious response even to myself.

When, at forty-two, after a few years of this laissez-faire attitude, I did not have a child, I finally saw a gynecologist for tests. Time, I knew, was short. I was accompanied on that visit by an actress friend in the full bloom of her eighth month: she sailed along, caftan flying, belly first, a walking promise of what was to be, possibly for me. Yet, in my heart, I did not believe I would soon be as she was. I couldn't say why.

The woman doctor gave me a few routine tests. Her initial check indicated that I was just fine, and the early blood test showed hormone levels that kept me in the running. I left the doctor with my pregnant friend, listening to the beat of her baby's heart, and went back up to the farm to start my official summer vacation.

Was it a few days later? A week? I think it was seven days after I saw that woman gynecologist in the city that she left a message on my answering machine at the farm. I saw the light blinking when I returned from a two-mile run. I was feeling fine, wearing a tee-shirt and shorts.

I stood in the kitchen, drinking water as I played back the messages. Then I heard the doctor's voice. The *doctor's* voice. Not the nurse's. Could I call her office as soon as possible? My heart, already beating hard from the run, pounded. I called her back, and she got on the line and said not the words I'd dreaded all my life but a sentence I couldn't have invented: "We don't like to call this cancer." *Then don't,* I thought.

I listened as she said that my tests had come back with some abnormal results. I had failed my prenatal tests in several directions. I didn't get all the news that afternoon, only the beginning. Still, it was enough to send me running up the steps and through the linen closet to the back of the house. I ran to the last room, the room papered in wild roses, and punched the walls.

It was such a beautiful day. A beautiful, beautiful day. If I had to say why I was so angry, I suppose the beauty had something to do with it—I knew, truly knew, there wouldn't be an endless succession of such blue-skied, luxuriant green summer afternoons. Even under the best of circumstances, there really are never enough days. But this was too soon. It wasn't fair.

After I punched the old papered plaster, made bits of the paper rip and the wall flake, some chill knowledge crept under my skin, beneath the trembling current of fear. It was so symmetrical. I'd long sensed there was a symmetry to most situations, and I hadn't wanted to acknowledge that this was the ending I'd feared most. The same age as Rosie. The very age at which she, unknowing, became sick. If God's a writer, why doesn't He have more imagination? Or is it DNA that can dictate only a single plotline? Was this my unspoken reason for not having a child? I could almost have laughed. Seeking news of fertility, I'd been handed my mortality—in spades. The following days and weeks were marked by the accelerating of my own bodily fear—the lurching descents and rises from brief sleeps. I felt as if I were suspended on a faulty cable to be yanked or dropped on a whim.

While my blood and heart raced, the medical pace was measured, with pauses. Appointments had to be made, tests taken. Fears I never knew I had were suddenly fulfilled: more results came in at weekly intervals—I was taken twice more by surprise. I failed not one but three tests. Within nine days, I was told that I had abnormal cells in three parts of my body. "We don't like to call this cancer," said doctor number two, "but we think it becomes cancer." With a constellation of problems, I was soon walking down the halls of the most famous cancer hospital in New York City. I thought of it as the Kmart of cancer, for its bright, overlit halls seemed to offer the same forced optimism, and too many choices. A red line was painted down the main corridors. I was instructed to follow the red line to the department I needed. I had to "shop" in more than one section.

The next few months were a whirl of surgical invitations. I had entered the dazzling brave new world of early detection. And my dance card was full.

There is something cool and creepy to early detection; although, mind you, I'll take early rather than late, any day. But it's disconcerting to schedule surgeries while feeling better than fine. I was bouncing around the hospitals in my running shoes, the "picture" as they say of good health. That is, if you didn't study the picture under a microscope.

Everywhere I went, I was congratulated. I was lucky. Yes, I was. "More good news" was how I was generally greeted after tests and biopsies were performed. The only tiny negative was that so much surgery would have to be performed to keep me as lucky as I was.

Nothing had prepared me for what I think of as "cancer lite," or the nouvelle malignancy. Certainly, there'd been enough of this disease in my family to give me a lifelong dread of it. But I'd been braced all along for the "big C" not the "little c." I'd known people and read histories of so many people with cancer, and it was always a terrible emergency: they were rushed into surgery immediately; then signed on for long programs of radiation or chemotherapy.

For the "little c" the protocol is better. Diagnosed in August, I was told I had a one-hundred-percent cure rate, but the doctor could not guarantee that if I didn't have my operation before Christmas. "Let's do you after Thanksgiving," he said in a pleasant tone.

In fact, I ended up having a double date for the operating room: two surgeons escorted me—one would work above the waist, the other below. They each held my hand as we walked into the operating room.

I wondered about this "two-for." They swore it was a terrific thing—and would save on anesthesia. I never knew if the surgeons operated in tandem or took turns.

There is a phenomenon, close to scandalous, of what is known in the trade as "awareness." Awareness is when a patient, immobilized on the operating table, is not sufficiently under to be oblivious. She hears or is vaguely aware but cannot speak or announce, even by the smallest gesture, that she is at least partly conscious for the proceedings.

I recall at least one such instance of awareness. Possibly my fault. There was something in me so afraid to let go of being conscious that I know I fought the anesthesia. I had, after all, the memory of my mother, who went into a hospital and never came out.

And so I stayed too aware of this new, unnatural world, this space capsule of molded Formica and steel; the gray tube where I now seemed to travel, perhaps about to be rocketed straight to outer space, or to nothingness beyond. This was science against nature: inside my body, nature had grown out of bounds, flowered into paisley smears I could see on my slides as I carted them from one hospital to another. The trick was to nip it in the bud.

"Catch it early" was a lame expression in my mother's time. No one seemed to be caught early enough. The style in those days, even for those lucky enough to exit the hospital, was to be booked soon for a return, and not necessarily a round-trip.

Matters are different now. Cool and creepy as that chill gray world of early detection may be, it seems to have saved me. Or—trickier question—was the investigation too thorough and did it uncover what might have forever remained nascent? Maybe I could have outraced my cells in my running shoes after all. No one can ever know.

So I did the prudent thing and had everything cut out and off. But my "awareness" did not end in the operating arena. I passed through my three hospital stays in a state that seemed half dream, half nightmare. *What was happening? Was this real?*

The custom of scheduling surgeries for dawn accentuated this response. To be awake at that hour is, for me, a sacred sensation. Under these circumstances, it was more than usually stirring to see the sunrise. It became more than an observance from my hospital window; it became a visual form of prayer: *May I see you rise again.*

The contact with the medical people was odd and dreamy, too—they must also be closer to their subconscious selves. Some dawns, I had a sense of communion as the attendants prepared me, the surgeons briefed me, and the anesthesiologists began their slow drip toward what we hoped would be only a transient nirvana.

I remember one of my surgeons standing by the window of my room. He was watching the sun rise, red over the East River. I sensed his escape into his own thoughts. It struck me as odd and intimate, having an impact from a man's mood on such a day. Then, both our trains of thought were interrupted by the sudden push of the gurney, as I rolled, resisting unconsciousness all the way, down to the stainless steel table and the scalpels that were supposed to save me from my nebulous fate.

I kept thinking, *I just want to go home, I just want to go home*. And I knew which home I meant—not my city apartment, which by creepy coincidence was on the same street as the hospital, but the distant world of Willowby, which I pictured, waiting, serene under snow, waiting for me to come home.

There were blizzards on my return to the farm. The snow had drifted over the walk. My husband suggested I wait in the car; he would shovel a path. No, I said, I didn't mind seeing my footsteps lead back into the house.

There was something in that soft white world of winter Willowby that reminded me of the near-forgotten thoughts I'd had in the similarly cottony atmosphere of the OR.

Whatever my fate, I had sworn to myself in the twilight of awareness, if I emerged, I would not have a child (not advised now, anyway) but find one who was in danger; save a life, not create one. It was a deal I made on the gurney, and I have kept it—twice.

twenty-three

My husband and I began almost immediately after my medical problems were resolved, to try to adopt a child. My first thought had been to find a baby in need from a foreign country. For reasons so mysterious that I cannot explain them even to myself, I'd long had a near-conscious image of myself with a small Chinese daughter. But in 1989, Chinese girls were not easily adopted. At that time, the Chinese consulate only allowed Chinese nationals to adopt the many baby girls in that country's orphanages.

At the same time that I learned this bit of news, I was overwhelmed by another international story involving orphans. The government of Romania had been toppled in the revolution of December 1989. The dictator, Nicolae Ceauşescu, had been executed. He had led the country into economic ruin. Rumored to be insane and syphilitic, Ceauşescu had outlawed all forms of birth control and abortion. He had dreamed of a super state with a large population. The result had been tragic: Romanian women bearing babies they were unable to care for. Many of these children ended up in orphanages that, in the winter of 1989–90, became notorious for their dreadful conditions. Babies were sick, starving, tied two and three to a crib.

The horror struck me, but the news story that made me leap to my feet was the first of the more joyful tales of the small children being taken out of the institutions and flown to new homes and families. I remember the first television image—a little girl, toddling across the tarmac at Orly airport to meet her new mother. The expression of eagerness on the child's face as she looked up at the woman who bent to lift her made me rise, tears in my own eyes, to take the series of actions that would lead me to Eastern Europe within a few months.

By summer, my husband and I had flown to Romania. We had not waited for the final U.S. immigration papers. We were told that if we found a baby, we could finalize the "unidentified orphan visa" at the consulate in Bucharest. We had no idea if we would in fact be able to leave the country with a child; at that moment, all was chaos, and adoptions were taking place one day, canceled the next.

In the interim, we had undergone the pre-adoption ritual of the home study. A woman social worker had walked through The Inn and inspected the nursery-to-be. She had examined the new crib, the changing table, the fresh wallpaper covered with a tracery of flowers and vines, and she had seen the domino motif of the cows grazing outside the nursery window. "I can't imagine a nicer place to bring a child," she said. Neither could I. But would we be successful?

The Romanian woman who translated our documents warned against our including a bucolic description of the cows and chickens. "They will think you are peasants," she said. "Tell them how many bathrooms you have." I laughed but followed her advice. *Peasants.*

A few weeks later, when I boarded the Romanian plane at JFK, I could see what she meant. The flight was packed with post-peasants—Romanians flying home with pots, pans, televisions, more carry-on luggage than I had ever seen. The plane seemed to heave at takeoff. The women passengers wore babushkas, smiled without teeth. The stewardesses seemed heavy-hipped as they served seven meals during the eight-hour flight.

This journey represented a round-trip for me. My family had fled this part of the world in 1907. They had lived in Russia, in the region closest to the border with Romania. I would be the first descendant to return to Eastern Europe.

After the dreamlike transition of flight, I awoke in what appeared to be another century as well as a separate continent. In the taxi from the airport, I stared out the window at peasants bent under their burdens. Horse-drawn carts rattled along beside us on the road. I felt as if I had returned to the world my grandmother had fled—exactly as she had left it, nearly a century before.

This impression deepened as I traveled north to the Carpathian Mountains, to the village in Transylvania where my husband and I had been told that there was a baby waiting to be adopted. As the train rode the racketing rails, I felt too numb to anticipate anything, afraid to believe in the actual existence of this baby girl. In the passenger cabin, which like most of Romania was poorly lit, it was possible to believe I was still in a dream, a dream that could perhaps turn to a nightmare. I held my feelings in check against disappointment, against despair. I looked out the window.

My heart leapt at the beauty of the passing mountains. The rivers rushed silver, the gorges plunged. I had never seen a landscape so unmarked by commerce—there were no billboards, no signs, no neon to distract from what nature had intended. The result was pristine, as spectacular as the Alps without the hoopla. I was reminded of home, of the Shawangunks, but, of course, the Carpathians were on a magnified scale.

We arrived at the Transylvanian village at night and were driven to the summer cottage that belonged to our translator's family. This was the Romanian version of the dacha, a mountain chalet, their place in the country. The stone-and-stucco cottage seemed a century or two old, heated by pretty porcelain stoves built catty-cornered into the rooms. There was no running water, but a tiled bathroom with washbasins. The beds were handmade, with rope springs, and when shaken, the duvets sifted what seemed like ancient dust. The furnishings, back home, would have qualified as country chic—the plain cupboards, bureaus; the lace tacked to the shelves. Everything was pretty enough to grace a Ralph Lauren ad, yet I sensed the hardship of the lives lived here—drawing water from the pump, carting wood or coal for the stoves. The beauty triumphed over the inconvenience—this was a place I would love to stay in for a long, long while, I thought.

I lay on the hard bed, too excited to sleep. Not only was I in the deepest country of my life, at dawn I might become a mother. The baby's doctor began his rounds at six A.M., and was to rendezvous with us soon after on the main road that cut through this mountain village. I stared out my window at a midnight sky more startlingly lit by stars than any I'd ever seen in my life.

You have to see true blackness of night to appreciate the difference. The heavens were illuminated by constellations. The moon cast a natural floodlight into my bedroom. I dove in and out of near dreams. I rose with the dawn to see a world more vivid than any I could have imagined. Very few of the villagers drove cars; horse-drawn carts moved slowly everywhere. The mountain village tilted at a steep angle, steeper than the Bronx cliffs of my childhood.

As in a waking dream, I walked beside my husband on a cobbled street. The doctor waited down the road, a silver-haired man with a handsome Roman profile. His smile kindled my own. His eyes crinkled. I felt the beginning of hope, the possibility of bliss. Such a doctor could lead me to my meant-to-be baby.

I got into the doctor's car, an ancient Mercedes, and we drove through an Old Masters landscape. Here was agriculture unchanged since the 1500s. Everywhere, cowherds, shepherds, and goatherds tended their flocks. Often, our car had to wait while hundreds of animals passed, led by men carrying staffs. What struck me was the sweet silence. How quiet the past must have been, before the advent of the engine.

As if to compensate, the Romanian doctor drove full speed, roaring around hairpin curves. The frequent sight of charred car hulks did not give him pause. We sped past farmers he called "cow men" who crouched in the field beside their cows. They milked from classic three-legged stools. How different, I thought, from our dairy barn at home with its milking machine and ceiling-hung conduits, its buzzing pipes and automated suction. Yet the cows seemed to look up at me in a kindred way, and I was comforted by their bovinity. My daughter-to-be, I was told, was the baby of a shepherdess and a cow man. Even as I strained toward my first sight of her, I felt a flicker of familiarity. I would be taking her to at least a version of a life she was born to have, to afternoons of play in the hayloft, of chasing chicks and petting ponies. She would have the childhood I had yearned for on those flat paved streets. She'd pick the flowers that had, for me, bloomed out of reach.

As we approached her birthplace, my future daughter's homeland turned more exotic by the kilometer. The villages and fields gave way to forest, black with evergreen, shadowed by mysteries and apparent danger: "VINOTUL!" WARNING! signs screamed. Warning of what? The signs were illustrated, giving face to fear: a snarling, fanged giant brown bear. "URSUS!" THE BEAR! The bear was here; he was everywhere—behind the trees, hidden in the rock dens. I felt as I did for the bears I had encountered at home—more thrilled than scared. Something there is that loves the bear.

My future daughter's history would be forever linked to the alleged maneaters. Her ancestors had, for centuries, been the forest-keepers, assigned to keep watch for the bear. They had patrolled these forests that held a cathedral shadow even as day broke. After several miles, the shadow lightened, gave way again to pasture, dotted with sheep. The long-faced mutton looked at me through their narrow eyes, as if to ask, *Who are you? What are you doing here?* They stood still on thin ankles, looking to me like New York women wearing bulky overcoats, regarding me with what I took to be a patient skepticism.

I was skeptical of myself. What *was* I doing here? We drove through a veil of fog and into the light of the new day. The village boasted a few streets and stores and at its center, a square, Soviet-style hospital. The hospital, too, seemed from another century, not so much in its exterior but in the formality and style of those inside. The nurses wore uniforms that dated back a few decades. Women patients wore babushkas and skirt-and-blouse ensembles that showed a daring chic in their clash of color and pattern. Most of the gypsyish women suckled babies at their bared breasts. How dare I trespass in this world and presume to be the mother of a baby born here? I knew I was crossing more than one border.

There was no elevator. My husband, the doctor, the translator, her friend, a male nurse, and I hurried up the stairs. My heart hammered. In the doctor's office, a surprise. A nurse had observed our arrival from an upstairs window, counted the number of our party, and now waited, proffering demitasses of Turkish coffee on a linen-draped tray. This was the human touch—and the caffeine—I needed to face the most dramatic moment of my life. I waited several more minutes to meet my daughter.

Then, suddenly, she was carried in, howling, her face framed by what looked like a nineteenth-century gauze baby bonnet. *Yowl! Here I am!* she seemed to squall. Everyone smiled. The baby had a full head of black hair and wide brown eyes that seemed to regard me with full recognition.

That night, my husband and I celebrated with Romanian home-brew, the fiery *tuica*, which we tossed back in tiny shot glasses, with the local toast, *"Noroc!"* To luck! I felt the liquor course down my throat, charting a warmth that seeped to my heart. I recalled the euphoria my grandmother had attributed to the wild plum brandy her family had brewed back at the dacha. I sensed that I was tasting the past. We laughed, ate, drank, and celebrated the most joyous event of all—a birth and an addition to a family.

In the following weeks, I spent time in the mountain home of the baby's birth family, getting to know them. They seemed relieved. The little baby girl whom they felt they could not offer a future was now going to that distant promised land, America. I memorized the details of their farm life to someday tell my daughter. I sat in the yard of their family compound and sipped the best coffee I had ever been given. The wash was done by hand in troughs in the yard. A woodpile was stacked for the coming winter. Cooking was performed outside or in a separate little kitchen to prevent the farmhouse from catching fire. A few animals stood in a corral observing me. A rust-colored pony and heavyset sheep.

On our final visit with the baby's family, the husky gentleman who was the baby's maternal grandfather did not understand our response when he invited us to dinner. We tried to decline—we had a plane to catch—but he misinterpreted our smiles as acceptance, and before I could say no, he had led a sheep out of its fold and brought it over to us. The grandfather produced a long, sharp blade, and I thought he meant to demonstrate shearing the sheep, but instead, with one sure stick, he pierced its throat, and down the sheep went.

The translator cried out, "No, they can't stay for dinner!" a second too late. I'll never forget the grandfather's face, how it fell. The translator babbled back and forth to the grandfather and to me. He had killed the sheep for a celebratory dinner. He had intended to build a fire pit and roast it all night long.

"But we can't stay," I said, feeling more embarrassed than I ever have in my life.

The sheep—now an inanimate mass of woolly torso and blank face, with poking, upturned hooves—lay in front of me like the biggest faux pas ever committed. As I stood in that farmyard, so far from the farm I call home, I realized one of the great distances between us— between the old country and the new. I would never be a genuine country person; the immobile form of the sheep was never something I could accept as a fact of my everyday life. I was capable of celebrating, even of eating barbecued mutton at fireside, but I could never be part of the routine rituals of real farm life, which automatically and naturally include slaughter. I will forever be a hybrid—a city person up to her ankles in the mud and dust. I would tiptoe through the manure to enjoy the scenic, but I would never truly be of the farm. I was transplanting my baby daughter from the world that would have been hers to my own version of rustic life.

"We can't stay," I told the Romanian grandfather, gesturing to the translator to somehow make this all right. "Can you have the sheep anyway?"

"Well," said the translator, "they'll have to. This is the sort of thing they might do once or twice a year, for a wedding or a festival." The grandfather smiled and kissed me good-bye. A roast sheep would be a roast sheep, and, thank God, they seemed to feel there was reason to celebrate.

And so did I as I carried my new daughter home to the United States, home to the farm in the Shawangunk Mountains, far from her birthplace but near to it in spirit. We arrived in the afternoon, and she took her first nap in the nursery. She smiled up at the view from her window, the living mobile of the maple leaves. The season had turned while we were overseas. The leaves were now golden against the gray of the early-autumn dusk.

Later, I carried my baby in my arms to meet her new neighbors, the true farmers who share our land. It was a clear night, and the stars sparkled almost as brightly as they had in the Carpathian Mountains, on the other side of the world. The Bowerses offered the hay wagon for a night ride around the farm. We climbed in, and I lay back, comfortable in the natural chair made by the baled hay. I looked at the sweet face of my little sleeping daughter, her long lashes against her cheeks. She held one small hand up, curled near her chin in a gesture I now knew as characteristic. We traveled the borders of the farm, escorted all the way by the Bowers' leaping dogs. Every few minutes, we scared up more deer, saw first their fire-dot gaze, then the flash of their white tails as they bounded ahead. Eventually, on our return to the barn, we were trailed by the herd of Holsteins, who lowed their approval and gave off great yeasty gusts of silage scent. Off in the distance, high on the ridge, I could see our own house. Its lights burned brighter as the night grew darker. I couldn't help but notice that the light was different now, more lemon-colored, and it spilled from the windows, inviting us as that long-ago farmhouse in the city had beckoned to me as a small child. *Come in,* the house seemed to say. *Come in and be right at home.*

twenty-four

Every autumn, Cecil Green had stood in the cellar and explained the workings of the furnace. "In case I'm not here next winter," he'd say. I always replied, "Oh, no, don't say that."

But Cecil would shake his head. "It will happen," he would say, "and you should know how to bleed the pipes, where the heat goes, to all the zones."

I appreciated his logic but never could accept the idea that one morning, he would not appear in his green uniform and cap. He brought the *New York Times* with him every morning, a nicety I felt guilty in accepting. In summer he appeared with neat bags of his own cultivated raspberries. They differed from the wild berries I had loved in Tuxedo Park, but they offered up their own sweetness. In a way, the raspberries had marked the difference between Tuxedo Park and Willowby. Tuxedo's fruit had been untended, taken for the picking in the wild, at a cost of welts and scratches. The berries had been tarter, possibly even more perfect to my taste, but they'd been gathered in prickly glens inhabited by snakes and stinging wasps. At Willowby, the berries were domesticated, part of the bucolic way of life. They appeared on groomed rows of bushes, tended by Cecil and presented by him with silent pride. His berries and, later in the season, his home-grown tomatoes, were the bounty he was accustomed to proffering to whoever lived at The Inn. Both berries and tomatoes were gifts from a more gracious past; Cecil himself was an emissary of the estate's glory days.

Cecil was such a part of Willowby that he seldom left the actual property. He traveled just a quarter-mile outside the stone-bordered entry on his daily rounds—the post office, the corner store. He seemed to have slowed the passage of time to the speed limit of Willowby, which was posted at fifteen miles per hour (during the eighties, Lord Hodgson lowered the limit to ten miles an hour in an attempt to put the brakes on changing times). I would look out the bedroom window every morning and see Cecil's maroon Pontiac in its silent crawl from the property and then its equally snail-like return. Stewart Lee, who for more than a decade sat and stood at Cecil's right hand throughout the work day, told me once that Cecil's car had to be put in the shop "for too little use." "You have to run 'em so's they work good," was Stewart's diagnosis.

Only a doctor's appointment or a rare outing with his grown children would draw Cecil more than the quarter-mile off his established route. He once confided in me during one of our basement consultations, "It's better not to leave the property." Cecil had been at Willowby for more than a half-century. He'd arrived in 1933 as a twenty-year-old seaman from England. He had jumped ship and traveled upstate to work on the estate. The person who straightened out his immigration and citizenship was none other than Hilary Talbot's aunt Mab.

Cecil Green, the name said it all. He had more than the proverbial green thumb, he was green through and through. Everything Cecil touched, grew—the raspberries, his famous tomatoes, the flower garden that bordered the drive to the Manor.

Everyone loved Cecil. The Hodgsons' son, Richard, wrote a school essay about Cecil, the gentle gardener who was so at peace on this place. Lord Hodgson and Lady Marguerite of course valued him, and the late Miss Talbot had deeded Cecil's "life lease" to his home in the carriage house. Cecil would never have to leave the property until he died—and not even then, it turned out. Lord Hodgson dreaded "losing Cecil"; he predicted it would be nothing less than "the end of life as we know it."

It was easy to love Cecil, his baby face and child's sweetness, but he had a grown man's shrewdness about the animals, plants, and machinery that made up the workings of the great estate. In his first note to me, Lord Hodgson had written "Cecil is the Brain," and so he was. He was also the heart and soul of Willowby.

And what was Willowby to Cecil? More than a place to work; surely, the property was his life. He had met his wife, Ida, here. She had arrived in 1933 as the nanny to the children of a visiting baroness. She and Cecil fell in love, and she returned to have her wedding party in the Casino. Ida, a pretty, outspoken woman from Copenhagen, had given birth to their two children in The Inn. In fact, their first home on the estate had been the Inn. They had lived on the first floor, without many amenities. "Our wedding present was a ton of coal," Ida remembered, "and it was a good gift." She and Cecil had lived in the house without running water or electricity. "We used Aladdin lamps," Ida recalled, "but they went out." It hadn't mattered much to be plunged into early darkness. "We were in love; we just went to bed," Ida told me.

The shorter the radius of activity, the deeper Cecil's pleasure seemed to be. I often reflected on Cecil's adage "It's a better day if you don't leave the property." My husband and I had joked about not leaving the property for an entire weekend but the truth was, it restored us not to leave. On many a Monday morning when my husband had had to return to work in the city, he'd envied Cecil. On one especially beautiful Monday, my husband was driving out when he saw Cecil kneeling by his roses. Cecil had sat up, trowel in hand, and given my husband a tiny smile. And it hit my husband then—that he had to leave and Cecil didn't. So who was really the caretaker and who the gentleman of the estate? That is a question that can have complicated and ever-changing answers. We suspected the quality of Cecil and Ida's lives might be somehow better than ours; surely, it was less wearing. I often recalled that Edmund Talbot had died during his weekend commute. Only the caretaker got to remain. It was he who clocked in every sunrise and sunset, who had the satisfaction of watching each day's progress as the buds and shoots bloomed according to plan. It was he who reaped the literal harvest, carrying the first and best of the fruits back to his own very charming carriage house, which looked upon the estate from a more modest but no less beautiful vantage point, than the Manor's.

But the caretaker could rarely leave. It was his duty and profession to oversee and to correct all the disasters that befell a country place. There could be no separation from his life and the life of the place. So, in exchange for the tedium of commuting and the burden of ownership, Cecil won the right to remain, to be salaried for the privilege that the alleged residents of the estate paid to support. But Cecil, like all family retainers, true old-style caretakers, would never be free. The daily rounds—boilers in winter, gardens in summer, the year-round mending of fences, replacements of screens—went on, endless, each season's duties supplanted by the next. The rhythms of Willowby suited Cecil, but Lord Hodgson once hinted to me that "Ida would have preferred a gayer life."

I've known Ida for nearly two decades. She reminds me a little of Jeanie in Tuxedo Park. Ida actually resembles Jeanie—the same white ringlets, china blue eyes, pink cheeks, a prettiness undiminished by age. But Ida's match was happy, and if she required more diversion, it didn't ultimately tell on her. Now, she is ferried from the estate to bingo games and other senior activities.

"What was it like in the nineteen thirties?" I once asked Ida.

"Well," she said, "there wasn't much to do; there weren't very many people. Miss Talbot came and went. Often, Cecil and I were here alone. When I had my first baby, I *ironed* the diapers—that's how it was then. I would walk up with the baby to the Manor. There were orchards then, and a long grape arbor." She remembered summer days walking the path, passing under branches hung with ripe peaches, the bunches of grapes, the fragrant berries. "It was quiet," she summed up. "It was very quiet."

For almost sixty years, Cecil maintained his schedule—the rounds to town to fetch the newspaper and mail, the tour of the buildings on the property. In summer, he carried his fruit offerings, the famous Cecil tomatoes.

Because of Cecil's hearing loss, I had to shout out my questions to him. Cecil always answered in his soft voice. So our relationship evolved as we stood in the flooding cellars (I recall one duet on paint cans) or on the stone-strewn earth of my failing garden. For all the years I knew him, I blared forth my need to know more, and he gave me the answers I craved. I especially loved his story of the little ser-vants' house that had stood over my cistern. "Corrupt overseer stole the house. It's sitting now on Cottekill Road," Cecil told me. The lit-tle yellow house had been tugged by horses, pulling a flatbed, to its new resting place. Cecil was excited by any innovation on the property and far from resisting such changes as my swimming pool, he seemed pleased and excited. The day it finally held water, Cecil nearly ran to see it.

Because I knew Cecil only as an older man, I was forever holding my breath when he executed any footwork on wet stone steps or tried to descend to the basement when it was flooded. One rainy spring morning, he did slip—falling as he tried to turn on a faucet outside the porch. He tumbled down to the old carriage step, where the guests of the original Shawangunk Inn had alighted from their horse-drawn carriages. He lay still for a moment, breathing harder than usual. I checked him, in silence, to see if anything was broken. "I'm all right," Cecil said, and he was.

More and more, Stewart Lee did the demanding physical work. And toward the end, Stewart took over the driving, too. Stewart Lee was, as the Hodgsons described him, the "young one," ten years Cecil's junior. Stewart was powerful, even at seventy-nine. He could lift a fallen maple limb itself as big as a tree; he could chop wood all day and then plow the snowy Avenue in the wee hours. Unlike Cecil, Stewart held other jobs: he opened the corner store every morning at five and acted as a part-time caretaker at other properties in the area. But assisting Cecil seemed to be his primary role, and at least for the last ten years of Cecil's life, I can't remember seeing Cecil without him. They worked as a team at the many two-man jobs on the estate: "You hold the door while I hang the hinge," that sort of thing. Stewart had been on the property almost as long as Cecil. He arrived from Maine after World War II and like Cecil, he had once lived in "my" house.

So it fell to Stewart Lee to report the reason, one gray autumn day, that Cecil did not appear at his side as usual. "Cecil's in the hospital," Stewart told me. "It's his lungs." I thought of Cecil's pipe, permanently clenched between his teeth, and guessed at the diagnosis. The constant draw on the pipe, the smoke he inhaled. I had become accustomed to the sound of Cecil's labored breathing, though it had always concerned me. I felt a belly clutch of fear.

Within days, the dread words were spoken: there was a malignancy. Then there was pneumonia. But Cecil would be coming home, I heard. He wanted to, and there was the possibility of time.

Cecil Green did return to Rock Ridge, but not to the property as he had wished. Instead, he was taken to the family-owned funeral parlor just a few hundred yards off his regular route. The funeral parlor was in a private house, but somehow the children's toys in the yard and the other accoutrements of life did not cheer me as I drove up.

"He went quick," Stewart had told me the first morning he brought the newspaper, now officially on his own.

"Poor Cecil," said Ida. "He didn't get to come home." She had not known what to do; there had been the promise of more treatment. I told her it was impossible to know in such situations. But on this point, she could not be consoled. "Poor Cecil, he just wanted to come home."

A crush of well-wishing mourners soon warmed the funeral parlor. It was comforting to see how many people had known Cecil. And everyone who had known him wanted to pay their respects. I stayed back from the open coffin. I had seen only my late father-in-law in this situation, and the waxy cosmetics and embalming had had the opposite of the intended effect. I had strained to retrieve a memory of that good man's face. But Cecil was indelible in my mind. I see him still, his blue eyes tearing in the cold, coming slowly up the stone porch steps, bringing the news and the comfort of his own presence. I, who cherish my privacy, had always been glad to see Cecil Green. He was a person who didn't invade privacy, he shared it with you.

Lord Hodgson spoke at length on Cecil's life and what it had meant to us all. I agreed with His Lordship that Cecil's passing was more than a man's death; it marked the end of an era, an era from which I had reaped benefits not usually experienced in the 1980s and 1990s. Cecil had been my escort into the place's past, and a beloved one at that. Because of Cecil, I know windmills once stood behind my house, that potatoes grew in the yard, and that the foundation that walls my tennis court was once part of a great dairy barn. "Mice chewed matches" was how Cecil explained the fire that burned down the barn long before my time.

Cecil remembered when the farm was worked by horses, how a

mare once fell into the cistern and had to be hoisted out by ropes tied to a wagon, pulled by a second horse. Cecil showed me the ruins I might have missed, covered with vines in the woods that separate my land from the lord and lady's. There, under fallen branches, lie the foundations of chicken houses and barns, a caved-in root cellar. It was Cecil who told me how the plantation met almost all their needs.

Cecil had attained a good age, almost ninety. After his funeral, he was cremated and his ashes placed where he had wanted to return, "on the property," overlooking the garden he had tended every season of his adult life.

t w e n t y · f i v e

Sometimes, destiny acts on a delay. Two years after applying to China and being told Americans could not adopt there, I received word that the People's Republic of China had changed its policy and would now allow foreigners to adopt the baby girls left in Chinese orphanages. This news arrived a year after my Romanian daughter. But why refuse this offering of fate? Our application was now accepted. Another daughter might already have been born and be waiting in another crib on the other side of the globe.

I responded without hesitation: yes. Of course I still wanted that baby. I thought of all my years as an only child and all the silent rooms in The Inn. Sasha was asking for a baby sister or brother. One can always find a reason not to do something—I already had the baby daughter of my dreams. But the tug toward China triumphed. Why not a second baby girl? And so, two years after adopting Sasha, my husband and I boarded a flight to Shanghai in the face of gale force winds. The nor'easter that blasted the plane that December day was later dubbed the Storm of the Century. The plane shivered, taxied twice back to the hangar before it finally made a shuddering liftoff into a gray, frozen sky. It is testimony to my anxiety regarding the purpose of this journey that I felt no fear of flying. I carried with me an empty infant car seat (aptly named the Dream Ride), a three-week supply of diapers, baby wipes, pediatric antibiotics, bottles, and disposable nipples.

Why was I more frightened this time? My first trip to Transylvania, in Romania, had been an odyssey that exceeded all my expectations. My daughter, Sasha, was now a two-year-old with heart-shaped lips, a sweet giggle, and bright, believing eyes. My friends' dire prediction—"Your life will change"—was a warning bell that never tolled for us. Sasha was my dream baby. She seldom cried or fussed. She enjoyed sitting on a play quilt beside my desk. I know it seems implausible and perhaps even smug, but she was so good that I didn't need to hire the baby-sitter or nanny I had imagined I would need if I were to continue to work.

The truth was that, as a mother, I fell into the "didn't know I was thirsty until I was given something to drink" category. I had not been consumed, as had so many of my friends, with maternal aches. I liked the idea of a baby, but I was not especially driven to have one. I would have said my life could go on, fairly happily, without my becoming a mother. But I would have liked to be a mother if fate made me—by whatever means. Being adopted in a sense myself, I had taken easily to the idea of not giving birth but embracing a baby who was already here.

Looking back, I see that I was the same age as my mother was when she died, when I became a mother. Was it that obvious? Had I waited to pass that fatal milestone? Or was I hoping to trade, to exchange life for death? I didn't examine my motives. I knew only that when it seemed, medically, I should not bear a child, I considered adoption at once. It seemed fated, effortless. At Christmas, I saw the scenes on television of the Rumanian Revolution; in August, I had a baby, born of that turmoil, in my arms.

Why, then, when I had been so blessed by the adoption of my first daughter, was I shaking with fear as I prepared to take a second child? Was it the double responsibility? Knowing I had a lovely daughter whose fate would now also be affected if something went awry? Perhaps I was feeling the tremors in a marriage that was destined to crack.

There were omens of profound change. Two nights before the flight to China, as I drove my older daughter to a relative's home, where she would stay for the duration of my trip, I witnessed, for the first time, a total eclipse of the moon.

Driving east around a bend on a mountain road, it seemed as if I were headed straight into the luminous orb. Then, directly in front of me, the shadow of the earth obscured the moon until I faced a glowing blackness. I drove alone; my husband had stayed in the city to work. Aware of my two-year-old, sleeping in her baby seat, I felt the full force of being part of the universe in a way I hadn't since that night so long ago when, as an eight-year-old who had just lost her mother, I looked to the stars above these same mountains and hoped, somehow, she could still see me here on earth.

That night I slept in a narrow guest bed in my sister-in-law's house. The bed felt alien, and I could not descend into a true sleep. The next day's journey was on my mind, and my heart raced. Curiously, my little Sasha, who always seemed to sleep deeply, woke up also—not to cry but to look into my eyes. I will never forget the expression, so knowing and mysterious, on her small face that night. She looked at me as if to say, *Everything will be all right.* Our shared gaze had the intensity that midnight encounters do—as if our souls met in a sacred silence. We held each other through the night.

In the morning, I left. My daughter's gaze had calmed me. But by the time I took my seat on the plane, the fear had returned, rushing in my blood. It is said that we all have an inner voice, and I had refused to listen to mine for some time. What that voice was saying, first in a whisper, then in a scream, was that the man at my side, my husband of so many years, would not be with me too much longer. We had often been separated by our work, and now the gap was widening. As a gauzy snowstorm whipped around the plane and take-off was delayed, I watched a couple across the aisle reach out for each other's hands. As if from above, I could see my husband and myself, seated side by side, flying into this blizzard, embarking on this significant journey to the other side of the earth for a wonderful purpose—to save a child. My husband had wanted both girls, but I could also see that we were no longer close, that we were hurtling toward the final break.

Why was I going? Knowing almost consciously what lay ahead, wasn't I tempting fate to try this twice? My husband wanted this child, too, but I sensed we would soon divorce. What did I have to offer this baby but the shattering of my own life? Fear and doubt swirled around me as I was propelled through those opaque skies. I felt compelled to complete the journey, even as my concern edged toward panic.

The orphanage had sent a fax (yes, in the new China, orphanages send faxes): "We have a baby for you. We would have taken her picture, but it was too cold." So, somewhere on the other side of the globe, this faceless infant waited. Faceless, but not voiceless. With the false intimacy that technology brings, I had heard the baby's voice when I telephoned the orphanage. After a staccato Chinese untranslated by the woman who answered the phone, I had heard the sound of footsteps—the hard, clacking steps, of someone crossing a stone floor—and then I'd heard a door open—in China!—and the cries of babies had traveled through thousands of miles of cables, across continents and under oceans, to sound in my ear as I stood on the wide pine boards in my kitchen, surrounded by the cheery domestic clutter of the life I'd lived here for so long—the old copper pots hanging from hooks, the plants stretching toward the paned windows, the long harvest table heaped with fruit and fresh-baked pie for Thanksgiving. Those voices, the thin, piteous wails of the abandoned babies, sounded right here, in the home that could be one child's, if I were willing to make it so. How could I not go?

The infant mortality rate in the orphanage was fifty percent. There was a baby who was already labeled mine. How could I not claim her? Yet I continued to tremble with doubt. I already had one perfect daughter; my marriage seemed precarious. A million babies are abandoned each year; I could make a difference for only one. Was I over-reaching my capacity to take responsibility for another life? My concern—if one can articulate a gutslide of panic as concern—was that this time my luck would fail, that I would jeopardize Sasha, the life that I had. What if I did not feel that rush of certain feeling for this new child? Wouldn't I risk the delicate structure of my first daughter's new life? I knew I would go through with the adoption, but would it be out of some grim sense of decency? That didn't seem fair, given the ecstatic experience in Romania. But everything was different now. The single constant was the nursery waiting back at The Inn, the little room papered in delicate flowers, the crib empty and ready for a second baby.

The flight to China took twenty-seven hours, and my husband and I arrived in Shanghai at night. The first sight to impress itself on me were the illuminated fruit stands; I saw the bright orange dots of thousands of clementines as the taxi carried us to our hotel. The city was even more intense than New York. It was ten P.M. on a Saturday, and high-rise construction was under way; hard-hatted men dangled from bamboo scaffolding wherever I looked. Stores were open, and the thoroughfares were clogged with bicycle and pedestrian traffic. The only cars seemed to be taxis. The crosstown drive, only a mile, took nearly an hour. We moved at a walking pace. The air reeked of exhaust. China's agrarian past pedaled by—old men on bicycles with caged chickens balanced on the back.

The orphanage did not open for official business until Monday, so the agony of suspense extended over the weekend. On Sunday, we visited the tourist attraction nearest the hotel, the Temple of the Jade Buddha. Inside the ancient building, a dimly lit corridor of polished wood led to a large stone buddha. "That is the buddha to whom the new mothers pray," said my guide, a thirty-five-year-old woman named Ms. Zhang, who was employed by the orphanage as a paralegal. She would walk me through the doors, literally, as I picked up my baby and made the round of offices to obtain her emigration papers.

Ms. Zhang was lovely, long-faced. She confided that she shared a room with her grandmother. She also murmured that she was celibate and someday hoped to adopt one of the baby girls herself.

I quizzed Ms. Zhang about the baby: How old was she? What was she like in temperament? The answers were a Chinese riddle: "She is very special." But how big was she? "What size clothes have you brought?" Ms. Zhang asked.

I thought on my feet. I had brought a variety of sizes, but I hoped for as young a baby as possible. "Little clothes," I said, holding my hands a span apart.

"You pray to this buddha," she said. "This buddha helps the new mothers."

The buddha glowed in the dimness of the temple. I have never been a follower of any organized religion, but I knelt before that statue. Half Jewish, half Southern Baptist, all doubt, I knelt in earnest prayer: *Let the baby be the one I can truly love. Let me be the mother this baby should have. Let me bring her safely home.*

At nine sharp the next morning, my husband and I walked into the courtyard of the Children's Welfare Pavilion, the orphanage where the babies were kept. The structure dated back to the early 1900s, and the architecture reflected the colonial French influence. The buildings formed a compound around a central garden, where bamboo grew and laundry lines were slung with still-gray wash. If the buildings had been maintained, they would have been pretty, the garden a centerpiece. As it was, all was begrimed and dirty; the red tiles of the roof were falling, the paving stones loose. Even the bamboo appeared dead, tall gray stalks jutting into the yard.

Inside the main office building, there was no heat. On this December day, the temperature inside the orphanage registered forty-six degrees. I could understand now the sentence in the fax: "We would have taken her picture, but it was too cold." Too cold to unwrap a baby.

"Look out the window," Ms. Zhang said. "You will have a choice." I looked. Through the dead garden ran two women in blue institutional smocks. Each woman held a bundle, a baby swaddled in heavy quilted bunting. The babies' heads were covered with towels, one pink, one blue-gray, their faces hidden.

"You will have a choice," she repeated. There were two babies.

I stood, numbed by the cold and the surprise, wearing my hat and coat indoors, while the women ran into the office, offering their bundles for inspection. Five women surrounded me—the two nurses holding the infants; the director of the orphanage, Dr. Han; Ms. Zhang; and two other women employees. Everyone chattered in excited Chinese.

Ms. Zhang translated, "Everyone wants you to take this baby." She gestured to the baby whose face was covered by a pink towel. "She is a very special baby. We have put her aside for you. She is very unusual. Very healthy. Very pretty." The nurse uncovered the first baby. She was, as described, very healthy, very pretty.

They tickled her chin, and she gurgled. But my eyes were riveted to the second baby, whose face was still concealed.

I asked to see her face. Everyone said again, "You must choose the first baby." The second infant's face was then revealed, almost as an afterthought.

As she was uncovered, the baby swiveled her head to look at me. Her face was thin, piteous; her low-set ears stuck out. Her color was a sickly near-green. She looked like a poor, sick elf. Her mouth turned down in sorrow, her eyes were wide with apprehension. She was eight weeks old, the same age as the first baby; she was half her size. She did not laugh and smile, she wheezed.

I felt in the pocket of my winter coat for the vial of pediatric antibiotics, carried on the good advice of a friend. As my hand closed around the medicine, I got a grip on myself as well. I had no choice. I also had no doubt. My husband whispered, "The one with the big eyes." Thank God, we agreed.

I took the tiny green baby, gasping and wheezing, into my arms. I noticed that she had a bald spot from lying unmoved in her crib. The back of her head felt flat in one place, another sign that she had seldom been picked up and held.

My earlier fear and indecision blew from the room like a fetid draft of disease and poverty. Was it another case of baby love at first sight? I knew in that instant that we stood at the start of our journey together as mother and daughter.

The first baby, the favorite of the nurses, was carried away to await adoption by another American woman who was expected to arrive in two weeks. She would live to be taken into that mother's embrace. The baby I carried out of the orphanage almost certainly would not have lived to that next date with fate.

My baby, named Sou Mei, meaning Celebration of Long Life and

Everlasting Beauty of the Flower, was placed on the orphanage's office table and undressed. The damp blue-gray wraps were removed, and she was dressed in the new fleece suit and down baby bunting I had brought along for this hoped-for purpose.

At the hotel, she was bathed in the sink. The water ran black from her small body. She never cried; she seemed not to have the strength.

Love can overtake you at odd moments. A few nights later, I was trying to collect the urine sample required for Sou Mei's medical tests. The doctor at the Shanghai hospital had told me to hold her over a rice bowl after her bottle feeding. It was late, after her two A.M. bottle. My husband slept, but it seemed the baby and I had been awake for hours in the Shanghai hotel bed. I held her little purple fanny over the rice bowl for what seemed an eternity.

To keep away the cold, I drew the blankets around us like a tent while we waited, silent, until she took a tinkle. Sou Mei's eyes met mine, and I felt the same depth of soul-searching that I'd shared with my older daughter back in America. I knew then that Little Miss Ears Stick Out with Tears in Her Eyes was going to be fine.

Within twenty-four hours the antibiotics had taken effect. She turned ivory pink, her eyes cleared. She exceeded all expectations— exquisite, a luminous old soul with contemporary wit. I gazed at her and saw the fatefulness of every mother's choice. It is not the beautiful baby who is chosen, but the chosen baby who becomes beautiful.

Within days, Jasmine (Sou Mei became her middle name) bloomed into the smiling baby she had a right to be. We sailed through her medical test, the official interviews, the passport offices. At the hospital, where she was given her final medical approval, a giant (six foot four) Chinese doctor answered my questions regarding her background.

I could never give this second daughter the complete answers I will someday have for my older daughter's questions—who am I? where was I born? who was my first family? Jasmine Sou Mei's records, like the records of most of the Chinese orphan girls, state only the address where she was abandoned. My baby's papers read "Quan Dong Road." Where was Quan Dong Road? "It is near the hospital," the doctor told me. But it may be that is not where she was found. He pointed to her umbilical cord—"surgically cut and tied." Most of the baby girls in the orphanage, he said, were actually born in hospitals, but the birth mothers fled as soon as they could run out of the building. In China, it is a crime to abandon a baby girl, but it is also a tradition. The baby, the doctor went on, might not even have been from Shanghai. Women came from the outlying provinces to give birth in the city or to leave their babies here to avoid detection. So I was left with my baby daughter's heritage, a mystery to match my own.

Before leaving China, I took a day trip to the ancient city of Suzhou. From the window of the 1940s train, I could see the swirling green circles of the rice paddies, the Chinese farm workers carrying straw on their heads, water buffalo straining against the plows. Was this the China that had produced my daughter? Or was she a child of that jagged city we had just left?

My husband and I visited a family compound, the ancient home of an illustrious citizen of Suzhou. The rooms were decorous, featuring stiff-backed carved chairs and high, throne-like beds. I absorbed as much detail as possible so that my baby might someday have my first-hand description of this part of her life.

At this house, with its dark, polished beauty, I saw the garden that the orphanage had failed to maintain. Beautiful stands of bamboo, rows of trees, reflecting pools. The curator, an elderly Chinese man, explained that in another century this had been the country home of a writer, that the place had been given to him. "A writer can write without meat, but not without looking out at the bamboo," the curator said.

I couldn't help thinking at that moment of the yellow house and garden that waited on the other side of the earth. Of the view from the room where I would write this story: a window that looks out at rolling pasture, grazing cows, a world alive with the cries of birds and the flight of iridescent butterflies.

I would take this baby girl there, to whatever waited for us, to the beauty of the place, and, I hoped, to health and safety, to fulfill her Chinese name: a Celebration of Long Life, Everlasting Beauty of the Flower.

twenty-six

At the moment when I believed I had more to be grateful for in my life than ever before, that life shattered. My husband and I had come through so much together. After a series of hospitalizations I had undergone over the past two years, I had never felt more truly married. We had been together since I was eighteen and he was twenty-four. It may sound incongruous, having had a marriage that endured so long, twenty-seven years, but I'd never counted on it lasting until the end. There was an uneasiness and sometimes a distance, often actual, between us. Work took us away from each other, and the mystery that may be every marriage was never solved. Only at the worst times, when I felt I might be facing death, did I lose my doubts. As my husband held my hand throughout the round-trips to the various operating rooms, I had felt certain that we would stay together, that we could endure anything. I believed our love had triumphed over the tensions that had sometimes torn at us. It was fortunate that at the time I didn't know I was mistaken.

Life seemed sweeter to me after my medical ordeal, and I felt blessed to be given my first daughter. But by the time we flew to China to adopt my second girl, I knew in my heart that we were finished. I felt no love from my husband, and I didn't truly know why. Was it the stress of suddenly becoming a family? Or some faultline that had run beneath the marriage all along? Was it him, or was it me? Of course, we would always view what happened differently. I knew only that by Jasmine's first birthday, our house was filled with hate, and the atmosphere had become unbearable.

Divorce came swift as sudden death. Some mornings, in the grayness of the new day, habit recalls almost three decades of marriage, and I vaguely imagine that my husband is still here. But when full consciousness returns, I can understand that he is gone and, along with him, the rage that came between us.

When I searched for my home, I had not wanted a "divorce house." I had seen the destruction everywhere. The marital Waterloo, the strewn toys, the emptied bottles. I'd often wondered how couples could wage war in idyllic surroundings. Now I know.

The rose-papered room we shared at The Inn was a too-charming stage set for the final, bitter fight. But the walls had seen similar sorry stories enacted. When I thought back on it later, I was perhaps the third person to end a marriage in this room. Hilary Talbot had returned here, leaving her prominent husband in England. And here, even earlier, her own father, Edmund Talbot, had spent the last night of his life, estranged from the woman he had once adored. Later, a historian turned up a deed from 1888 and the will of a certain gentleman who specified that "my wife not inherit this house." So, in the end, no place could bestow immunity, no life could be so charming as to distract from pain.

Now I find relief in and am reconciled to the fact that I had to end my marriage. I take comfort in knowing that despite our division, my husband and I did rescue two baby girls from dramas far worse than the one we staged here. I trust that this beautiful, if broken, home is better than any orphanage. Certainly, it is the best shelter I can provide. As time passes, I reflect more on the laughter and beauty of our shared lives than on the sorry end. I do remember the raspberries.

t w e n t y - s e v e n

Sometimes you can pinpoint the exact moment of a lifelong commit-ment. That second when you know how much you care, how far you are willing to go to ensure the well-being of someone else. My uncle Len's moment had occurred more than thirty years ago: that night at Camp Ava when he took his place beside me on the basketball court.

He knew and I knew—the instant he took off his trench coat and wrapped me in it, to keep the cold from me—that he would be re-sponsible and loving for the rest of my childhood. And so he was. Uncle Len remained in many ways mysterious. He never abandoned his slouch hats, his shades. His only luggage remained the manila en-velope containing its "classified documents." I knew when he was plan-ning to visit me because a package containing his size-thirteen shoes would arrive. The Len style—"I have to travel light"—dictated that anything of any weight had to precede him.

As the years passed, Len resumed the solitary style of his exis-tence, moving from hotel to hotel and eventually settling, to the ex-tent that he could settle, in Palm Beach. Even there, he preferred transient accommodations and only at my insistence rented the kumquat cottage, which was his home for the last years he remained on the island. As always, he balked at owning furniture—"Possessions possess you," he said. So almost all his things were rented. He seemed content with his new existence, retired from an occupation about which he had been characteristically vague; "something in confidential government" was all he would say. If he weren't my uncle, I would say Len had been a spy. But for which side? He loved intrigue, anything that made the everyday seem significant, rife with important secrets. "It's all in the details," he might say. He continued his mystery side trips—to the Keys, to Bermuda, to Jerusalem to visit his brother. My uncle Gabe had married the caterer he met at the first hotel on his initial visit to the Holy Land.

My uncles' divergent views on life and love led them to take separate paths. Gabe had long been the fervent suitor. Was it any wonder the women declined? "I've been spurned," Gabe would report to Len.

Len would sympathize but remark, "What do you expect, with a word like 'spurned' in your daily vocabulary?" He tried to teach his kid brother what came naturally to him—to be elusive. Len was very elusive, and it was absolutely for real. He was not playing hard to get. He *was* hard to get. As a result, from the time of my childhood when I could first note such matters, Len was pursued by women. They followed him on foot, stalked him at parties and dances. He had an unlisted phone number, and yet the phone rang. He was always courtly with women, but he would never "declare." "That remains to be seen" was his response to an insistent woman's pressure for commitment. He was gallant but as hard to spot as the yeti. Like Big Foot, one saw mostly his track.

Len did, however, escort his brother down the aisle, holding him by one arm. When Gabe was fifty-four, he wed the caterer in a synagogue in a basement in the Bronx. Gabe was given away by his two brothers, who half carried him down the aisle. Norm, the only married brother, supported Gabe by hoisting his other arm. "I'm swooning, mooning over you," he might have sung to the bride had he not been what he was—speechless.

Norm's wife, Barb, a woman who used more eyeliner than Nefertiti and turned a hard profile, too, said, "Oh, that Len. He's got a secret. He's got a secret. I know, Len. He's got a girlfriend." Later, she pinned Len against the *shul* wall and repeated her suspicions. "You got a girlfriend, you got a secret." Len smiled the noncommittal Len smile and backed out the door.

Gabe moved to Israel with his new bride and what he called "a semblance of normalcy." Len traveled and ended up, as they say, in Palm Beach in the kumquat cottage, a block from the sea he had always yearned to cross.

When I visited Len, he took me for long, mostly silent strolls along moonlit beachfronts. We "infiltrated" large hotel lobbies and stayed "incognito" at tropical Art Deco bars. He walked five miles a day and kept in shape, if someone that tall can be in shape.

Then, without warning, at age seventy-nine, a stomachache became too severe. During one of my visits to the kumquat cottage, I happened to glance out the window and see Len walking an agonized course in his garden. He held his abdomen and would pause, then resume, the agitated circling.

Still, he did not indicate anything was "serious"—on the contrary. He would be fine. But I saw something in his eyes, an uncharacteristic distractedness. By one A.M. we were admitted to the local hospital's emergency room. A few tests were performed.

The doctor told me he would have to operate immediately, that Len had internal bleeding and would die before dawn. The doctor's name was Shasha. Len and I both laughed. "You mean it's time to go *shasha?*" It struck us as grotesquely funny in the neon night. But then the pain worsened, and nothing was funny.

Len refused the surgery. He lay on a gurney, wearing a hospital gown and shower cap, and said to me in a level voice, "Laura, I suppose it's my time to die. I don't want to go in there and be cut up and go out that way." I refused to let him refuse. It was two A.M. Dr. Shasha was waiting. I had no idea whether he was a wonderful surgeon or an awful one, whether I was depriving Len of a peaceful exit or sending him, as he stated, to a botched, bloody death. But I could not say good-bye.

He signed on the dotted line. We've never talked about it—not right after, not since. But I knew I had taken his life in my hands, gambled with the awful potential of pain. I could not let him go. Not then. Not now. Not yet.

At dawn, in the deserted hospital hallway, Dr. Shasha said Len would recover. In that nightmare territory walked by seemingly somnambulant surgeons in green gowns and paper slippers and masks, it was almost hard to accept even good news. Was it true? I sat beside Len's bed, held his hand, said words he couldn't hear. I knew that from that time forward he was in my care, instead of the way it had been before, that old as I was, I had until that night been the child and he the adult. It was Len who intervened for me between myself and all manner of danger. How nice that he was a giant in every sense. His great heart kept me from doubting that I was loved, cared for; he was always there, someone to turn to, who assuaged every doubt and fear even when he fell silent.

Len recovered and for a time considered staying on, living the life he had established in his cottage by the sea. But as I postponed leaving him there, it became clearer, at least to me, that he had reached the end of his solitary existence. He would return to our family home, not the rented house.

I remember the minute the decision was made. I'd taken him to the hospital for a follow-up visit. The nurse called his name. I watched him rise, in sections, it seemed, his great height being an encumbrance at this stage. He held his medical papers in, of all things, a manila envelope. But he had thought to pack the files that would not fit in the envelope in an airline flight bag. The flight bag was labeled with an exotic name, Air India or Kathmandu Air or some such, but I knew Len had selected it as part of his lifelong wish: that carry-on was the receptacle of his unfulfilled dreams. He was the world traveler who had stopped at the home port to take care of a small girl so long ago and had lost his momentum in the consideration of family. Len's life had not materialized as the mysterious adventure he had imagined; instead, he had written his own history of devotion. He had exchanged the exotic for the mundane, but brought to our every day the illusion of adventure.

I jumped up from my seat in the hospital waiting room, steadied him by the elbow, and walked him to the door. I took hold of the Air India bag, which turned out to hold his Medicare cards and a change of clothes. "Come on," I said. "We're going home."

Nine years have passed since that day in the hospital. Len has lived all this time in The Innlet, the little guest house attached to The Inn. For intrigue, he has the secret door that connects his house to mine—one downstairs, the other, upstairs, through the linen closet.

Len is not a country fellow, as he'd be the first to admit. His feet pounded pavement for so long that when he walks here, he avoids the grass paths and favors the hard asphalt of the tennis court. For years, he has walked that court. We kid about it being his prison yard.

Inside the house, he is hilariously unimpressed by the colonial details. The wide floorboards, the fireplace mantels. He still refers to the house as the "apartment." The single great compliment he gave the house was in regard to the electricity: "So many outlets." When one of the frequent power failures occurs, he maintains his urban attitude: "When will the hot water come back on?" He doesn't grasp the fact that I run the show here and the hot water will come back on when I start the generator. There is no super to summon, although Stewart Lee, Len's contemporary, surpasses anyone in that role. Mostly though, Len revels in his grandnieces—his grandchildren in love and role—my little daughters, Sasha and Jasmine. He has, he admits, gone into "over-*kvell*." His speech is a run-on sentence of endearments.

"Has anyone told you yet you're adorable?" he asks each little girl every morning.

"Not yet," they answer, saucy on purpose.

The summer sunsets are our best times, when our world is seen as if through rose-colored glasses. Even the cows turn pink. Our actual roses bloom in a thick hedge in the front yard. The air is perfumed. Jasmine tends her "butterfly bush" and flutters after the Monarchs and other exquisite butterflies that swoop in to visit. Hummingbirds pause, too, in a stationary frenzy. We all laugh at their comical whirrings. Our porch is draped with hammocks. There are enough rocking chairs for all. How good it is to watch a day end this way.

"What an old age!" Len says, laughing. I watch Len play with my two daughters and remember another little girl, and her mother, and the long search that somehow led us here.

twenty - eight

Many marriages end on holidays. The pressure to be joyful, the availability of liquor, the rush to buy presents—all factors in the implosion that occurs in so many homes. My marriage ended during Christmas week 1993, concluding as the New Year began. The punctuation was painful, perhaps so painful that it has cauterized the nerve endings and I have no wish to recollect the events that occurred or to inflict them on anyone else.

I do remember the Christmas that followed, the first on my own. Although, of course, I was not on my own; I was living with my two-year-old baby girl, Jasmine, and her four-year-old sister, Sasha, and my seventy-nine-year-old uncle Len. It seemed to me that we huddled together for warmth that winter in a way that I had never experienced, even in the near-arctic conditions that had characterized life in Tuxedo Park.

There were seventeen blizzards that season. The snow blew into the house itself, needling under the window sashes, accumulating in narrow drifts inside. Outside, the great pasture that connected my land to the Manor was snow-swept into scalloped hills and valleys. Even the wooden snow fences could not hold back the drifts. Snow settled, obliterating the Avenue. The road to town became a lunar canyon, walled in white, a channel that narrowed with each passing storm. Inside the house, my radio played on, accompanied by the howl of the wind and the sting of sleet against the windowpanes.

This was the only winter when the snow exceeded Stewart Lee's capacity to remove it. Every morning at four Stewart drove, hunched over the wheel of his truck, his red plaid cap pulled down, the flaps over his ears. The plow attached to his truck cut through the snow, like the prow of a ship through continuously forming icebergs.

It was this winter that Stewart Lee became my savior, refusing to charge money to remove the drifts. I'd long appreciated Stewart Lee, as did so many people in Rock Ridge. He offered his services—"a dollar a day"—to maintain the country homes of city people. If you were gone, Stewart Lee was there, checking the cellar, testing for frozen pipes, defunct furnaces. If you were there, his presence seemed lifesaving. He got you going. He kept you warm. At seventy-eight, he was still strong. He never failed to pull the rip cord on the generator. "Got that sucker started" was all he'd ever say.

Stewart had lived his life combatting perverse machinery. He drove a truck loaded with replacement batteries, odd tools, and parts. He called all faulty pieces of equipment "sucker," and he never would quit till whatever sucker he fought had been brought into compliance. If I conjure an image of reassurance through that frozen season, it is that of Stewart's truck's headlights, twin golden beams, illuminating the ever-falling snow. He drove in long before dawn and made repeat investigative journeys down the Avenue, "just to check." If there was a sound that calmed the palpitations of my heart, it was the hearty roar of his truck engine and the stuttering start of the generator.

I felt too much chagrin to watch a man his age battle the elements and the engines alone, so I often wrapped myself in a heavy shawl or donned my old green parka (guaranteed to withstand temperatures of seventy degrees below zero), to stand beside him in the biting dark. I was almost useless at such moments, although, in a pinch, I did help him lift the two-hundred-pound generator; my arms were stronger than I knew from carrying my two children. Mostly, I kept Stewart company at such moments, and it was during these chill intervals, as we waited for sparks to catch and engines to kick, that I learned what I knew of him—that he was originally from Maine, that he had served in the Navy during World War II, and that he had visited New York City once. ("Went to Yankee Stadium to see the game, didn't want to go any farther.")

Stewart Lee had a verbal tic of saying "Yes, yes" in response to most remarks. "Yes, yes, the Manor is froze up"; "The road is bad, yes, yes." The stubborn sucker of the moment—the furnace, the hot water heater, whatever refused to catch or lay cold and sullen and plugged up under a layer of carbon—that sucker, yes, yes, was giving grief.

This time, it was the transformer. I'd witnessed its demise earlier in the day as I stared out my kitchen window. There had been a sound, an almost festive *pop!* rather like a premature Christmas cracker. There was a flare of fire and then smoke from the pole near the house. That sucker was gone, yes, yes. And so I found myself on Christmas Day standing in a house suddenly gone dark. The furnace shuddered to a halt. In an instant, I felt the warmth begin to ebb. The December wind infiltrated the clapboard walls and I felt the sudden truth of how frail a barrier stood between my family and the elements.

And the generator would not start, yes yes, that sucker was broken. Stewart and I heaved it into the back of his truck, a truck so filled with spare parts, ropes, chains, and other miscellaneous tools to combat disaster that the rear door would not close; it had to be roped shut over the bulge of the generator. Stewart drove off in search of repair. I packed the children into the car and coasted over the snow to town. I was wondering what I would do about Christmas dinner. As it happened, it was also Chanukah, so we were faced with the prospect of missing out on both holidays in one frigid swoop. The image of my goose-pimpled naked turkey in mind, I scouted the main street for an open café. The windows were black, the "Closed" signs were posted.

Only the corner store was open. Resigned, I carried the girls over the icy parking lot toward the fluorescent box of the convenience store. On the way, we encountered Rock Ridge's single homeless person, Wild Vern, the only other person around. Wild Vern was not a comforting sight. He was filthy. His matted dirty blond hair hung down to his shoulders, and his parka had the sheen of grease. His pants dragged over the backs of his splayed-out running shoes. Wild Vern's expression, viewed through the parted curtain of his mane of unwashed hair, was not encouraging. Neither was his history. Several years before, he had poured gasoline around his former home and threatened to set it afire. The house had been sold as a result of his parents' divorce, and "new people" had taken it over. Wild Vern was not making the transition. The police stake-out ended with his departure for an institution. But now he was back, rumored to be living in the woods or in an abandoned school bus behind the supermarket.

Stewart had told me that Wild Vern appeared regularly at dawn at the corner store, often staying until it closed, near midnight. His constant presence had evolved into a sort of job—he swept the store, crushed cartons. I had seldom heard him speak. On this evening, however, meeting him in the thickening grayness of Christmas, I ventured a weak, "Merry Christmas, Vern," and he surprised me with a reply: "Yeah."

Yeah. I drove the girls back to The Inn, where Uncle Len sat in the growing dark by the unlit Chanukah menorah and the white-skinned turkey. The girls began to whimper, they were cold. As we stood wearing our hats and coats indoors, the phone rang: Abner Bowers, down at the dairy farm. They had power and were inviting us to share their Christmas dinner. I accepted with a laugh.

We lit the first candle on our menorah and used it to light the others. I said the blessing, a napkin draped over my head. Then we headed down to the dairy farm. In the cobalt light of evening, the snowfall seemed to slow, relax. The horizontal wind changed direction, and lacy flakes fell, large and separate.

We stopped at the cow barn. The Holsteins stood at the ready for the evening milking. The lead cow turned and gave me a long moo in greeting.

"Look," my older daughter cried. I followed her gaze. There stood a bandy-legged newborn calf. Betty had shown us how to nurse the babies with a nipple-tipped bucket. We all took turns feeding the calf. She almost knocked Jasmine over in her eagerness to slurp from the bucket. I touched the calf's mouth, and, of course, she sucked off my glove.

Abner Bowers and his son Nate spread the green hay out as bedding—the scent of summer filled the barn. From the shadows cats emerged, tails up and mewing for milk. They were served, as they were every evening, from a wide dish on the barn floor. The cats and their kittens gathered, ringing the dish. Most of the cats were typical tabbies, tiger-striped. One little kitten was gray and fluffy—"That's the mean one," Abner said. We all laughed; the kitten seemed too tiny to be mean.

We left the light and heat of the barn to walk across the iced barnyard to Abner Bowers' cottage. Through its windows a golden light spilled onto the snow. Inside, we found the Bowers family waiting at a long table set for their Christmas dinner. The family was large, larger than the dimensions of the normal dining table would truly accommodate. This table actually comprised several tables, and the seats were supplemented by benches, whatever was handy to hold the increased number of diners. I was relieved to see places set for us anyway. We squeezed in to take part. Betty was still cooking; the kitchen windows steamed.

As Uncle Len, Sasha, and I took our seats (I held the baby, Jasmine, on my lap), I looked around at the faces of the farm family. Nate and his wife, Kelly, sat together, their three children lined up across from them.

Although I'd known them for more than twelve years, Nate and Kelly, both quiet, remained a mystery. I had interpreted their silence as shyness. Over the years, I could almost count the words we'd exchanged. There had been a single exception. One September in the early eighties, I'd returned to Willowby after a long stay in England. On my first morning home, I'd found Nate trying to salvage hay in my pasture. There had been a drought; the grass was scorched. As he stood there, studying the brown grass, Nate reminisced about a school trip he'd taken some years before, to Scotland, how intrigued he'd been by the country, the people, the landscape . . . how much he'd wanted to see more.

Nate had stared off at the visible boundaries of his world, Willowby. I saw something for the first time—that the barriers that protected Cecil and the lord and lady and me might imprison Nate Bowers. It seems that people who live within a restricted place either relish their isolation, using it to magnify the minutiae of their lives, or, as perhaps Nate did, they chafe at the redundant rhythms and limited vista.

Seeing Nate at the holiday table, I thought what a good life he had. But did he think so? I remembered the only occasion on which I had seen him explode. It had been a spring day, a heavy rainstorm. The cows had kicked open the gate and gone gallivanting up to my house and the open field to the Manor. The heifers were almost dancing, kicking up their hooves and nibbling the wet grass shoots. It had been a job to herd them back to the barns. I'd run out to help, joining the soaked circle that had included his wife and kids. Nate had bolted from the group, shouting as he departed, "If I had a gun, I'd shoot them all!" He'd marched back to the farm alone, his boots squishing through the muck.

"Write it down," his wife, Kelly, had said to me, "then show it to him later to remind him." What had been happening between them that day? I couldn't have known. Kelly, who looked like her name— she had green eyes and red hair—had always been reserved with me. While I had so often sat in Betty's kitchen and felt free to come and go from her cottage, I had yet to set foot in Kelly's house. It hadn't mattered, because the older Bowerses entertained for the entire family, setting up picnic tables out in the barnyard or holding parties in the barn. (They were known for the Halloween party that featured ghosts hanging from the beams and witches tucked into the straw.)

Over the years, I'd gleaned only one or two insights into the younger Bowers' marriage. The first had been under the tragic circumstance of a nearby farmer's suicide. That farmer, a man in his forties with a wife and several daughters, had been found hanging in the barn. He did the milking, cleaned up, went up to the loft and jumped, according to local farmers who described his death. I had attended the farm auction that followed. Nate and Kelly had been there, too, and had stood near me. "You tell me if it ever gets that bad," Kelly had said to Nate.

The second peek into the young Bowers' life had been more auspicious. They had taken their first vacation in years, attending a "marriage encounter" weekend. They had returned holding hands. They had three children, two girls and a boy. Kelly herself joked that she gave birth every Memorial Day. "I never get to stay for the picnic," she said. "I always have to excuse myself to go to the hospital."

Over the years, I'd attended the Memorial Day picnics, which always included at least three birthday cakes. Perhaps it was the volume of birthdays, but I'd been struck by the way Kelly had always walked alongside the party table, holding a trash bag open as the gifts were unwrapped. The paper and boxes disappeared instantly, and Kelly's trademark neatness prevailed. Her behavior seemed perhaps overly efficient, but I didn't question it. My husband had once held Kelly up to me as an example of a model wife. "She stands by her husband," he'd said, pointing out Kelly's silhouette as she drove a tractor in the distance.

Also at the Christmas table: Betty and Abner's daughter Ruth, her husband, and her three sons. The boys were familiar to me—handsome teenagers who wore plaid flannel shirts and worked part-time "helping Grampa" in the barn. Ruth was the easiest of the Bowerses to know. She had gone back to school and earned a degree in library science. We overlapped in the area of books. Ruth had married young, and her marriage had buckled under the strain of three babies in four years. Her husband had left and they had divorced, but Ruth's good nature had prevailed—even her divorce healed. Dave, a somewhat idiosyncratic fellow most often seen on a mountain bike pedaling straight up to Mohonk, had reconciled with her, and they had long ago remarried each other. They represented the word most often used to describe the family: "solid." The Bowerses were solid.

So I had felt myself steady a bit as I sat at this family table and took part in the holiday meal Betty had prepared—roast beef, potatoes, and gravy. As we ate and talked, the snow continued to fall outside. By the time my uncle and I and the girls rose to go to our own house, our power had been restored. Walking uphill, we could see the kitchen lit from within and the menorah in the window.

That year, we celebrated the Jewish holiday along with the Christian. I saw no conflict. The goal of both holidays was peace. The girls and I had picked out a Christmas tree from our own driveway, a little cedar that had trespassed between the giant maples and would have to be cut anyway. I had thought the tree the prettiest ever. It was feathery and gave off a scent of resin. "That's the kind of tree my family always had," Betty had said. "We never bought one." I followed Betty's example and decorated our house with grape vines, holly, and bitter-sweet from the woods and the fencerows. That night, as I walked my family home through the woods alive with unseen presences, I felt under the spell of the double holiday. The dual celebration had deepened the joy in our hearts as we left our neighbors' home for our own. One faith informs another. We had all felt the descending peace.

The snow continued, thickening, a curtain to our annual drama.

twenty · nine

In nearly eighteen years at Willowby, the lay of the land had remained remarkably intact. All around us, though, malls were replacing mountains, spawning satellite strips like lunar landing stations, almost overnight. Modular houses popped up, mushroomlike. What is called light pollution had already blanched the night skies over the nearby little city of Kingston. The fluorescence and insomniac glow was leaching into the night sky over Willowby. Already, the distant diesel decibel level had risen, and if you listened hard, there was no longer such a thing as a truly silent night. But "progress" like this had at least kept its distance from the property.

The great change, as I came to regard it, was carried on the current of two rumors, twin harbingers that the status quo was about to be challenged. As there were whispers that a Wal-Mart was coming, there were murmurs that "swamis are returning to Willowby."

Over the years, I was aware that devotees made annual pilgrimages to Willowby on July 4, the anniversary of the death of the original Swami Vivekananda, the Hindu monk who had visited Willowby in 1895 and again in 1899. He had been close to Edmund Talbot and Sara Jenson Talbot, the grandparents of the current Lord Hodgson. In fact, in Hilary Talbot's book, her parents' wedding was described as being "attended by an Eastern sage." Every summer, the devotees, clad in tra-

ditional peach-colored robes, would gather around the Manor to lay offerings of flowers and pray at the foot of a giant tree, the "Prophet
Pine," that was sacred to the dead monk's memory. Then they left.

But now the Manor was for sale. "A thousand a month to mow the
lawn," His Lordship lamented. "How is one to live?"

"It's impossible," said Lady Marguerite. The upkeep of the Manor,
its outbuildings, and the eighty-three-acre estate had become prohibitively expensive. Money gushed like the floods that filled the cellar of
the Casino, which, it turned out, had been constructed on an underground river.

"Why did they choose such a site?" I asked the lord.

"We don't know," was his answer.

The result was continuous upkeep, the digging of canals and
drainage ditches. A sump pump could be heard sucking and gasping in
its ongoing attempt to imbibe the gush in the Casino's basement.

The Manor itself, so beautiful, a perfect example of an English
country home, suffered the wear and tear of time. A paint job cost
more than forty thousand dollars. The Manor's lovely roof tiles had a
habit of slipping, its Jersey cream paint of flaking. Its high, wide screens
could be penetrated by intruders. One summer night, a drunken youth
crashed straight through the great meshed-in porch and was discovered
asleep on a sofa the next morning by the lord and lady. He left a gap-
ing hole.

Everywhere, there were holes. And frozen plumbing and burst
pipes. At one point, one of the lord's pretty daughters was seriously ro-
manced by the son of a plumber. The lord objected; I thought he was
being a bit shortsighted. The truth is, mansions become monsters with
time, their upkeep impossible except for the truly wealthy—software
executives, rock stars, movie actors. The average lord cannot stem the
tide.

And so, periodically the Manor and its grounds had been put on the market. There would be rumors that a movie star was going buy it. But in the end, the most serious and possibly the only interest came from the followers of Swami Vivekenanda.

There turned out to be several bands of followers, some more respectable than others. All the groups claimed to want to own the Manor because of its connection to the Hindu monk, even though the monk never lived at the Manor. Legend had it that he had slept in one of the other houses, but nonetheless, it was the Manor and its grounds that were declared sacred by the swami's followers.

I wondered why—the monk had spent far more time in huts in Calcutta. Why were his followers not anxious to acquire those shanties? Why did they have to acquire a bona fide mansion in which he had barely brushed his robes and taken a few meals? To make matters more controversial, their interest climaxed at a time when cults like the Hale-Bopp crowd were receiving a great deal of negative publicity. The Vivekananda leadership professed they were not a cult, but a religious society. Still, there was no way to establish what they were until they bought the Manor and moved onto the property.

It happens that since living at Willowby I have had that recurrent nightmare in which I wake and look out my bedroom window and see not the rolling pastures empty save for the occasional deer or cow or other critter but a sea of people. Rather like Strawberry Fields in Central Park on a busy summer Sunday. Hundreds and hundreds of people with picnic baskets and boom boxes walking straight toward my house. A Woodstock redux, in my yard.

The word "ashram" rang a warning gong in my brain. Even my friends who go to ashrams did not want to live next to one. "But this won't be an ashram," the lord assured me. "This will be a holy shrine. With only a few celibate female monks in residence." I tried not to voice my panic. Even the "celibate female monks" sounded threatening to me. Did I want all that celibacy close by? I was beginning to live in fear of celibacy.

"It will be fine," His Lordship said.

Negotiations went on for two years. The lord kept me apprised. He had given the followers an option: the Manor was off the market, but they would have to raise the money by a certain date or forfeit the option. "It doesn't look like they'll be able to raise the money," the lord told me as the deadline drew near. Then, one spring day, just as the Avenue burst into chartreuse bud and songbirds were tugging worms from the earth, His Lordship called me to say, "It looks like it's going through." A few weeks later, he phoned again to tell me that the new incoming swami's business manager would like to meet me. "You've probably noticed him in front of the Manor? A Burl Ives type?" The next thing I knew, I saw the Burl Ives type looming over the knoll of our dividing pasture. As he came closer, I made out his reddened features and the blue of tattoos on his exposed arms.

I went outside to meet the business manager, and he introduced himself as a former Marine and now a follower of the swami. To clarify matters, he said he was not himself a swami, or even celibate. "Wherever we go, we try to please our immediate neighbors," he said, avoiding my gaze. I tried to give him the benefit of the doubt and served him tea on the porch.

"We will be invisible," he promised. "That is the word most often used to describe us—'invisible.'"

"Good," I said. "I like the word 'invisible' to describe you." I decided to be direct. "I am here for my privacy. I have been meditating in my own fashion here since 1981. I would like not to be intruded upon, and I'm concerned, because of the way the boundary is cut, that the followers of Swami Vivikenanda will come close to my house and interrupt my train of thought." That would not happen, Burl promised.

In spite of the eccentric angle of the property line, that weird cut made near my front yard, the followers would stay back, far back, on the main part of their eighty-three acres.

"We have eighty-three acres, why would we bother you?" he asked. He promised a buffer zone and even offered to plant trees or construct a fence.

We walked a line ten distant acres from my house, and I rose to what I thought was his gracious intent. "No, no, if you're that far from me, why go to the bother and the expense?" I said, and added that I did not want to trouble Farmer Bowers, who was accustomed to haying that pasture and would be bothered by any dividing plants or fences. So we shook hands, Burl Ives and I, as we crossed the meadow on a perfect summer Sunday.

As he turned back toward the Manor, Burl remarked, "Oh, and Swami A, who will move in soon, will want to put in a shrine trail."

"A shrine trail?" I said. "What's that?"

Burl described a Hindu version of the stations of the cross, a procession path that would include ten stops for worship at the statues of deities. "But don't worry," he said. "That's a religious trail, and it would be on the part of the estate that is hidden from view." He pointed toward the Manor and the shadowy glen I knew lay hidden behind it, which was already served by several winding footpaths.

"If you have a shrine trail," I said, "please make sure it doesn't lead to me."

"Of course not," he said with a barky laugh and departed, sweating and huffing.

The deal went through. By fall, the new swami was rumored to be in residence, although by a quirk in the contract his presence would not mean the departure of the lord and lady. "We're staying on as curators of the estate," His Lordship informed me. Well, that was good, I thought.

I caught my first sight of the swami himself at a welcome party the day of the closing. The country squires of Rock Ridge were to meet and greet the new resident at a neighbor's estate. Everyone was curious to see him and the two "celibate female monks" who were rumored to attend him.

My uncle Len, who seldom strayed from the grounds of The Inn, left for this occasion. I drove him the short distance to the other mansion. There, as cars were being parked, Len pointed out an unfamiliar figure, an American man of perhaps fifty years of age, dressed in an almost clichéd country-squire fashion—tweed jacket with elbow patches—and escorted by two slim blondes, who were also costumed in correct *Town and Country* attire—sweaters and long plaid skirts.

"*That*," someone whispered, "is the swami, and the girls are the monks." Swami A, as he likes to be called, was born in the southern United States. He is a pleasant, fairly ordinary-looking man, save for his ears which are set unusually close to his head and which, with the length of his face and the angularity of his frame, give him an appearance a bit reminiscent of Mr. Spock, the Vulcan space traveler on *Star Trek*.

The swami spoke slowly, with elaborate cordiality, in an accent that was vaguely Indian and slightly British. The swami smiled and said yes a lot, between pauses. With my eyes closed, I could have believed he was Peter Sellers returned to us through reincarnation.

The swami asked about a dining table I have in my possession at which the original swami was said to have been served meals during his stay in 1895. "I would like to have the swami table," the new swami said.

I smiled. "I'm curious," I said. "Swami Vivekenanda and his followers were dedicated to a spiritual rather than material life. Why is it so important to obtain all the furniture they used?"

"The energy is left in it," Swami A said with a smile.

I agreed to talk about the swami table at a later date. It was impossible not to like the new swami. He did not seem to take himself too seriously. He even smiled and laughed about being a swami. "He could be a vacuum cleaner salesman," said a man who lived up the road.

There followed a brief season of détente. I sent flowers to the official opening of the shrine and attended the festivities (after erecting more "Keep Out" signs on my property). The followers, at least as they appeared at the opening, were an eclectic group—American, some wheelchair bound, many elderly, a few younger men in golf jackets, several slim, vegetarian-style girls with curling hair and misty gazes.

No actual Indian swamis appeared, but they would come later, at the inauguration. At that event, the swami discarded his tweed jacket and appeared in apricot-colored robes. A few women wore what looked like lap robes over their shoulders. They sprinkled water and burned a bit of incense and distributed a prospectus that appeared as glossy as one for a real estate development. They advertised the need to raise more than a million dollars to complete the shrine at Willowby. Even the curry the swami's followers served seemed bland. I also noted that although the group was supposed to be vegetarian, an enormous chicken salad had materialized on the buffet. The Burl Ives type reappeared, with a massive-headed dog that ultimately had to be chained and later earned the nickname Devil Dog for his growls at the non-celibate. At this event, Burl Ives ran around wearing a Willowby tee-shirt, passing a platter that he referred to as the *"prasad,"* which included Halloween candy corn and mini Mars bars.

I returned to The Inn, the only one to walk my path. At worst, the swami and his followers seemed tacky. And so I was lulled into not protesting the change of use as it was presented at our local town planning board in a series of two meetings.

The first meeting was not alarming. The swami and Burl Ives discussed handicapped ramps and parking spaces. I heard nothing to arouse my suspicions. But that night I received a phone call from a hoarse-voiced woman who warned me, "Stop Vivekenanda. They are dangerous." She identified herself as Rita and said she had some personal experience with the group. In what way were they dangerous? I wanted to know. "You'll see," she said. I didn't know whether to take her seriously or not. I did a bit of research but could uncover no scandal connected with the group. I did discover that they had received their tax-exempt status only the year before and were legally registered in North Hollywood.

Still, I was somehow unconcerned. I arrived five minutes late to the second town planning board meeting. Jasmine had been a bit fussy, and I'd taken the time to settle her with the baby-sitter. I was not worried as I had been the last time I'd attended the town planning board meeting; nothing of import to the Vivekenanda situation had been discussed until well into the evening. On this night, though, everything was different. I ran in, took my seat in the front row, and felt an electric prickle of tension in the room.

The board sat on a blond wooden dais inscribed with the town motto, "To Trust, Be Just," and an insignia of twin leaping stags. I had slipped into a seat beside a woman I didn't recognize (Rita?). She nudged me and hissed, miming her alarm. She indicated a map displayed on the far side of the courtroom.

"Your house," she whispered. *"Look."* But I could not see anything from where I sat. I didn't realize that the forces of Vivekenanda had just presented a map of the estate, depicting exactly what they had promised not to do—they had placed the proposed shrine trail close to the diagonal cut of my front border. The next thing I knew, the gavel thudded. The public hearing was closed, the change of use granted.

I ran over to Burl, the swami, and their lawyer. "I'd like to see the map," I said. "That looks like something near my house."

"It's not that close," their lawyer snapped, rolling up the map.

I insisted. The lawyer showed it to me, and it was my nightmare unveiled. "What?!" I cried, feeling like the naive fool I was. "But this isn't what you promised at all!" They promised to come down to the property the next morning.

"It's a mistake," said Burl. "We forgot to tell them when they drew the map. Don't worry."

It was January. We met in a needling sleet storm on the site of the proposed trail. The swami wore a cap pulled far down over his ears. Burl dropped all pretense of civility. "That's too bad, if you don't like it," he said. "You represent an equivalent problem to the followers of Vivekenanda."

"I do?" I asked, incredulous.

"Some of us would be disturbed by the sight and sound of your children playing in front of your house," Burl said. I looked at him and the swami for a long minute as the sleet stung us and my feet numbed in the mud.

"I don't think that's a very spiritual thing to say," I said.

A storm of legal consultation followed. I retained a lawyer who then also stood on the proposed shrine trail while the swami and his lawyer refused to move the trail to where they had previously indicated they would.

I appeared at the next town meeting and read a letter, along with another neighbor who adjoined the estate, describing how we believed we had been misled. We asked the town board to reopen the public hearing, and were refused.

The swami and I have discussed the shrine trail a few times since. I remarked that I had given them the benefit of the doubt, not opposed their change of use, and that now I felt I was being punished for it. He apologized for the way Burl's remarks about my children had sounded and assured me Vivikenanda liked children.

So far, no shrines have been erected on the shrine trail and no one other than the swami and his dog has walked on it. One day, I thought I detected a commotion on the trail and ran out to see who was there only to discover the resident thirty-eight wild turkeys scurrying toward the Manor.

Perhaps there just is no demand for the trail; maybe the swami's followers have decided not to invest in the ten-foot statues. I may even find myself a bit disappointed never to have used my ultimate protest: "Get those deities out of my sight!"

At present, I have no grievance with the followers of Swami Vivekenanda. The autumn after he moved into the Manor, Swami A himself began to metamorphose into something more familiar, when he appeared, riding a leaf blower, trying to recapture the ton of foliage that falls from the trees that so scenically line our shared Avenue.

One night, as a light snow fell, I walked up the diagonal cut of my front lawn to the spot where my land now met the shrine trail. I could not imagine I would run into anyone out there, at night, in the snow, yet a lone figure walked toward me. His gray shape became defined as we reached each other. It was Lord Hodgson, now curator of the shrine at Willowby. I could not resist asking him, "Why *was* this border cut on such a weird diagonal?"

"I had to be certain," the lord answered, "that the view from my windows would never change. This is the angle at which I look down at you."

thirty

Maybe it was because I focused so much of my worry on the swami and the potential for trouble at the Manor that I missed the warning signs at the dairy farm. I fairly skipped down, milk can in hand, one summer evening, only to have Abner Bowers greet me with the news. "I hate to rock your boat, Laura," he said, "but we're going to sell the farm. Someday, we'll tell you why."

"We'll tell you now," Betty said. We walked outside the house, around the corner, so the children wouldn't hear. I watched the Bowers chickens scratching the dirt. "It's Nate," Betty said. "It's Nate and Kelly."

As Abner and Betty spoke, my mind scanned recent memory. The oldest Bowers grandson had gotten married a few weeks before. The wedding had been held in a mountainside chapel, a plain wooden structure from the early 1800s that the family had decorated themselves with bouquets of wildflowers. The bride had had to ascend a steep, stony incline, lifting the hem of her wedding dress to make the climb. It had been my little girls' first chance to attend a wedding. Jasmine had stood waving an American flag and holding a bunch of gladioli. When the bride walked down the aisle toward the groom, who waited at the altar with his two brothers, Jasmine said in a stage whisper, "Does she get to choose?" and everyone, including the bride, had laughed.

But now I remembered Kelly Bowers, how she had looked that day—the unfamiliar delineation wrought by cosmetics on her usually scrubbed face, the tightness of her short black dress. Her face and figure looked suddenly younger and more glamorous; only her eyes, seeming to sink each day in their sockets, betrayed some ancient fear.

As if their lives had been suddenly pushed into fast-forward, the Bowers made plans to sell the farm: in the face of imminent divorce, Nate had declared he would no longer work on the farm. The atmosphere at the farm, long so comfortable and open, changed at once.

I prayed that somehow the farm would be saved. Farms are notoriously hard to sell. A realtor explained it succinctly: "Farms involve a lot of demolition"—the destruction of the barns and all the outbuildings. I recalled two houses I had "bought" but never closed on. So many things can go wrong. We passed the summer in limbo, hoping for a reconciliation that would leave the farm intact.

A few days after Abner told me the farm was for sale, a cow wandered into the pond and sank up to her black-and-white kneecaps and could not be freed without a tug from the tractor. I heard the cow bellow and went running down to see the two Bowers men, father and son, not speaking, hauling the cow from the slime.

By Thanksgiving, the farm was sold. It would operate for a few weeks more, but the dismantling would begin soon. The date for the auction of all the milking machinery and the tractors was set for March. After that, the cows and chickens would be sold. The world of the farm next door would disappear. It was purchased for just over a million dollars by a psychiatrist from Riverside Drive who had paused the fall before, lured by the promise of "pick your own pumpkin."

For eighteen years, I'd been smitten by the cows and the life of the farm that revolved around them. I'd felt that every morning I woke on the farm. I started my day at the kitchen window, sipping coffee enriched by the milk of the cows I watched. As I gazed at the herd, I listened to public radio, the classical station of the Hudson River Valley, the motions of the cows accompanied by Mozart or Mendelssohn. The combination of the mooing and the music, the distant movement of the farmer corralling the cows for breakfast, induced in me a caffeinated euphoria: bucolic bliss.

So was it any wonder, as I headed north to see the dawn milking for the last time, that I was mentally screaming "No!"? I paused at Eighty-fifth Street and Broadway at a twenty-four-hour café to tank up on latte for the hundred-mile drive. I accepted my warm paper cup and recalled the first time I saw Nate Bowers. He had been lightening his coffee by holding a mug under the teat of the lead cow.

Sipping my latte, I drove up the West Side Highway, past the dark façades of Riverside Drive. I thought of the psychiatrist who bought the farm. He was somewhere up there, sleeping presumably, oblivious to the upset he was causing. He could not have appreciated that he was not merely purchasing a place, he was ending a way of life.

I drove nonstop, over the speed limit, as if I could overtake the future. I shot up the black abyss of the New York State Thruway, then scooted down the back roads, taking shortcuts it had taken me years to discover. I skidded to a stop at the entry to the dairy farm.

I parked my car and entered on foot. I arrived on time. At four forty-five, I was, in fact, early. The farm was still unlit. The night was dense, black, sharp with invisible sleet. The cold March air defined every breath I took. Underfoot, mud and manure had hardened into a corrugated crust. I stepped over the frozen tire treadmarks of the tractors. I tried to walk silently so as not to alarm the families asleep in the farm compound. From the back snow fields, a coyote howled. Then another, and another, a chorus of indignation. The first house that I passed, the 1710 stone colonial, was occupied by Nate Bowers and his teenage son. A row of wooden name plaques decorated the outside entry. There were five name tags, but three were no longer relevant. Kelly Bowers and her two daughters had already left.

I walked by the stand, an open shelter that held fresh produce pulled from the earth every summer. In winter, the wooden racks were empty but signs offered crayoned invitations to the goods within: eggs, maple syrup. Inside, in a refrigerator, sat a cigar box filled with cold cash. The farm ran on the honor system. An irony to the farm's up-coming finale was that the past few seasons had been the most successful. Raspberries, peppers, greens, and tomatoes had been trucked into the city's greenmarkets along with organic chickens and eggs. Sweet corn, pumpkins, even an abundant weed, purple loosestrife, had sold out. The sugar shack had produced a record number of gallons of syrup. The milk was sold to a local cooperative that turned it into a superior sour cream that could support a spoon vertically. All had appeared abundant, rich almost. Even milk prices, formerly a source of woe, had swelled to a record high—sixteen dollars per hundred pounds. With fifty milkers, that meant eight hundred dollars a day in milk earnings alone.

Past the stand was Abner Bowers' cottage. I'd known Abner and his wife, Betty, long and well enough to know that their door was always open; that it was always all right to come in and sit at the kitchen table and have a cup of hot tea. Their home was not a candidate for *Martha Stewart Living;* it was an authentic farmer's house, which meant it was filled to the gills with reproduction antique furniture, stacks of mail order catalogues, and knicknacks. The centerpiece of the small living room was a large color television and an old recliner positioned to face it.

Years ago, when I first entered, I was struck by the authentic smell of old, wet dog. Now, I almost missed the odor and the dog. I viewed the Bowers home with the acute love one feels for something about to vanish—Betty's canning racks, her rows of hot pepper jelly, the pies and breads she was forever pulling from her oven, even her politically incorrect "Aunt Jemima" apron, slung over a hook on the back of the kitchen door. I'd grown familiar enough with Betty to have visited with her in her bedroom as she sat at her sewing machine. I knew how the Bowers bedroom seemed to be set below the level of the earth outside. With the windows open, the room felt like an extension of the field beyond. Their view upon waking was of the furrowed soil, or, in late summer, the rustling, live curtain of corn.

Abner was now seventy, Betty a few years younger. They'd been married since she was eighteen and had raised four children. They had met on her family's farm in Iowa, where Betty was the youngest of thirteen children.

Although he had a temper (he was known to yell at the cows), Abner also had a big smile. I'd come to care for him, in spite of the fact he squawked at me for walking too near a wild goose nest and charged me fifty cents extra for the gladioli among his cutting flowers. He'd been a farmer all his life, and farmers count the value of everything, down to the penny. Each year, although I allowed him to tap all my sugar maples, he would give me only a single quart of the syrup; I had to buy more if I wanted more. I'd have liked it better if he hadn't kept track, but he did, and I liked him anyway.

Betty, on the other hand, would on impulse hand you a loaf of fresh-baked bread. Having known her almost twenty years, I'm tempted to say that Betty is just plain good. But I'm a city person and a cynic, so I shy away from saying a person is as sweet as Betty is, even when it's so. She could be tart, too, like her hot pepper jelly, and she's strong enough to present herself just as she is. "Come in. I'm in here, vomiting," was her greeting one day. Her and Abner's habit of addressing each other as "Mother" and "Father" no longer startles me. *How many eggs today, Father? Forty-eight, Mother.*

As I drew near their house, in the predawn, it remained dark. I watched, waiting for the light cue that it was all right to enter, but they were still asleep in their king-size bed with its view of the frozen earth. I heard some motion in the barn, so I turned that way and walked across the hard chest of the barnyard.

In the fenced enclosure outside, a few heifers stood, regarding me. They appeared quizzical—*What are you doing here, at this hour?*—but intrigued. I have often had the impression that cows get bored and welcome a fresh face or a change in routine.

"Good morning, girls," I said. They regarded me, liquid tinsel dangling from their nostrils, eyes rolling. They executed the cow tango, two-stepping forward and back. Beside them, a single bull with black bangs that looked like a bad haircut, glowered. His eyes were smaller, redder. He had none of the females' benign charm.

This bull was a young bull. I remembered Astro, the senior bull who reigned on the farm when I first arrived, eighteen years before. His bull pen was torn down, but there was still a raised rectangle of earth, bracketing the spot where he once stood. Astro had offered his power and his potency, and that was all.

Astro's maleness may have cost him his life. Although, to my knowledge, he never attacked anyone, his potential had been too great. As soon as the Bowerses mastered artificial insemination, Astro had been shipped, replaced by a placard nailed to the barn door: "Member A.I. Collective."

For years there were no bulls, but in recent times, they had returned. "Their fertility ratio is better," admitted Abner. "If the A.I. doesn't work, most often the bull will." I found something heartening in that—the old-fashioned way was still the best.

I heard a deep moo from the open pasture. Again I was amazed by how sustained some moos are; they seem to be projected with the entire force of the cow's body. Walking past the fence, I saw them, out in the pasture—the milkers, the queens of this operation, the cows who deliver more than fifty pounds each of the product every day.

The milkers were still lying on the frosted ground, collecting crystals on their furred faces. I have never caught a cow asleep. They seem to wake when they feel your gaze. Now they were resting as if on their elbows: their bellies splayed out on the ground. Vapor rose from their bodies, creating a mist that met the sleet. A black cloud scuttled across the face of the already fraying morning moon.

I heard the steps of the farmer's son Nate as he entered the yard to fetch the cows for the milking. Nate wore a heavy padded jacket, a cap, waterproof boots. The cows looked up as he approached, a dark silhouette. The milkers rose up with effort, like overweight people who have lain too long. Once on their feet, the anticipation seemed to excite them. They snorted and moaned. Then they were off, almost prancing, following Nate, who in the darkness opened their gate. Nate led them to the upper barn, where the milking would take place. A few stray cows farther out in the field were summoned by the call I'd overheard all these years: "Come Boss, come Boss," "Boss" being short for "Bossie," a cow nickname from long ago. "Come Boss, come Boss." And so they came, a few cows slipping on the cement walkway, like ladies whose high heels have given way. They filed into the barn, lined up in two rows, each cow seeming to recognize her station. All the cows wore single ear tags, with their number. Each cow stood below a placard declaring her name, number, sire, dam, and whether she had been served by the bull or A.I., and if so, when.

The barn was cold until the cows entered. Their bodies heated the low-ceilinged room. On entering, I felt as if I were walking into a tropical atmosphere, humid with their yeasty breath, sweet from the scent of silage. There was a collective burping and communal expulsion of air. I heard the gush and gurgle of their unceasing digestive function. I walked down the center aisle, a rectal gauntlet. On each side, the cows were extruding spools of manure, releasing cascades of urine.

Somehow, the torrents of excretion were not unpleasant. The end products recalled the source—sweet grass and fermented hay, alfalfa, grain. I remembered one of my first barn chats with Abner Bowers. He had been talking to me while kneeling between two cows, and they had both given way at the same moment. As his face was framed by the twin flumes of cascading urine, he'd grinned and said, "It's not all glory."

The cows turned in unison to regard me as I worked the push broom, shoving feed on the tiles below their front position. Their neck chains jingled as they lowered their faces to the floor and gobbled what I served. Feeding and milking occur simultaneously—to music. The barn boom box was tuned to a country station, and we all moved to the soulful lament of Johnny Cash's "Ring of Fire"—*I stepped through a burning ring of fire I went down, down, down, but the flames went higher Oh, it burns, burns, burns that ring of fire.* Abner arrived by five forty-five A.M., pushing the wheelbarrow loaded with feed mix. He flipped a scooper as I followed with the broom. *Oh, it burns, burns, burns that ring of fire.*

I followed Nate to the milk room, where the "machines," looking rather like inanimate squid, hung on racks. There were four units.

At last, the suction tubes, like metal fingers, were attached to the teats. I could almost read relief in the milkers' faces as they felt the draw on their insides. Full udders swell and any delay causes the cows discomfort. The cows regarded me, chewing their cuds, as they seemed to listen to the music.

In their state of bovinity, the cows didn't know that their barn had been sold, that they too would soon be shipped to another dairy, most likely to the north, the direction in which the margin of country seems to move.

The barn pulsed with the music and the movement of the milk, a white current running along the conduits that paralleled the ceiling. I followed the flow back to the milk room, a white chamber with a nostril-tingling scent of chlorine and disinfectant. I watched the stream of white milk pour into the clear glass Laval Swiss container, where its temperature begins to drop on the way to the big metal cooler. "The trick is speed," Nate told me. "Cool it down quick, keep out the bacteria." Several long-haired tabby cats sat near the heat source: the compressor and pump that powered the milk conduits. The cats purred along with the vibration, waiting, as we did, for the end product, which they would lap from a wide dish set on the barn floor.

We'd been working since five A.M. The milking, shifting the four machines amongst the fifty cows, took two and a half hours, the feeding and cleanup another two and a half.

"Come on," invited Abner. "I'm going to the pit." The pit was a bank of silage stored a few acres away, down the bumpy farm road. Over the winter, the silage was protected by a cover of black polyurethane held down by discarded tires. Now, in March, the silage had been dug out by tractor shovel so that Abner, in the plastic-walled cab of his John Deere, rode into an open-roofed cave of the compressed feed.

He seemed to be diminished, hunched at the wheel of the tractor as he entered the pit. I ran alongside and went into the pit on foot. The pit's walls rose ten feet past my head; I was enclosed by its ochre-yellow sides. Abner scooped up load after load, then drove the full bucket, held aloft, back to the entrance to the barn. There, Nate scooped the silage into another bucket, attached to a little yellow mechanical cart called a side steer. Riding the side steer, Nate, traversed the aisle, depositing more feed.

Again, I ran the gauntlet, this time pushing a hoe-like manure scraper. The goal was to clear the surfaces before the next feeding / milking. Essentially, we cleaned the barn so that the fifty cows could reenter in the afternoon, and let it out, lavalike, only to repeat the process again for the morning milking.

How clean we got the barn floor. How pretty the fresh green hay, for bedding and for eating, looked, fluffed under the drained cows. It was ten thirty A.M., and I felt I'd worked a day. Abner Bowers had yet to have breakfast. We walked together to his cottage, where Betty waited with hot coffee, muffins, and green pepper jelly. Because it was Sunday, there would be a rest. "On other days, we do other things, like breed the cows, repair the machinery," Abner said. But today, he would take a nap before the next milking. He suggested that I go up to my house and do the same.

I ran up the hill to my house, entered and collapsed on the sofa. I stiffened, still wearing my parka, into a dreamless sleep that ended when I rose and went back down to the barn.

Outside, the sleet had turned to an ice storm. I had enjoyed the first milking—but then it hit me that I had to do it all over again. I thought of the farmer, of this routine, twice a day, 365 days a year. Farmers say, "It's the repetition that gets to you." Still, one of Abner's grandsons quit the farm to work on the outside, only to return after a few months. "Here," he said, "the shit is only shit." I laughed and agreed.

I moved along to my favorite chore—feeding the newborn calves. I staggered to the kindergarten, the corner kept for babies. I was weighed down by two buckets of fresh warm milk. The calves leaned forward and would have sucked off my gloves if I had let them. As it is, in their eagerness, they knocked over the buckets, vying for the spilled milk.

As Abner and Nate finished the second cleaning of the barn and the evening shadows deepened, I asked Abner, "Has it been worth it, to have spent all these years on this farm?" He and his sons haven't drawn a salary in years, yet they've enjoyed a place that would cost more than a million dollars to replace.

"It's a way of life," is all he said.

As I headed for home for the second time that day, my muscles aching in unaccustomed ways, I wondered what would happen next. After a life like this, what would it mean to rest? What would the farm be like without animals when the new owner "restored" the stone house and barns? Would there be pumpkin pine, buffed floorboards, a television concealed in a jam cupboard, pie safes, and other antiques fit for display in *Architectural Digest*? Would there be a perfect farm-house, but no farm, no life? I started up the old farm road toward my house and remembered how one year before, I'd been walking uphill and spotted a black-and-white detail hidden in the brush. A group of cows had circled the spot, and I soon saw what drew their attention: a lost newborn calf, a twin. Her sister had been discovered and taken to the barn, but this calf, too weak to walk, her existence unknown, had lain unnoticed. I called Abner and Nate, then walked out into the pasture to guide them, on tractor, to the spot.

That had happened exactly a year before, but last March had been warmer. The ground had thawed into a primeval muck. I wanted to get closer to where Nate was trying to extricate the calf, but when I tried to raise my feet, the suction held down my boots. I laughed, feeling foolish, but frightened, too. The draw of the earth was stronger than I had expected. I eased out of my boots and left them there, empty, in the position of the last step I had taken. In my stockinged feet, I scrambled to higher, drier ground and watched as Nate picked up the baby calf and was in turn lifted in the tractor bucket by his father. Abner drove them back down to the barn, son and baby calf held aloft, undignified but triumphant.

Not a living, perhaps, but a life. I had felt the blood race under my skin, a sense near ecstasy, when I showered off the mud. As I walked past the place where the calf had lain, half-hidden, I felt sad that an event like that would probably never occur there again.

According to Abner, the psychiatrist from Riverside Drive and his wife had not been interested in continuing to run the dairy farm, even though Abner had offered his help and had found a tenant farmer willing to keep fifty head in the barn. Abner had sounded excited about the young farmer. "He's Polish, he's young, he's across the river, working for his father, sleeping in a cot in the barn," he said. Why hadn't the psychiatrist wanted to keep the land in farming? "Well, he said he'd think about it in a year or so, after he's restored the stone house." But the farm auction would occur in a week. Unless that event was stopped, all the equipment would be sold, and it seemed certain the farm would be lost forever. To replace everything, from the milk vats to the last rusted nail, would be prohibitively expensive.

So on this gray evening, as I stepped over the frozen tractor tread of the farm road, I tried to resign myself to the death of this place. I could hear the protracted moo of a yearning heifer. In a few days, there would be only silence.

At the curve where the road turns uphill toward my house, I stopped and looked back down at the barns. For a moment, I couldn't see any cows in the dusk. Then, from behind the silver silo, a single cow appeared in profile.

That night, I slept, exhausted, inhaling the sweet scent of silage that seemed, even after a shower, not to leave my hair. I dreamed of the barn, of the breathing animals, of how they warmed the night air.

The sale happened as I had feared. Despite my own and my neighbors' last-minute efforts to find another way to save the farm, the farm auction was held on the last Saturday of the month. It was the warmest, sunniest day of the new year, and the cows, unknowing, lay in the pasture. They appeared to be sunbathing, watching the proceedings.

From my kitchen, a quarter-mile away, I could see the farm. Still a Tinker Toy, but now with so many moving figures. Two hundred men, their shadows behind them, walked toward the dozens of pieces of farm equipment that were set on the field like metal lawn sculptures. The auctioneer's caw carried upwind, and I could hear, "Do I hear a hundred, a hundred and fifty, two hundred?" I didn't want to go down, but I did, to keep Betty company. She didn't want to be there, either, to see everything they'd owned set out on the grass while the crowd, mostly men in tractor caps, bid on the pieces of her past.

The auctioneer, a man nearly as wide as he was tall, in a red satin jacket, megaphoned his message to the milling crowd: "These tractors were ready for this spring, they all start right up." From time to time, Abner or Nate was called upon to sit on a machine and demonstrate its roar to life. One tractor sputtered and would not start right up. Someone had pilfered the rotary, a trick played at auctions to keep the bidding low so that the perpetrator could swoop in for a bargain on the "broken" tractor.

The atmosphere was that of a fair without fun. The local 4-H club had set up a canteen in the machine shop and sold hot dogs with relish, cupcakes, and soda. Portable toilets stood sentinel in the field that might never again be plowed. The crowd, most of them apparently farmers, was attentive but somber; most were only too conscious that this could happen to them.

Only the few children who had accompanied their fathers were oblivious to the subtext of the scene. Tow-headed boys and girls crawled into the calf hutches that stood, like plastic igloos, across from the auctioneer. The hutches had long ago replaced the red wooden lean-tos that had been here when I arrived. The white molded plastic was yet another concession to practicality over rustic cheer; they kept the cold wind off the baby calves, that was the main thing. The children hugged the calves, who stood, wobbly-legged, tethered to the hutches. It was probably the last time on this farm that a child would put his arms around a baby cow and get a sloppy long-tongued lick on the cheek in return. We could kiss all this good-bye.

By dusk, almost everything was sold, much of it carted away. "We're holding on to one tractor and the manure spreader until the cows go," Abner explained.

Until the cows go. They would leave in two weeks. "They can go in a day," Abner said. "All it takes is one big truck."

Every morning since the auction, I'd woken with a belly clutch, held my breath till I looked out the kitchen window. *Yes.* They were still there, the fifty milkers marching out to munch at the outdoor manger. I tried to memorize the pattern of their black-and-white rumps, the chorus line moves of their entrances and exits. Some days they seemed to dance, to run and kick up their heels at the sight of the first dandelion. Then one Friday, I didn't see them. There was nothing but the blank wall of the barn, the long cement trough. On the radio in my kitchen, a Mozart requiem played. Then, to my surprise, as if summoned for a final call, the "girls" appeared, walking slowly, as if to the music, for the very last time. Even as they took their encore, I could see what they couldn't—the long line of the cattle transport truck as it drove into the yard behind them.

The truck was blue and gray metal. Behind its cab, the passenger cabin extended in two steel stories, like a sightseeing bus for cows. It was clean and gleaming in the sun, but there was something of a portable prison in the steel mesh and the bars.

We raced down to the barn, Jasmine and I, to say good-bye. My six-year-old swore to buy two cows with her allowance.

We ran, half afraid we would miss them. I was also anxious to see if Abner would be there. He had collapsed a few days after the auction, stricken with a kidney stone. He'd been rushed to the local hospital, screaming, "When was the last time you cleaned out the back of this car?" He was there, wearing a plaid flannel shirt and mud-stiff bib overalls, just as always. Abner and Nate were standing at the entrance to the milking barn. The truck was angled up to the door. A metal ramp, not unlike those used to board planes, was in position, and the cows were being asked to trot up it, one at a time. The driver and his assistant stood by with yellow cattle prods to be sure the cows went. Mostly, though, they did not have to use them. The girls walked up the ramp without rebelling.

I resist anthropomorphizing, but it seemed to me that once inside the caged truck, the cows moaned and issued moos that sounded like *no* . . . I turned away then, and took my daughter to town on our daily business.

Abner had told me the cows were being shipped to a dairy in Vermont, close to the Canadian border. For them, it was not a tragic end but a change of venue. So I tried to put them out of my mind as I went about my morning. An hour later, two miles from the farm, as I drove out of the parking lot of the town's only bank, at the rim of the major highway, I could have sworn I heard a moo. *I must really be undone*, I thought. Then I looked up and saw the cow transport truck poised at the stop sign next to the bank.

One cow poked her black-and-white face through the bars and gave her most sustained moo. From both levels, black-and-white-and-pink noses appeared.

I couldn't help but laugh, and found myself following them in my car. We all were heading north. I drove behind them for as long as I could. In a few seconds the details of the cow's noses and the shadows between the bars became invisible, and the truck streaked, blue and silver, up the Thruway, like an ordinary truck on an ordinary day.

t h i n t y - o n e

The situations on either side of me, at the Manor and down on the farm, continue to hurtle toward unexpected conclusions. More seemed to happen in the last year of our century than in all the previous years. For me, from my position at The Inn, the exact heart of what had once been the "great property," the effect was similar to being in the theater at the sudden end of a long run. I had only to look out my six-over-six-paned windows to watch as the set was struck.

One bright spring day another truck, a turquoise one, pulled up to Willowby Manor and began to cart away the *fuuurniture*. The truck made several trips in the following weeks, and each time more English antiques, some lovingly wrapped in protective blankets, like babies, were carried into the truck. This truck traveled in the same direction in which the cows had departed—north. The margin of country was being moved yet again.

Lord and Lady Hodgson had elected not to remain in the Manor as lifelong curators after all. "If only we could have had the kitchen," Lady Marguerite reported. "But we had no privacy. We had to stay in our two rooms upstairs." Whatever happened during those months that the swami and the lord cohabited is known only to them. The gold silk–covered walls will tell no tales, but both acknowledge that their relations became less cordial, and it was no longer feasible for them to remain manor-mates.

"We are moving to a *cond ohhh* in Fort Leslie," Lady Marguerite announced. "We shall have very little maintenance to do." After almost two decades, I had become accustomed to seeing her petite figure crouched near the shrubs that bordered the driveway, her pruning shears in hand, a basket for cuttings at her side. Could they really depart? Would Lord Hodgson be able to leave? He had never emotionally given up any of the property. How could he move away from the house that his grandfather had built?

I worried, too, over Abner and Betty Bowers. They had enjoyed life in their cottage since 1962. As the farm closing neared, I feared that Abner and Betty might find themselves in an unhappy situation. They had lived for so long in the beauty of Willowby—could they even imagine a life away from these beautiful green fields? Of course, they had no intention of truly leaving; as country people do, they had been able to hold back a few acres for themselves and ultimately they would build. But until a house, even one of the instant variety, could be constructed, where—and how—would they live?

I surprised even myself with the answer. They moved in with me. And why not? The Innlet had three bedrooms, a kitchen, and a separate porch and entrance. Under the circumstances, I thought it was the right thing to do. I heard myself say, "You move right up the hill until your house is built."

And so they did. On the first day of May, every vehicle in their extended family, vans and pickups, pulled up, and Bowers began to unload the contents of their cottage. Within hours, the downstairs of The Inn looked like a Smithsonian exhibit of their former home, down to the recliners, the TV, and the dog. It felt odd to walk in there—as if I'd somehow got turned around and was down the hill from my own home.

Within a few days, the scents of baking rhubarb pie and boiling hot-pepper jelly perfumed my home. Abner and Betty took their places on the porch and watched the renovation of their former farm. And what a show. The farm underwent a makeover in days, leveled by affluence. Machines that I might never have imagined, Godzillas with crunching teeth, came and devoured entire silos in one metallic munch. Another silo was peeled like an onion and taken away, a blue metal rind. Soon, Betty and Abner's former cottage sported a lacquered front door. "Oh my God," said Betty. "It looks like a weekend place."

The Bowerses settled into The Innlet and prepared to mark their own centenary of sorts. "Is it all right if my mother moves in?" Abner asked me one day. "She'll be a hundred in September."

"Sure," I answered. "Why not?"

And so it came to pass that I had a hundred-year-old woman in the back of my house. This past September, the Bowerses celebrated her birthday and their own fiftieth wedding anniversary. The Bowerses, at least, are in fact solid. But will they farm again?

I began to daydream aloud of cows and chickens. "I could have cows in my pasture," I suggested, "if we fixed the electric fence."

"Find another farmer," Abner said in his obliging way.

Well, in fact, I had. The night before the farm closing, I'd wandered down to the barn for a farewell look and bumped into a young farmer from up the road who also could not seem to let go. It happened that he had too many cows back on his own farm and was looking for a place to graze them. Mike Matthews appeared to be in his early thirties, tall, muscular, rather handsome. He was the first man with whom I've had an extended conversation while he was chewing tobacco and spitting. I was so cow starved, I was willing to do anything. But I controlled myself—*Don't let him see your desperation. Pretend it's for him.*

"I could help you out. I wouldn't mind a few cows, to keep down my pasture."

Oh, yes, he agreed, it would look like hell if I did nothing. "And besides, my neighbor hates their mooing," he confided.

"Hates their mooing?" I cried.

Our barnyard duet continued. "And he hates the lead cow's bell."

"He hates her bell?" I almost sang. "I love bells!"

"Well, we'll see," he said. "Maybe in the spring."

thirty-two

Because I continue to travel between city and country, every few days I reprise my life's journey. I often drive up to the country at night, and as I leave behind the crowds, the sparkling towers, and head into what appears to be a black abyss, I am left at the wheel with my memories and my reasons.

Each time, I pass the landmarks of my life. Manhattan, where I was born; the Bronx, where I grew up. I tend to take a route that parallels the East River so that I can pass Yankee Stadium, which can be counted upon to glow. I miss the old stadium and find the new one as romantic as a mixing bowl or multi-tiered parking garage, but the lights still cast an aura, and in summer, the crowd can be heard to roar. As I drive by, I note, too, the cliffs that drop to the river, cliffs I scrambled down as a child. I know the series of stone staircases, hacked into the sides of the hills, looking for all the world like remnants of some Incan civilization. In the distance are the parks I played in, the Cement Park with the mermaid fountain and the Dark Park with its shadowed glens.

I have returned to the parks on foot, and been shocked. The mermaids, chipped in my time, are now headless, a few marble breasts are missing. More startling is the diminishment of the parks themselves; the grass patches have shrunk, the trees thinned. Even the notorious Dark Park now looks merely hilly, with a few stout shade trees. Once or twice, I have actually stopped to walk the old neighborhood. I found the streets and buildings blackened and scary—the "garden" of my old apartment house, AnaMor Towers, a square covered with a mash of attack dog shit and broken glass. Coiled barb wire topped the fences I'd scaled as a little girl. For all the grim detail, I found the people friendly. Children waved to me from their windows, and the grownups smiled and said, "How's it goin'?"

Halfway between the city and my place in the country, I pass the Tudor gates of Tuxedo Park. It's been twenty years since I moved out of the "sportsman's paradise" and I have been back in the Park two or three times since. The last was ten years ago, when, on a hot night, I detoured on my way north and drove to my old jumping-off place at the dock on the lake. I took a furtive swim and was shocked when, expecting to be apprehended by the Park police, I was approached by a group of swimming snakes, heads above the water, glowing like metal under the moon. I scampered out like a coon, my nails practically scratching the dock, never to return.

The closer I get to my current place, the more crowded with personal signposts my route becomes. To the west lies the Pioneer Country Club. If I detour from the Thruway, and take a road called the Quickway, I pass within a mile of the country club where Uncle Gabe courted his steel-toothed rebbetsin. Once I tried to find the Pioneer, but I could not differentiate it from all the other white-stuccoed Jewish summer resorts. They all are abandoned now, silent, hidden in the sumac. The hotels have been deserted for decades. Raccoons and groundhogs congregate in the social hall.

Even closer, but harder to locate, is Camp Ava. For years, I tried to find the socialist camp where I was sent right after my mother died. Again, there were too many lookalike camps and bungalow colonies, all peeling white paint with blue trim. Then, two years ago, I was driven back to Camp Ava by a film company that had researched its location. I found it, too, to be hollow and unoccupied. Graffiti on the walls of the remaining cottages ended with the year 1971. "Susan" in red script still decorates the side of the social hall. Like the parks, the camp appeared smaller than in my memory, but it does sit sidewise, threatening to slide down the mountain. For the first time since leaving there as an eight-year-old, I walked the curved, steep driveway. The asphalt, cracked then, has broken up like the hide of an old rhinoceros.

The bunkhouse where I begged to have the cot next to my best friend has burned. But across the quadrangle, where each morning we raised the American and Israeli flags and sang "Oh say can you see" and "Ko-a-la-bohevoh pee-neeey-mo," the main communal buildings still stand.

When I returned, for the filming of a documentary, it was winter. The last time I'd been at Camp Ava had been in August 1955, and the social hall had been crammed with campers and parents; the walls had rung with Hebrew songs and a talent show took place on stage. Now, the social hall looked as if it had been abandoned at an instant's notice, as if in an air raid. A set and painted backdrop still decorated the stage. There was a music stand, the masks of comedy and tragedy, and a pair of platform wedgies that looked as if the performer stepped out of them in mid-dance number. Hebrew songbooks lay mildewed on the floor. There were overturned chairs.

Although I know the exodus of the Jewish vacationers was a gradual phenomenon that took place in the sixties and seventies, here at Camp Ava, departure appears to have been violent. As I stood remembering Uncle Gabe singing "Love Is a River" under a spotlight that glared off his eyeglasses, a hailstorm, complete with lightning and thunder, started. In February, this felt freakish. The social hall trembled and the remaining half of the roof seemed as if it might collapse. Hailstones, big as golf balls, struck the tin above my head, like shrapnel.

The storm ended as abruptly as it began. Under a blue sky, I walked outside to retrace my steps to the basketball court, where Uncle Len offered me the protection of his trench coat the night I boycotted the Bluebell bunkhouse.

The basketball hoop remained in place. The court itself had chasms buckling as if it had undergone an earthquake. I followed a footpath beside it, eager to find the old lake. The lake itself was still there, but the swimming end was gone. A dam had cracked and only a shattered cement wall remained. Again, the mood was one of devastation, as if there had been a war and this area had been struck by a bomb.

The year 2000 is upon us—the year that was so safely distant in the future that we could use it freely as "science fiction" in my single film epic, *Sin Sisters: 2000 A.D.* The set of *Sin Sisters* is close to my house; I could go there every day if I chose. But for thirty-four years, I stayed away. Then, without planning, one fall day, I found myself driving beyond Woodstock, wondering about that old farmhouse in the weeds, the "location." Could it still be standing?

After a few wrong turns, I thought I saw it—the detour to the old farm road. The road was gone, half covered with scrub. I braved the ruts and the high weeds in my four-wheel-drive sport utility vehicle. The drive covered time as well as distance. There at the end of the lane, sagging but unaltered, was the farmhouse. I got out of my car, made my way through stinging nettles and burrs that would later take hours to extract from my jeans, and reached the sagging front step. Perhaps the house had already been so decayed in the sixties that it couldn't deteriorate further. The door still swung on its single hinge. I walked inside, breathed in a familiar mustiness, the combined scents of damp wallpaper, wet wood, and ossified mouse.

I touched the wall in the kitchen and an odd thing happened.

The plaster behind the old faded green wallpaper disintegrated and went up in dust. The wall itself crumbled to powder, yet the paper stood intact, like a life-size blueprint, the configuration of the room that used to be. Later, I asked a contractor what could explain this phenomenon, and he said, "Carpenter ants." How many years had the wall waited for that ultimate touch? How many more years would it have stood had I not entered on a whim? Fearful that the floor, which had a sickening softness to it, would be next to give way, I backed out of the building.

I ran down to the river where I had waded with K and thought of that long-ago afternoon when I pushed him away. The seasons have turned so many times. More than thirty years have passed since I stood in this body of water. This time, I was here in early autumn; the river ran the brown-gold of a light beer and reflected the yellow of the maple leaves that still lined the shore.

I don't know why, but I gave way to impulse and did something I never did for the film or for K—I stripped naked and lay down in the shallows of the riverbed and let the current wash over me. The water, warmed by the heat of the dying day, glided silkily past, running as it has always run and will do for all time, from its source in these mountains toward an unknown conclusion.

This summer will mark eighteen years on the farm. Eighteen is a significant number in Hebrew; it stands for *chai*—life. In a sense, the eighteen years have flown by. In other ways, I have felt the passage of time. It took years to wear the deep grooves in the dirt lanes—the trails that lead down to the dairy barn, the footpaths that wind around to my favorite spots. More than decades for the trees that surround The Inn to tower over it. Now, each summer they cast a green gloom into the downstairs rooms.

My roots run deeper each season. I now know, from planting or occasionally having to dig up a tree, how deep roots run, how little is apparent on the surface.

I tell my time by the flowers. I know the order in which they bloom here each spring and summer. We begin with daffodils, old varieties that still rise up in clusters around the house and down the hill at the farm. Their sister jonquils, pale, with petals blown back, are gathered like delicate-faced screaming girls. Then the tulips and hyacinths reappear, loyally, in front of the Innlet's porch. For more than ten years, their strength was undiminished; now they poke up from the soil with effort, thinner, smaller each spring. The peonies are undaunted by time; they burst forth every June, into heavy-headed scarlet blooms. The lilacs, too, flower faithfully, even as their boughs grow tougher, overlong, "leggy." The trees that seemed to be mere bushes when I arrived now reach the second-story windows; I could reach out from my bed and pluck them.

Many generations of cows have been born on the farm. More wobbly-legged calves, more stately mothers wading through the high grass. Their processions carved deep trails through the pastures, narrow highways for the turkey and coyote to travel.

On a farm, you remember the hard years—the blizzards that broke the trees, the winter when we could not leave the property for four days until a rented Big Cat snow tractor could plow a new avenue in the world turned white. This past winter was mild, but a freak storm coated every twig with ice; the glass forest tinkled in the January wind; branches snapped and cracked. Eighty-nine was memorable: no power for five days. Ninety-four seemed Siberian, with seventeen blizzards to bury us, and Christmas, blacked out and shared with the Bowers family.

By now, the rhythm runs deep. I know when to dig the garden. I've lifted out so many stones, I have created small walls, yet the earth yields ever more. They rise to the surface like inedible potatoes. Each year the garden seems to be a more familiar place—where to put the tomatoes, how the cantaloupe vines can climb the fence. But each season, it needs more help—manure to replace what my vegetables drew from it the previous year, before being devoured by the local population of now completely gentrified woodchucks and deer. I have taught whole generations of wildlife to appreciate radicchio and frisee. I have also, finally, learned to hide a second, secret garden at my back door behind heavier fencing, close to the scents and sounds of our house. There, I can reap my small harvests—mesclun mix for the spring and summer, and herbs that even chipmunks disdain: thyme, rosemary, lavender.

I know the seasons by the chores I must perform. Uncover the cistern in May, patch its walls before calling the born-again pool contractor to restart the filter. I work with caustic chemicals, feeling more janitorial than I would have dreamed in my city life. I lug out the porch furniture (less each year, as I grow lazier) and leave rattan couches, covered by plastic, to sit out a season and see if they make it. This year, no wild wind tore the tarps off the outdoor couches and chairs. I got away with it—an exception. Generally, I've learned every oversight is instantly punished. A day late to drain the hoses, and pipes burst.

I recall individual years, too, by events of note. Forever, 1987 marks the year of the fox. A red fox kept a den somewhere behind my house. She gave birth to five kits and led them, as if in maternal display, on a parade before my front porch. All summer, I sat still and watched as the mother trained her babies to hunt and kill. She would appear, at a run, a groundhog between her teeth. In a frenzy, the young would devour it. Later, they ran behind her. My lawn was littered with bones that spring, and a sour scent of entrails rose. I called the environmental experts and asked what to do. "She will move on," they assured me. "Mother foxes stay only till the young can fend for themselves. So I settled back on my front row seat on the porch and learned that baby foxes bark and, surprisingly, box. They stand on their narrow hind legs and come at each other, playful pugilists. Like their mother, they had little fear of me, and would come quite close. I never made a move toward them, so each time the baby foxes drew a little nearer.

The mother eyed me in the shrewd way of foxes, sized me up as no threat and came to lie, relaxed, her haunches spread, like a dog, at the foot of my porch steps. I thought of her as *my* fox, and looked for her pointed ears each time I drove to the farm. And there, sure enough, she'd be, sometimes sitting up, as if to greet me.

Eventually, as the animal experts predicted, she moved on, part of the rhythm of the wild place upon which the farm stands. The beat of life is inescapable here—animals appear, sometimes die, right before my eyes. Young animals take their place.

In summer especially, when the hot wind blows and kicks up dust and pollen flies in my face, I catch more whiffs of that past. One afternoon, I sat on a fallen log, in a thicket, unseen by everyone but the animals, and watched the full progress of an August day. From where I sat I saw nothing that was not there two hundred years ago. I've spent more time here than any other place in my life. A city girl, I've logged more years in the country. I have never left the city completely; in a way, I need it to appreciate coming up here. The truth is, I boomerang between my two worlds—fleeing each when I need to. But more and more, the flight is to the mountains, the rolling meadows and this old house. As the passing of time seems to accelerate, I seek ways to slow it. Looking back gives me more pleasure than looking forward. Time is supposed to march on, but now it hurtles.

Only last week, another mountain seemed to disappear, decapitated by equipment that cleared the way for yet another mall. The old mall was bad enough—it sprawled across a plateau that once afforded 360-degree views of two mountain ranges.

As an antidote to change, I began to research the history of my house, to go farther and farther back in time. I had so long puzzled over the stone carriage step that read "May 8, 1849," and the initials "T.H.J." I could dig up only a few more facts on my own, so I turned to a local man famous for researching the past lives of historic homes. He arrived at The Inn one morning, a slight fellow with a full walrus moustache wearing vaguely vintage clothing and a string tie—a living daguerreotype. His name was Charles Cullen, but he preferred to be called simply Cullen. He seemed to have emerged from the past he promised to uncover. Together, we walked over to the carriage step and studied the mysterious initials. He promised to return in a few weeks with the facts. And so he did. He came back with a sepia-tinted brochure, "NOTES ON LAURA CUNNINGHAM'S HOUSE," and kicked off his discoveries by announcing, "This house is much older than you thought." He showed me a census listing—by 1810 the house was already built and occupied by a family, headed by one Jacobus Elting. The household had included a husband, wife, four children, and "one male slave, twenty-six to forty-four years old."

As I read Cullen's history, the facts confirmed what I had always felt—that my property's past was connected to my neighbors', that we were inextricably linked as a great farm whose borders had changed, fluctuating with sales of land over the years.

The "old plantation" that Cecil had remembered from his earliest years here had produced crops that were inventoried year by year. The income of "my" land had long been derived from eggs, cider, fruit, oats, and pork.

The initials "T.H.J." stood for Thomas Henry Jansen, the son of one Henry T. Jansen who acquired the property in 1843. It was at this time, Cullen told me, the house had been "modernized" and converted to an inn.

"Jansen didn't live here himself," Cullen told me later. "He owned it, but others ran the place for him as a business investment." Cullen took a dramatic step onto the porch as he prepared to leave me, sepia brochure in hand. "Do you know who owned this house the longest?" he asked.

I didn't. "Who?" I asked.

He smiled before he answered. "You."

Me? The little girl from the city streets who tried to buy a watchman's shack for seven dollars, who spent most of her youth coveting abandoned "haunted houses"? Could it be true that I was the person who had hung on the longest, planted her feet most firmly on the old pine board floors? I loved the idea, but I also knew better than to believe for a single second in any sort of ownership. Mortgage or no, no one owns a place. In the truest sense, all we do is pass through. Other people lived here in 1820; years from now, someone else may walk the porch, perhaps swing in the hammock whose hooks were positioned at the corner of the porch long before I was born. Someday in this new century, perhaps even this pretty old house will no longer sit square on the ridge.

For now, my family inhabits this place. I sleep in the bedroom where Edmund Talbot spent his last night on earth, where Sarah Bull, a devotee of the original prophet Vivekenanda, also slept. A series of women who wrote books occupied "my" room: Hilary Talbot; Nivedita, who wrote *Kali, the Mother.* In more recent years, the room was rented to an actress and to a woman who was famous for her ties to the Queen of England. They all are gone now, and I am here.

In the morning, I wake up to see the old rose-covered wallpaper. Sometimes in those gray moments between dreaming and waking, I confuse my present with the past. I hear a small girl cry for her mother, and for an instant, I imagine that it is I who am crying. "Mommy" still evokes Rosie, and the cry is an echo of a need that has never vanished. But these mornings, I am the one who must summon up the comfort and the answers.

Often, the dawn begins with my younger daughter's whimper of alarm. I hit the floor running to gather her up before she panics. The shadows of this old house surround us. I race, half-blind without my contact lenses, into the blurred atmosphere of a child's fears.

What does Jasmine dream of that frightens her so? I can never know; she is reluctant to tell. Later, she may say, in the light of day, "There were monsters." And how can I tell her there are not? Once upon a time, my night world was peopled with witches and bad monsters who chased me into daybreak. I can only try to outrun her fear and my own. Each dawn, I lurch into consciousness and retravel the road that led us here. My life repeats but also reworks the patterns that run through my family history. Like Rosie, I have come to motherhood rather late, and alone. I am now ten years older than my mother was when she died. My older daughter is eight, the age I was when I lost Rosie. When my little girls hold my hands, I can feel the warm clasp of my mother as she led me on those long-ago expeditions to find our dream house. I am thankful that I seem to be luckier, but I know too well from my own childhood that all safety is an illusion, and that only luck, fragile as a membrane, separates us at every second from disaster.

I stumble through the rituals of every day—"Hurry, brush your teeth, here are your socks," "No, you can't wear two different socks. Well, maybe you can, as long as it's on purpose." I am aware that downstairs, in the Innlet, my eighty-four-year-old uncle, city fellow to the core, is waking, too. More accurately, perhaps, Uncle Len is still awake, having never gone to sleep. ("I don't truly sleep," he claims, "I just rest.")

We are three generations under this old roof, a reprise of the way my life began.

For part of my childhood, my grandmother lived with me. When I was eight and she was eighty, we shared a room, dubbed the "Girls' Room." Etka had behaved like a child, an aged kid sister who swiped my jewels and clothes. She had taken much, but she also gave. She taught me how to say "I love you" in Russian, *Ya lblue Ya lblue tebya.*

She bequeathed me her precious past—the dacha, the memories of sweet cherries and plums. The rooms she had loved—"I had a white room and a white dog." My grandmother Etka from Minsk had been a figure of exaggerated pride and posture. It was easy to laugh at her grandeur. But sometimes, her gaze would clear and she would speak to me in a different voice, as if she were not elderly and I was not a child. As if we were exactly equal and I could understand. At one such time, she held my hand and said, "My life passes as a dream."

I began my life as one of seven people in three rooms. Now, we share, the four of us, twenty-odd rooms, in the center of many acres, surrounded by trees and grass. We have *Luft* to spare. We spend long days exhausting ourselves with pleasures. In summer, the girls sail a rubber boat on my homemade swimming pool. We catch frogs, caterpillars, and butterflies.

Now in winter, the farm offers its cold-weather consolations. As I write, the snow is falling. Looking out my window, it is easy to lose track of time, and I have. Music is playing, and I have fallen far deeper than usual into what F. Scott Fitzgerald called "the long empty dream of the day," the writer's trance.

The music is a Chopin mazurka, and as I listen I am also watching a small herd of deer appear, walking single-file, on tippy-toe. They cannot hear the music, but they seem to move to it, like dainty ghosts past a stand of evergreen.

Downstairs, my little girls call out for me. As if they can hear this sound, too, the deer startle and flee, white tails waving. The quality of light has changed, and the snowfall lessens, the flakes falling it seems individually. I must leave my desk now; I've promised the girls a walk before dark.

Bundled up, we start down the hill. We can see steam rising from the sugar shack. The air we breathe tastes sweet. We appear to be alone, but the path we travel is crisscrossed with the V-shaped prints of many deer and the wide-spaced footprints of the occasional leaping rabbit.

In the distance, our house glows as lemon-colored as that city farmhouse down my block beckoned to me so many years ago. Only now, it is my door that is unlocked and open for all of us, and it is my children who will run pell-mell through the center hall, shedding scarves, caps, and boots.

You could say I have ended up where I wanted to be, smack in the center of the circuit of memory. For eighteen years, I have walked this land, sometimes in circles, most often by myself. As laughable as this may sound, my long introspection at my country place has yielded this truth: what I sometimes mistook for moroseness was joy, a contemplation so sustained that it could be confused with melancholy.

Ah, nature—cruel, indifferent, dirty. Not all it is cracked up to be, but maybe more. I don't wander up and down my rutted path, worn now by my tread, to find answers. I go to remember or to let my mind wander ahead. What each day offers is beauty and, possibly, a surprise.

Tonight, we are lucky. The snow stops and the moon rises, the second full moon in a month. The "blue moon" does indeed appear blue, illuminating the snowfields, turning them blue, too. The moonrise seems a cue for action: an unseen pack of coyotes howl. Two herds of deer suddenly appear, seeming to chase each other across the pasture. And then, as we round the final bend to our house, there he is. The coyote. He is posed, perfectly still, directly in our path. I did not see him run or even turn. He is simply there, silver and buff, with his feral stare. His eyes meet mine, and there is an exchange of information. Then he turns and leaves, not fleeing, just departing. He is not scared of us. His tail is plume-like. He lopes easily over the snow toward the far pasture, to the woods, where his pack is waiting. They howl in unison, in response to a distant firemen's siren.

Oooooohhhh Ooooooohhh. He is beautiful, wolflike, as he runs on the diagonal. "Does he bite?" my littler girl asks.

"Not us," I answer. I don't want to tell them that coyote will surely kill tonight. They are still too young to learn the harder lessons here. Anyway, the coyote is not our enemy—he is the entertainment. We have more to fear from the glow of light on our shrinking horizon, the deepening roar of the highway. Just as, years ago, I walked to "the end of the city," it might someday be possible to reach the edge of the country. Cement might flow, a manmade glacier, right to our own barn door. But not now, not yet.

We walk up the final trail, retracing our footsteps in the snow. The closer we get to the lemon-colored lamplight that flows from every window, the quicker our steps. I pick up my little girl and hold my older girl's hand. And then I run, run toward that place I can call, in this blink of time, home.

Acknowledgments

First, I must thank my late mother, Rosie, for setting me on the long path to the beautiful place where I am today. And her brothers, my uncles, who took such good care of me and escorted me the rest of the way. I have gratitude, too, to my two daughters, Alexandra Rose and Jasmine Sou Mei, whose love continues to inspire me and who make every place our home. Many thanks to my faithful cousins, Richard and Betsy Weiss, who are great friends as well as relatives. And many thanks to my aunt Mary, who has carried on so gallantly and with good cheer all her life. In loving memory, too, of my great aunt Dora, who always came back from her "place in the country" with a present for me of a miniature wooden wishing well (the word "Wildwood" burned into the bark—and my brain).

Mispucha aside, I thank my enduring friends for their kind support. Suzanne Watson for staying for the whole trip—from college days through Tuxedo Park to where we are today. Nina Shengold for her good heart, keen mind, generosity of spirit, and all manner of help with work, and companionship in play. Elana Greenfield for almost two decades of delicate intuition and uncanny sensitivity. Becky Stowe for giving so unstintingly of her attention to this work while in progress. Lidia Dancu for guiding me to her "place" in another country and finding my beautiful first baby, Alexandra. Francine Shane and Eric Duffield for leading me to my darling second daughter, Jasmine, and staying the course as true friends in trying times. Thank you also to Frank and Ruth and the entire clan of Gilroys for being great and loving, more than friends, a second family, for more than two and a half decades. My gratitude to Kristina and Stephen Lang for their gracious and generous friendship—adding so much pleasure and inspiration, in recent years. And my abiding appreciation to John Patrick Shanley, whose journey so closely parallels my own and whose good heart and talent have always been a comfort. And thank you, too, to David Rasche for his astute eye on the work and for sharing an almost incomprehensible love of the dairy farm and theater, a great combination.

A huge thank you to Chester and Bonnie, for opening up their wonderful world to my family. For the good people who "take care," I almost cannot put into words how they make life possible and pleasurable—the stalwart Stewart Lee and, in loving memory, Cecil Green. And my enduring appreciation of Cecil's widow, Ida, who keeps the old spirit alive. Appreciation, too, for Pat and Andy. And, of course, my lasting thank you to Lord and Lady, for bestowing The Inn and the wider view of their wondrous "Willowby" upon me—it has never been taken for granted. To her young Ladyship, my "giggle twin," for all the fun we've had here, and whose world this also is. And, of course, Jill and David Rabe, who have shared this place, also, with all its expected and unexpected pleasures. Going back in time, I must thank William Bozzufi for his unending hospitality and consideration—his Castle doors were always open.

I must acknowledge also the invaluable help provided by my writer's group, which has included over the years Rebecca Stowe, Casey Kurtti, Scott Spencer, Zachary Sklar, Nina Shengold, Mary Gallagher, Ron Nyswaner, John Bowers, and Mary Louise Wilson, writers who listened for three years and in so many ways helped in the shaping and rewriting of this book. A bouquet, too, to Actors and Writers, my "other group," whose interests overlap, between plays and prose, and whose spring and fall festivals kept the soul alive. For new and true friends Frances Madeson and Joseph de Dominici, for their many kindnesses to me and my family. This book surely could not have been written in good time without the kind and diligent efforts of Toni Ahearn. A special thanks, too, to Karen Williams, who escorted me so kindly into cyberspace . . . and on deadline, yet! And my appreciation to Charles Cullen for his historic research.

My gratitude to my beautiful-in-every-way editor, Julie Grau, for her loving attention to each sentence. Her buoyant support has added so much joy to the process of going from page to print. And a special thank you to Dan Harvey for his strong and gentle support for this book. And thank you to Hanya Yanagihara for unfailing patience and sweetness in going over the daily work of this publication. And Elizabeth Wagner deserves acknowledgment for the painstaking copyediting of this manuscript.

A profound thank you to Deborah Garrison, who so gently and skillfully edited the version of *A Place in the Country* that appeared in *The New Yorker*.

My gratitude extends to Rosemary Ahern, for her shepherding of the earlier edition of *Sleeping Arrangements* and her enthusiasm for this work. And to Daniel Menaker, always an inspiration in his dedication to writing, as a writer himself and an editor. I also appreciate my former editor Joseph Kanon, now fellow author, for his continued caring attention and savvy advice.

And, of course, a big bouquet to marvelous Molly Friedrich, who "knows just what to do" and does it with flair, kindness, and good speed.

Laura Shaine Cunningham,
March, 2000

About the Author

Laura Shaine Cunningham is a playwright and journalist whose fiction and nonfiction have appeared in *The New Yorker, The Atlantic Monthly, The New York Times, Vogue, Harper's Bazaar,* and other publications. The recipient of numerous awards and fellowships for her writing and theatrical work, Cunningham divides her time between New York City and her place in the country.